8124

SPLINTERING THE WOODEN WALL

SPLINTERING T

THE BRITISH BLOCKADE C

NAVAL INSTITUTE PRESS   ANNAPOLIS, MARYLAND

WOODEN WALL
UNITED STATES, 1812–1815

Wade G. Dudley

Naval Institute Press
291 Wood Road
Annapolis, MD 21402

Library of Congress Cataloging-in-Publication Data
Dudley, Wade G.
Splintering the wooden wall : the British blockade of the United States,
1812–1815 / Wade G. Dudley.
        p. cm.
Includes bibliographical references (p.) and index.
ISBN 1-55750-167-X
1. United States—History—War of 1812—Naval operations, British.
2. United States—History—War of 1812—Blockades.
3. Great Britain. Royal Navy—History—War of 1812. I. Title.
E360 .D83 2002
973.5'25—dc21   2002006878

Printed in the United States of America on acid-free paper ∞
10 09 08 07 06 05 04 03   9 8 7 6 5 4 3 2
First printing

To my wife, Susan Marske Dudley;
to her parents, Art and Dorothy Marske;
and to my mother, Lois Hopkins

Contents

Foreword		ix
Acknowledgments		xi
Introduction		I
1	*The Royal Navy and the Practice of Blockade, 1642–1783*	7
2	*The Blockade in Theory and Practice*	23
3	*Assessing Maritime Potential*	35
4	*The Geography of the Blockade*	51
5	*1812: Birth of a Blockade*	64
6	*1813: The Grip Tightens*	79
7	*1814–1815: The Wooden Wall Complete?*	110
8	*Challenging the Efficiency of the Blockade*	131
9	*Comparison to Contemporary Blockades*	161
	Conclusion	183
	Notes	185
	Bibliography	213
	Index	225

Foreword

When I was a wee nipper I contributed my pennies to the rescue of the battleship USS *North Carolina*. Once it reached its final berth at Wilmington, North Carolina, I was among the first of millions of visitors to tread its decks, peer into its turrets, and marvel at this triumph of technology. Across the years I have walked other decks, from sailing vessels to modern aircraft carriers, but that sense of marvel has never abandoned me.

The reader may well wonder what this brief anecdote has to do with the blockades of 1793 to 1815. Aside from allowing me to use that wonderful expression "wee nipper"—a holdover from the age of sail when ship's boys would attach or "nip" the anchor cable to the capstan messenger so that the anchor could be raised—and aside from the fact that this incident led me to the study of maritime activity, such memorials as the USS *North Carolina* are to some degree indicative of the direction taken in the study and writing of naval history.

The *North Carolina* was built to stand in a line of battle, hurling 15-inch shells at its enemies. It floated at the apogee of a crushing offensive naval power, one directly descended from the writings of the nineteenth-century naval theorist, Alfred T. Mahan. For Mahan, the economic and political success of a maritime nation hinged upon the possession of a navy capable of quickly sweeping its opponents from the sea in time of war. Failure resulted in the interdiction or destruction of friendly commerce, the life blood of every nation.

Post-Mahan historical writing reflects this emphasis on the offensive and the clash of naval might at sea. Hundreds of books and articles deal with historic fleet, squadron, and single-ship engagements. Line after line chronicles glorious salvos, deadly torpedoes, and (perhaps more deadly) lapses in command and control. Word after word examines the theoretical projection of naval assets against the enemy. Yet only a handful of manuscripts are spared for the investigation of one of the oldest and most used of naval stratagems—the blockade.

From the Peloponnesian War of the third century B.C. to recent NATO efforts against Serbia, written records support the blockade as a cornerstone of naval activity. Why, then, have modern historians failed to address the evolution of blockade theory and practice? Perhaps the answer lies somewhere between Mahan's emphasis on the battle fleet, the dull and repetitive nature of blockades, and the difficulty in collecting the data needed to evaluate the success and failure of such maritime interdictions.

In 1995, I began research into the British blockade of the United States during the War of 1812. My findings were perplexing. Historians had invariably viewed the blockade as an iron fist tightly gripping American shores as early as 1813, but existing data failed to support that stance. In fact, many New England ports remained open through mid-1814, while some southern ports suffered interdiction for only a few weeks during the conflict (and even then, not necessarily during the closing months of the war). As troubling as the data itself was the lack of analysis of blockade theory and practice. Despite the fact that Great Britain established and maintained three national blockades during the late age of sail, neither contemporary nor subsequent historians had examined these central activities of the Royal Navy in detail, nor had they proposed a method of evaluating success and failure of the blockades.

This work is a first attempt at defining blockade effectiveness during the age of sail. Sadly, much data has been lost or is simply unavailable; thus the technique used in the evaluation is strongly subjective. Nevertheless, I hope that the results stimulate debate and additional research into a neglected segment of naval history. In conclusion, it is well worth remembering that three times in this nation's relatively brief history—during the American Revolution, the War of 1812, and the Civil War—significant numbers of Americans have experienced the misery inherent to a blockade. And it is well worth considering that the blockade remains a potential tool in every nation's naval arsenal.

Acknowledgments

Many are the hands and minds that contribute to any book. At East Carolina University, Michael A. Palmer, Carl Swanson, John Tilley, Lawrence Babits, and Don Parkerson (among many others) contributed helpful critiques and suggestions. The staff at the university's Joyner Library searched high and low for old tomes and wayward manuscripts that were always needed the day before yesterday—and they found most of them on time. At the University of Alabama in Tuscaloosa, John F. Beeler, Howard Jones, Marteen Ultee, and Harold E. Selesky (again, among many others) gave freely of their time, advice, and critiques.

My initial research progressed rapidly thanks to the support of the Naval Historical Center at the Washington Navy Yard. Those kind souls allowed me full access to documents collected for potential inclusion in their four-volume documentary history of the War of 1812. In particular, William S. Dudley (unfortunately, no relation), Director of the Center, Michael J. Crawford, Director of the Early History Section, and Christine F. Hughes were exceedingly helpful, not only with guidance but with reading various manuscripts prepared from the materials. Also located at the Navy Yard is the Naval Historical Foundation, and a special salute goes to David F. Winkler of the Foundation, who provided more assistance than he realizes.

My family, friends, and students have been extremely thoughtful over the past years. My wife, Susan, as well as my sons, Bill and Glen, daughter-in-law, Jess, and grandson, Wade, have endured my long absences (literally and figuratively) patiently. Dan Kornegay, best friend and fellow wargamer, has been denied far too many of our Friday afternoon gaming sessions (and his usual victories) as I submerged myself in blockade theory. Many of my students have encouraged me to expend even more effort upon research and writing—encouragement rooted at times, I suspect, in the delusion that such undertakings would make my assignments less frequent and my critique less painstaking.

Numerous other people and institutions have contributed directly or indirectly to this manuscript. All have my gratitude, and all have my assurance that any errors of judgment or research in the finished product reflect not upon them, but exclusively upon me.

Finally, to place the seriousness of the events of almost twenty decades past in perspective, I must acknowledge some of those who sacrificed their lives in support or challenge of the blockade of the United States, 1812–15: the officers and crew of the USS *Wasp*, sloop-of-war, lost at sea, October 1814; and the officers and crew of the HMS *Cuttle*, schooner, lost at sea, December 1814.

SPLINTERING THE WOODEN WALL

Introduction

The blockade is one of the oldest stratagems in naval theory. In the ancient and medieval worlds it was a tactical tool complementing siege warfare. By the late 1700s, changes in naval warfare had given the blockade a strategic emphasis. Entire coasts and nations could be interdicted for months or years as long as sources of resupply and repair for the blockaders existed nearby.

By 1812, the art of blockade had matured in the hands of Great Britain's Admiralty and Royal Navy. Militarily, it was a weave of defense and offense, protecting Britain's vital seaways as it projected force against an enemy's coast. When turned against an opponent's commerce, the blockade halted international trade and disrupted coastal traffic. The resulting economic dislocation injured the enemy and allowed alert British merchants to expand into the newly created vacuum. Finally, the threat of British blockade formed a political hammer held over the heads of all maritime nations. To anger Great Britain risked the hammer's fall.

On 18 June 1812, the United States, with full knowledge of British maritime capabilities, declared war on Great Britain. The causes of the conflict, viewed in the light of nearly two hundred years of historical analysis, bear a strong resemblance to the fabled Gordian knot. President James Madison, in his war message to Congress, listed three maritime issues—impressment, sovereignty, interference with commerce—and incitement of Indians as his reasons for war.[1] Most nineteenth-century historians concurred with Madison.[2] In 1905, Alfred Thayer Mahan added American military unpreparedness as a cause of war.[3] Twenty years later Louis M. Hacker introduced the American land hunger thesis to explain Canada as a military objective, while Julius W. Pratt offered sectional politics as a catalytic agent.[4] George R. Taylor and Margaret K. Latimer followed the two Turnerians with agricultural economics in the West and South as a basis of conflict.[5] During the 1960s, Norman K. Risjord and Bradford Perkins championed nationalism and the search for national respectability. Perkins also stressed the bipolar international situation as a major contributor to war.[6] More recently, Donald R. Hickey theorized that the Republican party deliberately led the nation to war in order to consolidate its power.[7] Though historians may have disagreed on what caused the war, many felt that Madison timed his action perfectly, at least in regard to the international situation.

Between 1793 and 1815, Great Britain was embroiled with revolutionary, then imperial, France. Through 1814, the only cessation of the war was the brief Peace of Amiens of 1802–3. It coincided with the break between revolutionary and imperial France, for Napoleon Bonaparte crowned himself emperor in 1804. Through conquest and political maneuvering, Napoleon brought most of Europe under French hegemony. By June 1812, only three European nations—Russia, Great Britain, and tiny Portugal—were resisting French control. Napoleon prepared to invade Russia with the largest army of contemporary times, while several of his best marshals faced the British Army in the Iberian Peninsula.

Well before this point, the British Navy had developed into the largest such force in the world. It had captured all of the once-numerous French colonies and maintained a constant blockade of the European coast. Few French coasting vessels risked the blockade, and the still-large navies of France and its allies languished in port, unwilling or unable to face the vigilant British vessels. The danger from French naval raiders and privateers had virtually disappeared, and the numerous French seamen confined in British prisons and prison hulks attested to the effectiveness of British naval strategy.

The Royal Navy, however, was stretched exceedingly thin. The blockade demanded the bulk of its resources, each convoy required escorts, and the few French raiders that reached the sea-lanes necessitated the maintenance of roving patrols. The British Army in Portugal, led by the capable Sir Arthur Wellesley, Viscount Wellington, requested constant assistance from the Navy, while the Admiralty often dispatched squadrons to support allied nations (in 1812, Russia received such aid). By June of 1812, the military assets of Great Britain were fully committed to the eventual defeat of Napoleon. Only a small squadron patrolled the coasts of North America, while a tiny regular army contingent garrisoned Canada. Madison's declaration of war occurred at a most opportune moment.

The American government planned on a short war of only a few months' duration. A quick seizure of Canada by the regular Army and militia offered the means to force Great Britain to recognize and correct the grievances put forth by Madison in his war message. If Britain failed to do so, the rich lands of Canada could always be retained as spoils of war. Unfortunately for the American cause, the invasion of Canada failed, and a stalemate developed. Instead of a few short months, the war lasted thirty-three long months, during which the coast of the United States came under British blockade.

At first glance, that interdiction should have been overwhelming. The Royal Navy numbered 607 active naval vessels, plus a few auxiliary cruisers, against the 16 ships of the U.S. Navy, aided by a few dozen gunboats designed for coastal defense.[8] Invariably, historians have recorded that the blockade proved highly effective, pinning American naval forces in their ports, destroying virtually all American commerce, and in essence rivaling the success of the Royal Navy's blockades of France.

There seems to have been little doubt among British historians as to which side claimed the laurels in the War of 1812. William James, writing in 1817, knew that his nation's victory rested on the invincible Royal Navy, though he used many of his paragraphs to rationalize its losses during the war. William Laird Clowes, shortly after the turn of the century, dodged the issue in his massive work by inviting Theodore Roosevelt to contribute the chapter on the 1812 conflict. Adroit politician that he was, Roosevelt countered a smothering blockade with American victories on the Great Lakes and called it a draw. During the 1940s and 1950s, Gerald S. Graham published two studies of the maritime struggles of the British Empire in North America. He doubted neither British victory nor the fact that the Royal Navy achieved that victory, despite its challenges in Europe.[9] G. J. Marcus, publishing his volume on the Napoleonic Era in 1971, depicted the years 1793 to 1815 as a clean sweep for John Bull and the Nelsonian spirit, observing that the coasting trade of the United States had been destroyed by late 1813.[10] In 1976, Paul Kennedy appropriately used the end of the war as an example of the stalemate potential inherent to conflict between a maritime and a continental power but carefully noted that "the United States was suffering the most by 1814."[11] Six years later, Ian R. Christie far less carefully claimed that "the overwhelming naval pressure the British were able to exert along the whole length of the American Atlantic coast wiped out American seaborne traffic and communications and gradually inclined the government in Washington to become more disposed to peace."[12]

For Graham, Marcus, and Christie, success depended on the strong British fleet and its blockade. Ironically, they, along with most twentieth-century historians of the War of 1812, used the research and interpretation of an American to support that conclusion. Their emphasis on the destruction of American commerce, the containment of the U.S. Navy within its ports, the deprecation of *guerre de course*, the disaffection of New England, and the drain of American specie reflected the work of an earlier historian—Alfred Thayer Mahan, who published *Sea Power in Its Relations to the War of 1812* in 1905. Virtually all naval historians since that date have accepted, used, and borrowed from Mahan's evidence and interpretations.

They did so with reason. Aside from determining international naval strategy for at least five decades (and he still has his adherents today), Mahan's research was thorough, while his interpretations flowed eloquently from the pen. He supported his views with profuse primary quotations and tables. Yet Mahan's bias toward a strong blue-water navy caused him to find a strength and effectiveness in the blockade of the United States that existed no more than his perceived "annihilation" of that nation's commerce.[13]

This study questions that perception of the effectiveness of the blockade, though this assertion should not be interpreted to mean that Britain's wooden wall collapsed, for it did not. That wooden wall, however, was severely splintered and the degree of effectiveness assigned to it by historians deserves challenge. Even the most widely read newspaper of Great Britain, the *London Times*, cried its concern in December 1814: "We have retired from the combat with the stripes yet bleeding on our back . . . with the bravest seamen and the most powerful navy in the world, we retire from the contest when the balance of defeat is so heavy against us."[14] Perhaps the *Times* exhibited journalistic extremism, but voicing such sentiments certainly implied less-than-total success for the blockading forces. Similarly, the *status quo antebellum* mandated by the Treaty of Ghent in December 1814 hints that the blockade was less than completely efficient. Finally, surviving writings of British naval officers serving in the war often aired feelings of frustration directed at the weaknesses of their own superiors, as well as at the American ships which so often evaded the blockade.

Among them was Lt. Henry Edward Napier, a youthful officer on board a British frigate. The youngest of several family members serving in the armed forces of Great Britain—all of greater rank and all having achieved a measure of distinction for their services—he often felt frustration at the lack of glory accompanying the blockade. In penning an angry journal entry, he unwittingly identified an aspect of the British blockade not usually addressed by historians:

> 10 June. Without some risk, some dash, very little will ever be done in the navy; prudence has never yet answered. Even if you fail, the attempt will gain you the applause of Englishmen.
> —Onboard H.M.S. *Nymphe*, off Scituate, Massachusetts, 1814[15]

"Without some risk" wrote Napier, as he considered the possibilities of burning American naval vessels in Boston Harbor; but British risk taking actually occurred on a far grander scheme than the tactical engagements envisioned by the lieutenant. From the Admiralty to each individual commander in chief of the North American Station, operating "without some risk" would have been a deviation from the norm. Too often, as the pages of this narrative will reveal, the choices made—the risks taken—at the strategic and operational levels, actually reduced the potential effectiveness of the blockade, a reality lost in the accepted historical view of the Royal Navy during the War of 1812. Certainly, too, failure did not "gain" these gentlemen "the applause of Englishmen."

Before examining the war proper, it seems appropriate to provide important background material. Chapter 1 offers an overview of the historical development of the blockade from the British naval perspective, while chapter 2 discusses blockade theory and practice in the waning years of the age of sail, a seldom-addressed arena of naval operations. This chapter also identifies the contemporary principles governing the success or failure of a blockade. Chapter 3 turns to those frustrated officers, the men they commanded, the technology at their disposal, and the naval hierarchies within which they functioned. A tour of the geography of the theater of operations, another oft-ignored yet critical aspect of blockade operations, is taken in chapter 4.

The examination of the blockade itself can be broken into three segments corresponding to the years of the war: 1812, 1813, and 1814–15. British admirals tended to suspend offensive efforts during winter's inclement weather, concentrating on preparing for a new campaign in the spring and summer. Use of this division, though necessary for purposes of presentation, is somewhat artificial as naval activity never completely ceased. Chapters 5, 6, and 7 address the three chronological periods of the war. They are event-intensive, detailing the activities of the blockade as well as the serious dilemmas confronting the Admiralty and British commanders in the North American theater of operations.[16] An analysis of the performance of the blockade throughout the war and discussion of the reasons for the Royal Navy's less-than-optimal performance are offered in chapter 8. Chapter 9 examines the British blockades of France, 1793–1814, allowing a comparison of the Royal Navy's performance during the War of 1812 to that against France.

1

The Royal Navy and the
Practice of Blockade, 1642–1783

Frequent conflict among European nations marred the second half of the seventeenth and all of the eighteenth century.[1] In a commonly perceived zero-sum universe of economics and power, each nation struggled for its share of gold, influence, and glory. Many wars assumed a global nature, following the shipping lanes across the Atlantic basin to the coasts of the Americas, Africa, and beyond. Colonies changed hands, colonials learned the methodology of war, and parent countries, their attention and wealth focused upon the great battlefields of Europe, allowed their administrative leashes to loosen. Somewhere between the neglect of colonial governance and the over-expenditure of fiscal assets, two great revolutions developed. Britain's American colonies initiated a long and bitter struggle for independence. The rebellion soon escalated into a European war as France, followed by Spain and Holland, extended support to the colonials. America won its independence, but Britain's European enemies paid a stiff price. They failed to humble Great Britain and amassed tremendous debts in the attempt. In France, national bankruptcy joined with threads of internal dissent to spark the second great revolution of the late 1700s, ushering in another two decades of intensive conflict. In this arena, encompassing over 150 years of time and all of the world's oceans, England's Navy guarded its shores and constantly

growing merchant marine. By 1793, extensive experience and technological advances had allowed the Royal Navy to develop a tactical
stratagem, the blockade, into a strategic tool.

England (Great Britain as of 1707) found itself involved in, if not
the focal point of, most of the era's conflicts. In addition, the nation
suffered periods of internecine readjustment: the civil wars of
1642–51, followed by the Glorious Revolution of 1689–92 and the two
Jacobite insurrections in 1715 and 1745. Whether the threat originated
externally or internally, however, insular England invariably turned to
its Navy as a primary military tool.

With the onset of civil war in 1642, the bulk of the Navy aligned
itself with Parliament. That government tasked it with interdicting
the Royalist line of communications to the continent, halting the
steady flow of military supplies carried in Dutch and French bottoms
to Royalist ports. Occasionally, the Navy physically blockaded Royalist harbors; more often, squadrons cruised likely approaches to those
harbors or the Channel itself. The Royalists at last managed to organ-
ize a squadron from loyal vessels in 1648, placing Prince Rupert in
command. The parliamentary Navy promptly blockaded the harbor—
a Dutch harbor, Hellevoetsluis—but could not maintain the effort
when faced with sickness and a shortage of provisions. Once the
blockade lifted, Rupert escaped to sea, raiding his way through the
Channel. Entering port in Kingsail, Rupert found himself again blockaded. As parliamentary land forces approached the port, a fortuitous
gale drove the blockaders away, allowing Rupert to regain the sea. The
Royalist squadron continued taking prizes as it looked southward for a
safe haven, welcomed at last by King John IV of Portugal. When news
of this event reached Parliament, it dispatched a fleet to destroy the
Royalist vessels. Attempting to ascend the Tagus River to attack
Rupert at Lisbon, the English vessels came under fire from Portuguese forts. Failing to reach accommodation with John IV, the parliamentary fleet settled into a blockade of Rupert's squadron which
lasted from March to September 1650. Only the ability to water and
purchase fresh provisions locally made such a lengthy interdiction possible. Still, the English vessels suffered from lack of repairs and fouling of their hulls by marine growths. When the annual Portuguese
Brazil convoy appeared in mid-September, the English admiral chose
to capture most of its vessels and return home rather than watch his
fleet sink under his feet from lack of maintenance. Rupert sailed as
soon as the blockade lifted. He continued raiding, for a time in the

Mediterranean and then in the West Indies, at last disbanding his squadron at Nantes in 1654.[2]

Three times Rupert found himself blockaded by an equal or superior force. In each instance, he observed the demoralization and deterioration of his crews caused by enforced idleness, diseases inherent in close confinement and proximity to an urban environment, desertion, and the failure to earn much coveted prize money. Twice he feared being forcibly ejected from his anchorage and directly into a battle with readied opponents—once by Cromwell's soldiers at Kingsail and again by possible edict of an irate John IV at Lisbon. Three important lessons regarding the blockade emerge from Rupert's experiences: a port is not a haven but a potential trap; a raiding force at sea is difficult to intercept, much less destroy; and blockades are impossible to sustain indefinitely without a nearby base—weather interfering where the frailty of men and vessels does not. It can be conjectured that Rupert actually took those lessons to heart in later years. After surviving the English Civil War, the prince returned to England during the Restoration. There he served as a flag officer in the second of the Dutch wars and as commander in chief of the fleet during the final months of the third Anglo-Dutch conflict.

As England's senior admiral, Rupert, in conjunction with French allies, attempted to establish a blockade of the Dutch coast in 1673 aimed at denying the United Provinces of the Netherlands' naval assets access to the sea. Rupert's plan included the landing of troops to seize the island of Texel as a local base for the blockaders. Fortunately for the Dutch, Adm. Engel De Ruyter (also spelled De Ruijter) sortied twice (First and Second Schooneveld). These actions, coupled with unusually stormy weather and dwindling food stocks, forced the allies to retire for repairs and provisioning. A repeat of the attempt to establish a blockade resulted in the battle of the Texel, an engagement conclusive in the sense that it prevented interdiction of the Dutch coast by the allies.[3] Regardless of Rupert's lack of success, this remains the first readily identifiable precursor of the national blockades of 1793–1815.

Economic warfare characterized the Anglo-Dutch Wars of 1652–54, 1664–67, and 1670–74. As the belligerents attempted to disrupt or destroy commerce, both turned in varying degrees to the convoy system, with massed escorts (squadrons and even fleets) protecting the unarmed merchantmen. Dutch shipping found itself particularly vulnerable, as all but the Baltic trade had to transit the length of the

Channel to reach its destination, while the Baltic fleet was subject to interception as it entered the North Sea and made for Dutch ports.

Historian Richard Harding made several important observations about the Anglo-Dutch Wars in his work on the rise of the battle fleet as the determinant element in sea power. The conflicts saw an increase in the use of privateers as a cost-effective instrument of national policy, especially by the United Provinces. Between 1665 and 1674, Dutch privateers captured 973 of the 1,135 prizes taken from England, France, and the occasional neutral. A dilemma, however, accompanied that success: the availability of seamen to meet the needs of the merchant marine, the state navy, and the popular and profitable private navy. The United Provinces resolved the problem by suspending privateering in favor of the public navy whenever the need arose. English privateers appear to have fared less well than the Dutch, though exact numbers are unavailable (other than a total of 1,022 captures by all parties). Apparently, the stringent Dutch convoy system, necessitated by geography, inhibited English *guerre de course*.[4]

Here, Harding identifies two additional points, both critical to the development of blockades. Dutch convoys with escorting fleets required the massing of English naval assets even to attempt to assail the merchantmen. Such attempts often involved concentrated fleets of eighty to more than one hundred warships. Even if a successful interception occurred, the size of the opposing forces guaranteed a long and frequently inconclusive battle from which the convoy could steal away. Perhaps more significant than the utility of convoys was the reality of logistical demands. Massed fleets required massed feeding, massed repairs, and a massive treasury. The crews of eighty vessels stripped a port bare of victuals and maritime stores in a few weeks, necessitating relocation or disbandment of the fleet. Logistics, as much as weather, seems to have encouraged the dispersal of vessels during the winter and their reassemblage for summer campaigns. As for repairs, the English dockyards did not possess a single dry dock until after the Third Anglo-Dutch War (the French, in contrast, had dry-dock space for sixty vessels at that time).[5] This series of conflicts served as a spur to the development of the royal dockyards, an investment which would pay handsome dividends by 1793.[6]

War is seldom cost effective. The strictly maritime conflicts of 1662 to 1667 nearly impoverished both nations, even though the Dutch initially were in sounder financial condition. English seamen deserted in droves when not paid in a timely fashion, but more important, fiscal constraints pushed decision making in both countries. Perhaps the outstanding example is the Medway raid of 1666. England's King Charles II, hoping to see the then–Dutch ally, France, pressure the United Provinces to accept a peace accord, fitted out minimal forces for the summer campaign (Charles also lacked the financial assets to do much more than that). Those forces proved incapable of stopping a Dutch fleet from ascending the Thames and Medway, stripping naval stores and victuals in the area, burning vessels, and carrying away several of England's best warships.[7] Two important observations regarding the study of the development of the British blockade relate to the Medway raid. First, fiscal constraints place a cap upon the projection of naval force (accompanying the logistical and manpower stops previously discussed). Every nation has its limits, no matter the breadth of its empire. Second, England is vulnerable even at its heart—what strategy would best relieve that vulnerability? One answer lay a century away.

Historian Peter Woodfine writes that British naval efforts against Spain immediately before the War of the Austrian Succession "sank into partial blockades and intermittently successful patrols."[8] Following the Third Anglo-Dutch War, the same can be said of the concept of a national blockade. Woodfine then clearly defines the problem associated with naval supremacy well into the 1780s: "To build up a reliable ocean-going navy, with efficient communications, and capable of keeping the seas in all weathers throughout the year, was not simply a work of great time and effort: in the 1740s it was impossible."[9] And without such a navy, blockades of the breadth in use after 1793 could not have been successful (this implies that Prince Rupert's attempted blockade would have dissolved without Dutch interference).

The most critical constraints upon any pre-1793 blockade, excluding the rather obvious finance and manpower, were disease, naval infrastructure, and vessel durability. Scurvy, caused by vitamin C deficiency, was the scourge of the Royal Navy, and unsurprisingly so as the standard naval provisions included little of that vitamin. Physician James Lind published *A Treatise of the Scurvy* in 1753, having discovered by experimentation that fruit and green vegetables, fresh or properly preserved, prevented the disease. The Admiralty ignored the recommendations of Lind and other physicians until 1795. As a result, a six-week cruise of the Channel Fleet in 1780 resulted in 2,400 cases of scurvy, while the sick list for the 100,000 men of the Royal Navy in 1782 featured 23,000 ill. Most suffered from vitamin C deficiency. By 1805, with lime juice and fresh fruit introduced into the standard diet, only 8,000 of 120,000 men appeared on the year's sick rolls. Other improvements in the 1700s—standards of cleanliness, quarantine procedures, proper attire for the men, and more and better doctors on board ships—joined with Lind's work to produce a healthier Navy capable of spending the months at sea required by long blockades.[10]

Daniel A. Baugh, in an article titled "Why Did Britain Lose Command of the Sea during the War for America?" observes that "the skills, facilities and resources that subtended effective and efficient naval power in the eighteenth century had to be built up and nurtured over a long period of time."[11] Penny pinching by the North government, he concludes, ultimately caused the temporary loss of command of the sea, but the Bourbons would have been hard-pressed to overcome the long-term British lead in maritime and naval infrastructure: yards and artificers for rapidly building and repairing vessels, a pool of highly skilled seamen to man an expanding Navy, and an experienced naval bureaucracy to coordinate maritime efforts. Thus Great Britain, between 1672 and 1780, developed a lead in naval infrastructure that could not be easily challenged by other nations. It was that infrastructure, nearing its peak of perfection for the age of sail, which was required to support the logistically demanding blockades of the Napoleonic era.

The greatest problem with the durability of British ships before the late 1770s resided in their wooden bottoms. Wood submerged in warm water was attacked by worms, which could completely destroy it in a few years. In both warm and cold water, barnacles attached themselves to a vessel's bottom, quickly followed by long strands of seaweed. The weed rapidly grew until its drag slowed the ship's movement. More important, this sea life actually forced its way into the seams of a vessel, opening it slowly but surely to the sea. Vessels often accumulated enough growth in less than six weeks at sea to slow movement, and in as little as three months it could become necessary to careen the ship (to tilt it by careening tackle at a dock or at low tide on a sandy beach), scrape its bottom, and recaulk its seams. The invention of coppering at last mitigated the problem. Attaching copper sheathes to ships' bottoms avoided the worm and vastly slowed sea growths, allowing ships to stay at sea without reduced movement for much longer periods of time.[12] It is difficult to conceive of the post-1793 blockades existing without the discovery of coppering.

The limitations imposed by ship durability and disease, as well as the growth of the British naval infrastructure since 1642, are clearly visible in the close blockade of Brest, May to November 1759, conducted by Adm. Sir Edward Hawke during the Seven Years' War. In an era of "partial blockades," its length of seven months made the interdiction unique, while Hawke's tactical deployments foreshadowed those used against French ports after 1801.

Sir Edward received instructions from the Admiralty on 18 May 1759, warning of an assemblage of French troops, ships, and stores at Brest preparatory to an invasion of the British Isles. The lords ordered Hawke to take his squadron to Ushant (some twenty-five miles off the French coast and sixty miles by sea from Brest) and to use appropriate forces to observe and harass the enemy. Then, the Admiralty allowed Hawke a choice: "You are to return with the squadron to Torbay, so as to be there by the expiration of fourteen days from the time of your sailing from thence, unless the attempts or operations of the enemy against this kingdom should make it necessary for the defense and security thereof to prolong your cruise or to take any other station near the coast of Great Britain."[13]

Hawke sailed on 20 May with twenty-five ships-of-the-line, thirteen frigates, and two fire ships, all well manned and fully provisioned.[14] Upon his arrival off Ushant, he dispatched ships to examine each of the harbors in the Bay of Biscay. Sir Edward discovered French ships in a high state of readiness at L'Orient (Lorient) and Brest, and decided to establish an inshore blockading force (initially four ships-of-the-line and two frigates) capable of defeating or delaying any squadron attempting to shift from L'Orient to Brest. He continued to cruise with the majority of his fleet off Ushant. His remaining frigates kept close watch on the local ports. On 27 May, Hawke advised the Admiralty, "I do not think it prudent . . . to leave them [the readied French ships] at liberty to come out by returning to Torbay." The lords of the Admiralty officially approved Hawke's close blockade of Brest on 1 June 1759.[15] Both admiral and Admiralty expected eventually to fight the French as they sortied from Brest, but neither party suspected that engagement to be six months distant, and it would have been amazing if anyone, British or French, believed an undertaking of the magnitude of Hawke's blockade could have continued across that span of time. The effort to maintain the blockade in its first weeks is best described in Hawke's own words:

> 4 June: The *Pallas* being very foul, I have sent her with this express into Portsmouth to clean with the utmost expedition and then to repair to Torbay for farther orders.

> 6 June: [Deterioration of ships, need for provisions, and weather forced Hawke to return to port.] For several days preceding my last [letter] . . . we had had very fresh gales with a great sea. Yesterday it increased so much at south-west, with a thick fog, as to make several of the ships complain [a twisting of the hull causing the seams to open], more particularly the new ships. As in this weather it was impossible for the enemy to stir [the wind direction pinned the French in Brest] and our own ships stood in need of a day or two to get themselves to rights, I bore away for this place [Torbay].

> 6 June: Being disappointed in my expectation of finding victuallers ready here to supply the squadron under my command, I am under a necessity of desiring that immediately on receipt of this you will order all the vessels you can procure round to me, loaded with beer. . . . Bread is likewise wanted, though not so much as beer.

> 8 June: Yesterday morning arrived here His Majesty's sloop *Tamar* with five victualling sloops, with 260 tons of beer. . . . At present we have as much as will enable me to keep the squadron out a month or five weeks. . . . [From this point, victualling ships were dispatched continuously to the fleet off Ushant, an at sea replenishment strategy made possible by short sailing distances between home ports and the blockading station. This letter also mentioned the need for replacement anchors and problems with sprung, or split, topmasts, both a result of adverse weather conditions in the Bay of Biscay.][16]

During the remainder of June, the blockaders became more and more aware that their most immediate enemies were not the French, but time and weather. Damage to spars and sails mounted, a ship-of-the-line being dismasted and nearly lost on 11 June, while opened seams forced another to port on the twenty-second.[17] By early July, Hawke realized that the blockade could last far longer than a few weeks. To maintain battle readiness, he thought to establish a system for the careening and refitting of his ships: "The operations of the enemy indicate a long cruise for the squadron. In order to preserve it in a condition to keep the sea, I purpose to send in two ships of the line to clean at Plymouth every spring [tide, not season]. I have begun with the *Fame*, who has got a very malignant fever on board, and the *Bien-faisant*, whose rudder is not to be depended on. They are both above six months foul."[18]

By the end of July, Hawke had abandoned the idea of rotation:

> The *Hercules*'s company being very sickly, I sent her in to heel
> [careen] and refresh her men ten days in port. For the
> disappointment I met with by the two first I sent in not saving the
> spring [that is, taking too much time] has induced me to alter my
> plan and give orders for no more line of battle ships to clean. If the
> enemy should slip out and run, we must follow as fast as we can. I
> have not yet received the supplies of butter and cheese, beef,
> pork, etc., in so much that I can not help regretting the want of a
> commanding officer at Plymouth to see all orders executed with
> the expedition and punctuality necessary.[19]

The Admiralty responded to Hawke's provisioning concerns by appointing a commodore at Portsmouth in August, but the fleet continued to be plagued by the poor quality of the food and beer provided by victuallers. Fresh beer was the greater necessity, as drinking water stored for days and weeks in a wooden barrel almost guaranteed dysentery. As for careening and repairs, the admiral decided to send vessels in as he felt they could be spared. At the end of August, six ships-of-the-line and two frigates—roughly a third of Hawke's available strength—crowded Plymouth's dockyard. [20]

As with the post-1793 blockades of France, the blockade of Brest was essentially defensive in nature, intended to thwart an invasion of Britain. That does not mean that the blockaders were passive. Frigates observed French ports on almost a daily basis, keeping an eye on the state of readiness of the warships within. The inshore squadron and patrolling frigates virtually eliminated Brest's coasting trade, denying the French much needed naval stores. Information gathered from local fishermen and captured merchantmen assisted Hawk in planning the best use of his fleet. Captains supplemented the Admiralty's provisions with cattle raided from coastal French settlements. They took soundings along the enemy coast, and cut out enemy ships whenever the opportunity arose. And always they battled the sea—patching canvas, fishing masts and spars, holding their stations until their ships made twenty-one inches of water in an hour.[21]

By November, Admiral Hawke's men and vessels neared exhaustion. Sickness began to increase as the summer's vegetables became a distant memory and the chill of winter appeared.[22] Yet Hawke showed no intention of abandoning the blockade. Driven into Torbay by a four-day gale on 10 November, he advised the Admiralty, "The instant the weather will admit of it, I shall get to sea again." He tried to do so two days later, only to be forced back to port with extensive damage to his flagship. On 14 November, Hawke managed at last to sail for Ushant.[23]

Well that he did, for the French fleet sortied from Brest for the safety of Quiberon Bay on that same day. Hawke received intelligence of the movement three days later. On 20 November, the tenacious admiral closed the French fleet, pursued it into Quiberon Bay in the midst of a gale, and ended the immediate threat of invasion. The French lost seven ships-of-the-line to capture or shipwreck; the British lost two.[24] The blockade, at much reduced strength, continued into 1760, losing men to scurvy and ships with their crews to storms. One can imagine the physical state of Admiral Hawke when he penned the following lines to the Admiralty on 16 December 1759: "I have now been thirty-one weeks on board without setting my foot on shore and cannot expect my health will hold out much longer. I therefore hope to be relieved."[25] In August 1780, remembering the hardship, Hawke opposed keeping fleets long at sea, writing to Adm. Francis Geary, "Six weeks is long enough in all conscience; any time after that must be very hurtful to the men. . . . I wish the Admiralty would see what was done in former times."[26]

In many ways, the blockade of Brest pioneered the way for the later blockades of France. The Royal Navy implemented or experimented with blockade tactics, at sea provisioning, intelligence gathering, and a planned rotation of vessels. Credit for its success must go to Hawke's leadership ability and the continuing improvements in Britain's naval infrastructure. Together, the Admiralty and its chosen admiral managed to overcome systemic and material weaknesses in thwarting the French invasion plan.

Historian Richard Middleton's "Naval Administration in the Age of Pitt and Anson, 1755–1763" identified several improvements in Britain's naval organization in the years leading to Hawke's interdiction of Brest. The introduction of the two-deck, seventy-four-gun ship-of-the-line provided the Royal Navy with a cost-effective, hardy, and handy alternative to the expensive three-deckers then forming the core of battle fleets. Similarly, new intermediate classes of frigates allowed the Navy to better fit light vessels to a multitude of tasks. The Royal Dockyards also underwent close scrutiny from the Admiralty, though both expansion and the elimination of wastage fell somewhat short of the ideal. Portsmouth, the subject of several letters by Hawke, received careful attention, resulting in both physical and personnel improvements. In lieu of expensive expansion of the state's yards, the Admiralty turned to private contractors for warship construction. It discovered that such firms not only built cost-effective vessels, but their ships were usually of high quality and often touched water in less time than those constructed on the Admiralty's own slipways. The Admiralty also established a process for the continuous maintenance of ships in ordinary, assuring they would not rot away before needed. Taken together, these changes allowed a rapid mobilization of warships at the onset of a conflict—an improved chance of seizing initial naval superiority. Still, the Admiralty chose not to listen to Lind's theory, and scurvy remained a grave problem affecting the availability of manpower. Nor could the naval bureaucracy find an answer for the underwater fouling which all too quickly returned vessels to port for careening. Finally, and to a great degree because of the Royal Navy's efforts over the past one hundred years, the Admiralty continued to enjoy one tremendous advantage: the rapid growth of the British economy and population. Part of this expansion meant ongoing increases in the size of the merchant marine, in the quantity of public sector slipways, and in the availability of maritime manpower.[27] Great Britain would need all of its advantages in the next round of war.

By the conclusion of the Seven Years' War, Britain had acquired new colonial territories, enhanced its national prestige, and accumulated a large national debt. It seemed only logical to king, government, and Parliament that the thirteen original North American colonies should help defray the costs of their own defense; thus Parliament placed new duties upon the loyal Englishmen therein. Whether the cultural drift evident between the settling of Jamestown and the growing penchant for tea parties in the 1770s produced a new breed of people—the Americans—or simply a better breed of tax resisters, by late 1775 a large number of decidedly disloyal Englishmen had united the colonies in open rebellion against Great Britain.

Initially, the Royal Navy performed three important tasks in the attempt to subdue the wayward colonies: safe transport of men and materiel to North America, interdiction of maritime supply lines from Europe to the colonies, and support of the British Army's actions against the rebels. As the pace of war increased and the colonials built both public and private navies, it became necessary to provide for the protection of British commerce. In 1778, France officially cast its support to the Americans (unofficially it had long been the primary supplier of arms and munitions to the rebels). Spain soon followed suit, and Holland eventually joined this alliance of the house of Bourbon. From 1778 to the war's end in 1783, the Royal Navy added to its missions protection of its far spread colonial holdings and defense of the homeland from invasion. All considered, the government required its Navy to establish and maintain sea superiority over its enemies. Thus the tasks placed before the Admiralty changed radically as the war progressed from a low-intensity conflict, requiring naval support not dissimilar to that provided by the parliamentary Navy during the English Civil War, to a multinational global struggle, a rehash of the Seven Years' War—except this time Great Britain lacked significant allies on the Continent.[28]

Initially, First Lord of the Admiralty John Montagu, Fourth Earl of Sandwich (formerly commander in chief in North America, 1771–74), desired to increase the number of warships along the American coasts in order to institute a blockade capable of denying the rebels both foreign support from without and the shipments from within which paid for that foreign aid. Adm. Sir Hugh Palliser wrote a memorandum in July 1775 estimating the extent of forces required for such a blockade (table 1.1), including assisting the Army.

"A less number of ships than the above," warned Palliser, "will be insufficient to perform the services expected." Suspecting that the events at Boston were but the first in a rising tide of rebellion, Palliser advised Sandwich that "in case the other colonies should become in the same state of rebellion as New England is, it will then be necessary to increase the above force considerably, and above all things to secure in each colony tenable posts, at least one at New York, Virginia, and Carolina, where the King's ships can lay in shelter, get water, receive and secure succours and supplies for the friends of government in those parts."[29]

One flaw certainly existed in Palliser's memorandum. He failed to allocate ships to replace those refitting. In a second memorandum, written in December, he suggested that less than 20 percent (opti-

TABLE 1.1. *Palliser's Estimate of Vessels Required for Blockade, July 1775*

Location	Fourth Rates and Frigates	Smaller Vessels	Total
Boston	12	10	22
Rhode Island	3	0	3
New York	5	3	8
Delaware River	2	0	2
Virginia	4	4	8
Carolinas	2	2	4
St. Lawrence River	0	2	2
Florida	0	1	1
TOTAL	28	22	50

Source: Memorandum, July 1775, Barnes and Owen, *Private Papers of John, Earl of Sandwich* 1:64–66

mistic, considering Hawke's experiences) of the vessels on station would be refitting or on other duties at any one time (the first mention that convoy escorts would also be provided from the station's ships). He also suggested that vessels sailing for home ports, whatever the reason, should be those most in need of dry dock or refit—an indirect acknowledgment of the lack of repair facilities in North America.[30]

Palliser's memorandums identified two issues critical to the success of any blockade, ship availability and logistics. Keeping in mind that the rebellion did, indeed, expand, British ship availability in North America during the first two years of conflict, when the rebellion could have been conceivably crushed without a European war, rose from thirty to only seventy-odd vessels. The latter constituted approximately 40 percent of the total vessels available to Great Britain in 1776.[31] Logistically, the Royal Navy depended upon its underdeveloped and distant dockyard at Halifax, Nova Scotia, and the American ports, particularly Boston, for support. None of the ports possessed a dry dock, and Halifax could careen only three ships at a time. Though some naval stores and provisions were available locally before the rebellion, most had to be supplied from England after 1775. The same held true for manpower and ordnance. With local ports available only when seized and garrisoned by sizable military forces (who then had to be clothed, fed, and supplied with munitions), logistics quickly deteriorated.[32] A third point, command ability, plagued early British efforts at a blockade. Sandwich did not have an Edward Hawke in Adm. Samuel Graves, and Graves's successors proved little better. Most noticeable in Graves, but perhaps having greater influence than has been credited by historians, is a fourth point: this was a civil war fought by people who were culturally and physically as alike as they were different. In 1775, Sandwich wrote to Graves,

> I think I should not perform the part of a friend, if I endeavored to conceal from you that the world in general has been full of complaints that the fleet does nothing; and that in particular fresh provisions are wanted at Boston, which the ships have it in their power to procure [through an effective blockade and raiding]: they say that you do not consider the rebellious colonies as a people you are actually at war with; and that though they take every advantage in their power in order to starve the navy and army, you seem to have delicacies about taking possession of whatever is wanted for subsistence or in aid of your operations.[33]

Between an initial shortage of vessels, constant demand by the Army for naval support, and a lack of command initiative, an effective blockade did not exist in the first years of the war.[34] Certainly, patrolling naval vessels ranged far and wide along the coast, but patrols alone do not constitute a blockade. An effective blockade continuously prohibits access to or from the shore along an assigned section of coast. Patrols proved a poor substitute for stationed forces, interrupting traffic only until the British vessels continued on their way. Had the Royal Navy followed Palliser's suggested deployment for blockaders, joined those points with patrols, and seized and developed proper dockyard facilities, then perhaps nine-tenths of George Washington's powder would not have arrived from overseas sources through 1777, and the war would have ended without overt European involvement.[35]

Americans quickly fielded both public and private navies against the British, who had clearly not planned for such an eventuality. Vice Adm. Molyneux Shuldham wrote to Sandwich in early 1776, "Your Lordship will be surprised and concerned to hear how fast the armed vessels of the rebels have multiplied lately; how many of our storeships and victuallers they have taken; and how successfully they have defeated all our force, vigilance, and attention by their artifice, but more by their being too early in possession of all harbours, creeks, and rivers, on this coast, most of which they have already fortified."[36]

By March, the British Army had evacuated Boston for Halifax, and logistics had dipped to a wretched state. As Shuldham recorded, "[The Army] almost totally subsists on what I have been able to spare from the naval stock of provisions, already so low that I am under a necessity of putting the fleet to two-thirds allowance of all species."[37]

In October, the Admiralty recognized that all stores being shipped to North America had to travel in heavily armed vessels or with large escorts, so great was the danger from privateers.[38]

Logistical problems, especially the occasional reduction in an already poor diet, aggravated another long-term ill. Scurvy and other diseases drained the ranks of the American squadron, necessitating a constant stream (usually appearing as a trickle) of replacements from England. Surgeon William Northcote, *Prudent,* addressed a fervent letter to the Admiralty in 1781, in which he claimed that two-thirds of the seamen on the North American Station had died from scurvy or related diseases. He reminded Sandwich that this had also been the case in the Seven Years' War, though even then the cure for scurvy had been common knowledge. Sandwich retained a copy of Northcote's letter—he did not bother responding to its plea.[39]

By early 1778, the blockade had become a rather obvious and embarrassing failure.[40] Secretary of State for America Lord George Germain provided the commander in chief in the colonies, Gen. Sir Henry Clinton, with new instructions in March, a copy of which went to Sandwich:

> If therefore he should find it impracticable to bring General Washington to a general and decisive action early, it was recommended to him to relinquish the idea of carrying on offensive operations within land; and as soon as the season would permit embark what troops could be spared to cooperate with the King's ships in attacking the ports on the coast from New York to Nova Scotia, and to seize or destroy every ship and vessel and destroy all wharfs, stores, and materials for ship building, in every harbour or creek which it should be found practicable to penetrate.[41]

Though Clinton did not fully implement Germain's instructions, the fact that they were dispatched at all blatantly admitted that the Royal Navy could not maintain an effective blockade of the American coast in 1778. The Bourbon intervention shifted the emphasis of the Royal Navy away from the blockade to fleet actions. That emphasis did not return until mid-1782. By then, the Royal Navy featured copper bottoms (introduced in 1778), allowing them to stay on station longer, as well as the new carronades (lightweight, short-range cannon), requiring fewer gunners to use and thus smaller crews. Numerous British privateers joined forces with the Royal Navy, and the losses to the

American merchant marine and private navy quickly soared—too late, however, to accomplish anything, other than, perhaps, vengeance for the failure of the blockade of 1775–78.[42]

The British attempt to interdict its rebellious colonies differed tremendously from the three blockades which followed. At the onset, it faced rebels who lacked naval assets, making the initial mission of the British blockade strictly antishipping. Once the rebels built, acquired, or converted numerous naval vessels, the Royal Navy responded slowly, the layered, defensive orientation of the post-1793 blockades entering into its final stage of development. Coppering did not cover all the fleet's bottoms until 1782; thus the British Navy lacked the benefits of tripling and quadrupling the time between refits during most of the Revolutionary War. The introduction of the carronade, with its reduced weight and smaller crew requirements, allowed a tremendous increase in the number of shallow-draft warships commissioned after the 1780s.[43] These vessels would prove to be invaluable to later blockades. Perhaps most important, the Admiralty's eventual implementation of an improved diet substantially reduced the ravages of scurvy. Without that single change, the 140,000-man Navy deployed against Napoleon and James Madison could not have existed. Finally, as Daniel A. Baugh pointed out, North's government valued fiscal conservatism over early mobilization—a mistake that would not be repeated against revolutionary and Napoleonic France.

The history of the Royal Navy's blockades has been one of change only when ratcheted by maritime expansion, new technology, dire necessity, and the occasional exceptional personality. Perhaps it is more appropriate to view the stratagem as slowly maturing, along with the naval infrastructure and the nation's assets, until it reached the point at which the complete blockade of an opposing nation could be successfully realized. Which begs a question: How did Great Britain define a successful blockade? Chapter 2 searches for the answer in the blockade theory of 1793–1815.

2

The Blockade in Theory and Practice

By 1812, the Royal Navy had refined the concept of blockading, constant effort testing an unwritten theory even as it shaped a well-documented practice. In fact, some type of blockade had been almost constantly in use against the French since 1793. As with any endeavor involving thousands of men and hundreds of machines, the blockade exuded complexity, and both its theoretical underpinnings and practice sometimes seemed obscure, even to contemporaries.[1] This chapter attempts to simplify the complexity inherent to blockading theory and practice. At the same time, it summarizes two additional convoluted issues: the changing objectives of the British blockade of the United States and the chronology of the blockade's development.

Central to British strategy was the warship: acres of timber, miles of cordage, and tons of metal carrying a highly disciplined crew and always at the mercy of the elements. These vessels existed to protect a nation's assets and to extend national policy into the international arena (much as the concentration of American warships in the Indian Ocean and Red Sea during the Gulf War was an extension of the policies of the United States). All naval options stemmed from those premises—whether to build a potentially aggressive cruising fleet or a nonthreatening coastal defense force, whether to assume a strategic posture of attack or defense, whether to raid or to stage amphibious assaults, and among still other options, whether to blockade. Of all the choices which have been made regarding the use of warships, the last-named seems to have been more appreciated and less understood than any other form of naval activity.

Naval historians have obviously recognized that four British national blockades (those of France and the United States between 1793 and 1814, and the blockade of Germany during World War I), as well as the Union blockade of the Confederacy during the Civil War, contributed to victories. But few scholars have attempted to quantify the contribution of blockaders to victory, and none have subjected blockade theory and practice to rigorous analysis and comparative study. Without such analysis and comparison, the question of exactly what a blockade accomplished, much less how efficiently it operated, remains elusive. Similarly, historians have often sought to evaluate the blockades of 1793–1815 in terms of economic damage inflicted upon Britain's enemy of the moment, forgetting that the Royal Navy's primary role was the protection of British ships, goods, and soil. Proper study must begin with an attempt to define the concept of blockade and its practice during the late age of sail.

A strategic, or national, blockade can be implemented only when four prerequisites exist. Geographically, two nations must have coastlines supporting maritime commerce or naval forces or both. In terms of numbers, the blockader requires at least a slight superiority in operational naval assets and must possess the infrastructure to maintain forces for an extended period of time off an opponent's coastline. Finally, diplomacy having failed, politics must be taken to the sharp point. It is here, before the first warship sails for the enemy coast, that questions of international law should be considered since blockades always have international repercussions.

By 1793, a plethora of legalese dating to the fourteenth-century *Consolato del Mare* (an attempt to protect the rights of neutrals) constituted the core of international maritime law. Complementing these cases and rulings, certainly attempting to create legal templates for their generations, were volumes written by a number of jurists, statesmen, and public officials. The works of Hugo Grotius, dating to the first half of the seventeenth century, and Emmerich de Vattel, published in 1758, received the widest acknowledgment.[2] Grotius's *Commentary on the Law of Prize and Booty*, written in 1604 amid the struggle by the Dutch for maritime hegemony, defined international law as the "common consent" of nations. More important, it identified legitimate prizes of war and suggested the use of legal tribunals (the precursors of Admiralty Courts) to ensure the legitimacy of captured vessels and goods. Grotius also addressed the transport of materials by neutral vessels. Such shipping had the right of access to blockaded ports unless carrying contraband: war materials or enemy-owned property. Later, he added that sufficient warning of blockades had to be given to neutrals in time of war to allow for adjustments in cargoes and trade lanes.[3]

Grotius's theories, incorporated in 1646 into *The Law of War and Peace*, faced competition for the place of honor in international maritime law by 1793. Vattel's *Law of Nations or the Principles of Natural Law*, as with *The Law of War and Peace*, addressed the entirety of international relations. It differed from that earlier work in several instances. Clearly an Anglophile (at least politically), Vattel presented theories of international maritime law that embraced impressment (every soul born to a nation owed service as required), allowed the search of neutral vessels even on the high seas (refusing the search made the vessel a lawful prize), disallowed indemnities for illegally seized vessels or goods (although they had to be restored), and opined that the expanse of sea patrolled constituted territorial limits (as opposed to "cannon shot," or the three-mile—one nautical league—limit). Inherent to his arguments lay the concept of national survival as a quasi-Machiavellian justification for desperate actions in desperate times. In general, Vattel favored the stronger naval power, the power most capable of instituting a blockade. It should go without saying that Great Britain—the strongest naval power of its era—also favored Vattel.

England, of course, had learned to flex its national maritime muscles in the international arena long before Vattel's book saw publication. The Navigation Acts of the mid–seventeenth century both protected and developed the country's merchant marine, specifically at the expense of the Dutch, though other nations suffered proportionally. Later, the Rule of 1756 mandated that a neutral barred from trading at a port in time of peace could not trade there in time of war (in essence replacing the blockaded merchant shipping of the enemy).[4] Though targeted against French colonial possessions in particular, this law far exceeded the internationally understood and accepted scope of search and seizure of contraband by a belligerent. It actually constituted an attempt to control routing of neutral shipping—and Britain successfully enforced it through 1815. Grotius's "common consent" of nations had devolved into a most singular "consensus of force" embodied within the Royal Navy. The great blockades between 1793 and 1815, as well as related naval activities, observed the niceties of international law only until necessity dictated otherwise.[5]

The traditional (meaning British) strategic blockade of the late age of sail served multiple purposes. It protected the homeland from waterborne invasion by the enemy. It sought to confine both enemy naval vessels and privateers to harbor, thus protecting friendly commerce. It isolated enemy bases by interdicting the coasting trade, thus causing severe shortages of maritime stores (along with civilian transportation woes within the entire littoral). The blockaders also preyed upon enemy merchant shipping, sharply curtailing national imports and exports. At the same time, patrolling squadrons monitored neutral shipping, seizing vessels to prevent contraband from reaching the enemy. Blockading ships served as platforms for raids, from the destruction of enemy batteries to frequent "cutting-out" expeditions. Finally, by confining enemy squadrons to their harbors, the blockade allowed the capture of their unsuccored overseas possessions.

Protection, interdiction, and harassment collectively constitute a *military blockade,* not because such activities are more or less warlike but because the actions of the blockading squadrons are confined to the militants or to military goods. The more precise terminology is necessary to underscore the difference between *limited* or *tactical blockades,* the post-1803 *commercial* or *economic blockades* of the Napoleonic era, and military blockade itself.[6]

The Admiralty experimented with two forms of military blockade against France, the *distant blockade* and *close blockade.* In the distant blockade, the major elements of the Royal Navy waited in English ports while light units observed French harbors, rushing to call the main fleet to battle when the enemy sailed. This method avoided the constant wear and tear on vessels and crews frequently incurred while fighting violent Channel weather. Unfortunately, response time was often too slow to allow engagement of escaping French squadrons and individual raiders, while idle sailors in harbor threatened such trouble as that occurring at Spithead and the Nore in 1797.[7]

By the second segment of the war against France, beginning in 1803, the Admiralty had embraced the concept of close blockade exclusively. In simplest form, close blockade meant stationing and constantly maintaining British fleet elements within sight of the enemy's ports, so that interception of hostile vessels could occur before they escaped to the open sea. Where this *linear military blockade* confronted large concentrations of enemy naval vessels, it rapidly developed into an *echeloned military blockade* because of the dangers to an inshore fleet precipitated by inclement weather and currents.[8] The first element of this system consisted of light vessels operating as close as feasible to the mouth of the enemy harbor. Their mission was to gather intelligence, visually and from such sources as local fishermen, to intercept weaker forces attempting to enter or exit the harbor and to alert the next echelon of vessels, the inshore squadron, if major enemy fleet elements attempted a sortie. These vessels acted at greatest risk of loss if the weather deteriorated, coastal charts were incorrect, or the enemy staged a surprise sortie aimed at eliminating the watchers.[9] The inshore squadron patrolled within signaling distance of the first echelon. It supported the light vessels (nominally under the command of the inshore squadron) and was composed of warships capable of delaying an enemy squadron until the main British fleet could arrive. The inshore squadron often operated close to the French coast and had to retreat to sea or risk abrupt (and terminal) landfall when threatened with inclement weather. Finally, the main British fleet comprised the third echelon of the blockade, sailing safely out to sea, usually in direct communication with the inshore squadron and never far away. In the event of severe weather, the Admiralty or the admiral on station set a rendezvous for each blockading squadron so that reforming could be accomplished rapidly, leaving the French port unblockaded for as short a time as possible.

The Royal Navy applied this echeloned system of defense to major enemy naval bases, notably Brest, Toulon, and Cadiz. The linear military blockade served for secondary ports—such as Ostend, Calais, and Ferrol—which lacked concentrations of enemy naval strength. From 1812 to 1815, the Admiralty employed the latter form of blockade in its struggle against the United States, American naval strength being far too weak to justify an echeloned blockade.

The Admiralty never envisioned a perfect military blockade: between weather, accidents of command, and just plain bad luck some enemy vessels always avoided the interdicting warships. Because of this practical limitation, the blockade constituted only the first part of a three-tiered defensive system. The second level consisted of aggressive pursuit of escaped enemy squadrons and patrol of major shipping lanes. Blockading forces seldom pursued individual enemy naval vessels and privateers, relying on the patrols or the final segment of the system to handle them. That final segment was formed by strongly escorted convoys. Great Britain maintained a convoy system throughout the Napoleonic Wars, and intensified it considerably in 1812 when the Americans entered the struggle. By the end of the Anglo-American conflict in 1815, British ships could not be insured on any of the world's major sea-lanes unless sailing in convoy. Even then, the Admiralty realized that vessels would be lost and gambled that the gigantic British merchant marine would accept minor losses as a cost of doing business—not that merchants had a realistic option of doing otherwise.[10]

Though the military blockade was the most common blockade used by the British in the Napoleonic era, a second type rose to prominence after 1805. The *commercial blockade*, or *economic blockade*, as instituted by Great Britain, was an offensive ploy aimed at enhancing Britain's trade while disrupting the enemy's economy. A military blockade allowed neutral trade to continue through enemy ports as long as it did not transport contraband. A commercial blockade halted all neutral shipping into an opponent's harbors, ideally isolating the enemy's economy from the outside world, ending any chance of supplying its colonies using neutral shipping, and turning neutral trade to Britain's advantage. The ideal state often proved impossible to reach because of international land borders and, more important, because of Great Britain's own pressing economic needs. In 1810, for example, Napoleon actually sold grain to a famine-stricken England, while American vessels transported American grain and provisions to Wellington's army in Spain, the British possessions in the Caribbean, and the Canadian Maritime provinces through mid-1814. In both cases a licensing system allowed the Admiralty to track the process and, it hoped, prevent abuse.[11] Theoretically, a second benefit should have accrued from the implementation of a commercial blockade. Stoppage of all trade, with a timely warning to other governments, should have eliminated complaints of illegal search and seizure. Unfortunately, many neutrals, especially American merchant captains, seem to have viewed eluding the commercial blockade of France as a challenge—with large profits as their potential reward. And when taken lawful prize, they invariably cried to their government for help.[12]

The actual mechanics of blockading seem simple—sail back and forth off the port, watch for enemy naval activity, and seize all legal prey in sight. Consideration of logistics adds additional complexity to the situation. A ship could stay at sea for two to three months without needing to replenish food and water. Even with local watering and provisions shipped as deck cargo on returning vessels, that time at sea could be extended for an additional two to three months at best before general wear and tear, especially to spars and canvas, forced a return to port. The reality was that as much as a third of any blockading fleet would be in port or in transit to or from port at any given time.[13] In other words, a blockading fleet of twelve ships some four weeks' sail from their logistical base would have only eight vessels on station at any one time, and several of those would be operating at less than full efficiency.[14] This mattered less in the Channel, where home ports could be reached in a day or two of sailing but became a matter of grave concern in the Baltic, in the Mediterranean, and on the American coast.

Blockading was a thankless and tiring business. For weeks ships sailed back and forth over the same stretch of sea, boredom relieved only by bad weather and new ships joining the squadron as worn ships returned to port. Smaller vessels ranged closer to shore, seeking information about the enemy within their harbors or interdicting coastal trade. Somewhat relieving the boredom of the crews of these small warships was the knowledge that a shift in the wind threatened a lee shore, while a tiny slip of attention placed the vessels in range of French 32-pounders. Officers suffered almost as badly as the men; boredom, as well as watching hopes of quick promotion disappear, was debilitating. Sir Edward Codrington, on the Brest blockade shortly after Trafalgar, wrote to his brother, "It is not fighting, my dear William, which is the severest part of our life, it is having to contend with the sudden changes of seasons, the war of elements, the dangers of a lee shore, and so forth, which produce no food for honor or glory beyond the internal satisfaction of doing a duty we know to be most important, although passed by others unknown and unnoticed."[15]

Another consideration, and a critical one by 1812, was the impact of years of blockade duty on the efficiency of the Royal Navy. Seamanship remained excellent, as did the often unmentioned skill of damage control—making rapid repairs and providing jury-rigs in the wake of storm- (or, infrequently, battle-) induced damage.[16] Gunnery, however, suffered. Between the lack of targets and strict Admiralty control of gunpowder wastage, including virtually eliminating practice firing, fighting efficiency diminished. Also, ships on blockade, continually under the eye of admirals with their impact on promotion, tended toward "spit and polish," an effect ruined by even dry-firing guns. With the reduction of gunnery drill, potential disaster loomed on the horizon.[17]

Of course, the amount of tedium depended to some degree upon the blockader's opponent. In theory, a nation faced with blockade had several courses of action available: do nothing, attempt to break the blockade, institute *guerre de course,* apply countercoercion, and seek diplomatic avenues (immediate surrender, by the way, has apparently never been considered as an option). Though these choices are examined individually in the following paragraphs, historically nations usually tried a mix of actions against their blockading foe as the conflict developed.

A nation with a weak or nonexistent navy could adopt the "do nothing" strategy. Hiding its merchant marine in well-protected ports while using gunboats and artillery batteries to defend coasting traffic, it attempted to outwait the blockaders. Such a scenario became a test of the viability of the nation's economy without external commerce ranged against the expense incurred by the enemy in maintaining the blockade.

A nation with relatively strong naval forces could attempt to destroy or drive away the blockaders. In international legal theory, a successfully broken blockade of a given port could not be reestablished for a set length of time. Thus the vessels breaking the blockade could then sail to free the next port along the coast without having to detach vessels to defend the port recently freed. Unfortunately for legal theory, a blockade has never been broken—at least not in the eyes of the blockader.

A nation, whether from naval weakness or in an attempt to damage the enemy while maintaining a fleet-in-being, could initiate *guerre de course*—raiding enemy commerce with single ships or groups of vessels. Small, fast naval vessels have often served as raiders, though most numerous have been civilian ships operating under government charters. Slipping from harbor in the dark of night or under cover of bad weather, these privateers usually eluded blockaders and often exacted a heavy toll from the enemy's merchant marine despite aggressive patrols and convoys.

The economic coercion of the blockade could be met by countercoercion—an attempt to gain leverage against the enemy, forcing the lifting of the blockade indirectly. Three potentially viable methods existed to force the blockading nation's hand. First, the enemy nation could be invaded, though lack of a land route offered numerous challenges against an established blockade. Second, colonial holdings valuable to the enemy could be seized; again, this became problematic without an overland route. The exertion of military pressure against enemy allies offered a possible substitute for capture of colonial hold-ings. Finally, a strong enough coalition of nations could theoretically apply sufficient economic coercion to force a blockade against one or all of its members to be lifted.

When material responses failed to end a blockade, diplomatic measures remained—if talks, with or without a mediating nation, could be established. Diplomacy also featured in attempts to rally international support, quite often by drawing attention to violations of maritime law by the blockader (historically, a fruitless endeavor). The enemy, of course, also vigorously pursued such support, while its blockading forces sometimes violated perceived international laws, necessitating the diplomatic smoothing of ruffled neutral and allied feathers. The importance of diplomacy cannot be underestimated: the lifting of British national blockades was evenly divided between defeat of the enemy (France, 1814; Germany, 1919) and a negotiated peace (France, 1802; United States, 1815).

Clearly, the Admiralty understood the power of the blockade, hav-ing thoroughly tested it against the French before instituting it against the United States. It constituted the primary strategic tool in the North American theater of operations in 1812 and 1813. Success offered much, and blockade theory identifies several potential meas-ures of the degree of success attained by British efforts. Seven princi-ples (all familiar to contemporary naval officers) can be isolated for evaluation:

1. The military blockade, as part of a three-tiered defensive system, holds friendly merchant marine losses to enemy squadrons and *guerre de course* to an acceptable level. Methods of measure include comparative losses, varying insurance rates, economic dislocation, and public outrage.

2. The greater the duration of the military blockade, the less effective the enemy navy becomes as losses experienced by raiders, inability to gain the sea, and the debilitating effects of prolonged, forced stays in port weaken it. This is best measured by the number of enemy vessels at sea across the duration of the blockade and by the performance of those vessels when in action.

3. The ability of the enemy navy to interfere with the tactical options of the military blockade is impaired or eliminated. The ability of the blockading forces to conduct successful raids, and the impact of those raids on the enemy, measures degree of success.

4. The enemy's coasting trade is virtually eliminated or severely retarded by the military blockade. Measures include percentage of normal trade occurring, reduction of enemy tonnage, diversion of potential cargoes to land transport, and public outrage.

5. The enemy merchant marine is held in port or destroyed by the military blockade. Measures are percentage of normal exports, tonnage lost, varying insurance rates, and public outrage.

6. A successful commercial blockade stops unfavorable neutral trade with the enemy. Measures of success include the elimination of imports and exports carried in neutral hulls, as well as the establishment of trade favorable to the blockader.

7. Successful military and economic blockades assist in causing visible dislocation to an enemy's economic, political, and even social infrastructures. This will be readily apparent at the end of the conflict, and the degree of blockade efficiency can be roughly measured by the terms of the peace treaty and the length of time the enemy nation takes to recover from its maritime losses.

These principles will be used in the final chapter to evaluate the Royal Navy's performance against the United States. They also allow a comparative evaluation of the three blockades established between 1793 and 1815.[18]

The actual implementation of the blockade in the North American theater, a blockade that mutated its way across thirty-three months of combat, was rather complex. It seems appropriate to summarize two important chronologies at this point—both treated in greater detail in chapters 5, 6, and 7.

The first concerns British strategic objectives during the conflict. Initially, Great Britain, strained nearly to the limits by its war with France, sought to secure a quick peace based on the repeal of its objectionable orders in council. By December 1812, such a result appeared doubtful, while the early American frigate victories aroused a strong feeling of resentment in naval-oriented England. Thus 1813 found Great Britain ready to fight; but, forces still arrayed against France, it lacked the resources in North America to do so effectively. The major objective became the tightening of the blockade and an essentially defensive action in the Great Lakes theater—a holding action. By 1814, the British government, repeatedly stung on the Great Lakes and at sea, adopted a hard-line stance against the United States. The impending collapse of Napoleon's empire freed Wellington's veterans and Royal Navy vessels for service in North America. With those assets, British planners envisioned a successful drive into the United States from Canada via the Great Lakes, the seizure of New Orleans by land and fleet elements, and a strong blockade serving as a springboard for punishing raids along the Atlantic seaboard. The United States, isolated, disillusioned, and—perhaps most important—physically beaten on land and at sea, would then have been the recipient of a dictated peace favorable to Britain. Such a favorable peace could have taken several courses. Most likely, Great Britain would have levied a large indemnity for damages to its trade. Certainly it would have forced major concessions along the Canadian border, protecting the St. Lawrence River and, possibly, seeking military control of the Great Lakes. Fishing rights and the possession of islands along the Maine coast would have been an issue. Finally, the successful invasion of New Orleans could have provided sufficient leverage to force the return of the Louisiana Purchase to Spain, curtailing the threatening westward expansion of the United States.[19] Unfortunately for the British, things did not work as planned.

The second chronology establishes the evolution of the blockade. On paper, the military blockade went into force with the first shots of the war and lasted until the final notifications of the peace agreement reached the blockaders. In reality, the blockade developed throughout the war as the Admiralty slowly vectored warships to the theater. Even at the end of the war, the Royal Navy proved unable to patrol regularly long stretches of American coasts, and several ports, among them New Orleans and Wilmington, North Carolina, had not been permanently interdicted. Throughout the war, both the Admiralty and the local command structure considered the New York to Boston area to be the most important target of the military blockade. Those ports supported the large American frigates and the bulk of the smaller naval raiders, as well as being the leading commercial centers of the United States.

Great Britain also instituted a commercial blockade against the United States. Like the military blockade, it was introduced in a piecemeal fashion, though not entirely for the same reasons. The availability of warships certainly played a part in the process, but the somewhat special status of New England and Amelia Island, and the need for American grain to feed the British Army struggling in the Iberian Peninsula, contributed equally to the uneven implementation of the economic blockade. The first segment of the commercial blockade, that of the Delaware and Chesapeake Bays, was ordered on

27 November 1812 and was reported implemented on 21 February 1813. The Admiralty ordered the next expansion, extending the economic interdiction from Long Island through New Orleans, on 25 March 1813. The order had been received and distributed to the North American command by 26 May, but it remained a paper blockade (without warships backing it) along the coasts south of the Virginia Capes through most of the war. Adm. John Borlase Warren extended the commercial blockade to cover the northern approaches to Long Island Sound on 20 November 1813, effectively ending neutral trade to New York. The New England coast remained free of economic restriction until Vice Adm. Sir Alexander Cochrane placed it under commercial blockade on 25 April 1814. In other words, this new form of interdiction did not completely encompass American coasts until that last date, and even then the Royal Navy lacked the vessels to enforce it along stretches of the southern seaboard.

Experienced with blockade theory and practice, and understanding what constituted an efficient blockade, the Royal Navy answered the American call to war in 1812. But the effectiveness of blockades hinges upon far more than theory, its practical implementation, and desired goals. The next chapter examines the ships, men, and administrative organizations on both sides of the conflict.

3

Assessing Maritime Potential

The strength and reach of both naval forces and merchant marine comprise a nation's maritime power. The quality and quantity of vessels, officers, and seamen considered in concert with national strategy determine maritime potential. In this case, the aspects of maritime potential to be evaluated are those of Great Britain and the United States—respectively, the greatest maritime power and the largest neutral carrier of the Napoleonic era. The following pages provide an overview of the ships, the naval establishments, and the merchant marines of the belligerents.

The warships of 1812 were the most complex machines of their age, built literally of acres of timber, miles of hemp rope, tons of metal, and gallon upon gallon of tar. By that date, a system of rating ships by armament had been in use for many years, a European standard also embraced by the United States (table 3.1 lists ratings, number of guns and decks, and appropriate comments). All rated vessels were ship-rigged (three masts, square sails), while the rigs of unrated craft varied tremendously (for example, a ship-sloop had three masts with square sails, a brig-sloop of the same hull size had two masts with square sails, a schooner had two gaff-rigged masts and a fore-topsail, a cutter possessed one mast with topsail over fore-and-aft rig, and so forth).

TABLE 3.1. *The Rating System*

Rates	Number of Guns	Number of Decks	Comments
First	100+	3	Used as squadron/fleet flagships
Second	90–98	3	Used as squadron/fleet flagships
Third	64–80	2	Most common ship in the line of battle
Fourth	50–60	2	Being phased out by 1812
Fifth	30–44	1	
Sixth	20–30	1	Most numerous of rated ships by 1812
Unrated	0–20	1	Many specialized types

Source: Lavery, *Nelson's Navy,* 40.

Limitations in construction forced the placement of a ship's batteries along the sides of the vessel (thus the term *broadsides* for massed cannon fire) and dictated a line-ahead formation during battle, preventing one ship from blocking another's fire as well as maximizing the concentration of firepower against the enemy. To control ships during combat (as well as for administrative purposes), navies developed squadron and fleet organizations during the seventeenth and eighteenth centuries, though contemporaries exhibited great flexibility in their usage of the designations. A squadron consisted of two to as many as thirty vessels of varying types commanded by a commodore or junior admiral.[1] The small American Navy used the term *fleet* in a generic sense of the Navy in its entirety or simply as a large grouping of vessels. British fleets were geographically based administrative units (the Channel Fleet, the Mediterranean Fleet) usually commanded by senior admirals. The number of vessels in a fleet varied tremendously (from ten to over eighty ships), depending upon the responsibilities and level of activity in the area of operations. Quiet sectors of the watery world did not rate fleets; rather, independent squadrons formed the upper command echelon (Jamaica Squadron, North America Squadron). These squadrons often controlled as many ships as a small fleet.

The most renowned ships of the era, the first through third rates, were those capable of standing in the line of battle. By 1812, the most common of these ships were the two-deck, seventy-four-gun ship-of-the-line; anything smaller simply could not survive the fire massed against it, anything larger was tremendously expensive to build and maintain. Designed specifically for the line of battle, these ships also formed the hard core of blockading squadrons, exhibiting certain strengths and weaknesses in that role. They discouraged enemy battle squadrons—unless in overwhelming strength—from attempting to force the blockade. Their massive firepower and strong construction allowed them to challenge, and often neutralize (at least temporarily), enemy shore batteries and fortifications. The large crews of the first through third rates, over six hundred men and officers on the smallest ships, meant that vast raiding forces could be put ashore or engaged in cutting-out expeditions. On the other hand, large crews consumed immense quantities of food, alcohol, and water, limiting the vessels' time on blockade without replenishment. The constant worry of British officers from first lieutenant to most senior admiral, however, was maintaining crew size in the face of continuous attrition. Squadrons on blockade lacked the luxury of impressing from passing British merchantmen or drawing from the established impressment apparatus ashore. Blockaders, therefore, like most ships of the Royal Navy, remained woefully undermanned throughout the War of 1812, especially when operating from foreign stations. These ships also exhibited two mechanical weaknesses relating directly to their large size. First, a deep draft prevented them from operating in shallow water; thus shallow-draft enemy coasting craft capable of maneuvering close inshore often escaped their depredations. Second, the length of the vessels and the amount of weight carried caused hogging—the sagging of the ends of the vessel below the plane of the keel—usually developing under the stress of heavy seas. Though all wooden vessels hogged to some degree, the severe failures associated with the larger ships sometimes broke the keel and often opened the seams between the planks to such a degree that the ship became unseaworthy. The constant battling of harsh weather on the blockade aggravated this condition.

If not the most renowned of vessels, the fifth- and sixth-rate frigates were certainly the most beloved by officers and public alike. They constituted the "eyes" of the various fleets and squadrons, leading those forces to the enemy. Frigates served on blockades, usually the vessels nearest to the enemy and often approaching harbors closely enough to count the opposition's masts and determine their state of readiness. Often frigates blockaded secondary ports alone or in concert with other frigates and unrated vessels. They also patrolled the enemy coast between interdicted ports and performed sweeps against escaped enemy raiders. Finally, frigates served as convoy escorts throughout the conflicts of 1793–1815.

For every squadron or fleet engagement of the era, British frigates fought over fifteen single-ship actions, seldom losing to the enemy.

Frigates specialized in the surprise cutting-out expedition and destruction of batteries by shore parties, especially in the later years of the wars against France when few enemy ships even attempted to sail from their defended anchorages. Their captains' dispatches, eagerly reprinted by British papers and journals, lifted civilian spirits, while victory after victory surrounded the frigates with an aura of invincibility in public and naval minds alike.[2]

Across the Atlantic, frigates constituted the largest vessels at the disposal of the U.S. Navy. The heavy frigates *Constitution, President,* and *United States*—hulls built as strongly as those of third rates and mounting a nominal forty-four guns—outmatched any fifth rates then afloat in durability, sailing quality, and weight of metal (the weight of shot fired from one broadside).[3] Their successes in ship-to-ship actions during the War of 1812 gained prominence in public eyes far beyond their designated mission as instruments of *guerre de course.* Those same successes came as a shock to the citizens of Great Britain. Two frigates lost and one taken as prize in the early months of the war shattered their Royal Navy's aura of invincibility.

As with the larger ships, frigates possessed strengths and weaknesses when on blockade. Good speed, reasonable firepower, and the ability to approach most shores closely made fifth and sixth rates ideal platforms for patrolling, raiding, or pursuing merchantmen; but that very flexibility tended to place them in harm's way. Often operating close inshore, frigates constantly faced the threat of a sortie by ships-of-the-line—a superior force from which they could only run or surrender. Their draft, though lighter than that of the first through third rates, still precluded closing the shallower areas where coasters maneuvered. The heavier British frigates were among the most livable (a relative term in wooden navies) of vessels, with the best living space–to–tonnage ratio of any ships in the Royal Navy. Crew size contributed more to this than design specifications, and size mattered little against the numerous but poor-quality crews of other European nations. Against American frigates with good-quality crews as large as those found on old British fourth rates, the difference eventually told another story.

Lacking both love and renown, the plethora of unrated vessels in the Royal Navy outnumbered its frigates by 1812 (table 3.2 contains the quantity of vessels per rate). Types included both combat and fleet support vessels as well as the tenders inevitably acquired by all squadrons on distant stations (usually prizes purchased on the spot and crewed from the squadron's ships). The lightly armed, swift, and

TABLE 3.2. *Comparative Strengths of the Belligerent Navies, July 1812*

Vessels by Rate	Number in USN (All Locations)	Number in RN (Americas)	Number in RN (All Other Locations)
First	0	0	7
Second	0	0	6
Third	0	3	94
Fourth	0	1	3
Fifth	7	15	119
Sixth	1	8	36
Unrated	8	71	290
TOTAL	16	98	555

Sources: Clowes, *Royal Navy* 6:25, provided the American list, with gunboats and unready hulls removed; Ships in Sea Pay, Admiralty Office, 1 July 1812, UkLPR, D, Adm. 8, Public Records Office, London, contained the data for the British forces. (All unarmed hulls, guardships, and vessels in ordinary have been removed.)
Note: British North American stations are Halifax, Newfoundland, Jamaica, and the Leeward Islands (Antigua).

shallow-draft tenders served as messengers, as inshore patrollers, and to extend the line of blockade. Support vessels included supply ships and troop transports, both armed. Bomb-ketches, mounting one or two mortars and specifically designed to reduce enemy fortifications, fell somewhere between the two categories. Combat vessels constituted a varied lot, the most common being sloops (ship- and brig-rigged), brigs, and cutters. Cutters generally served as messengers for the fleet, while the remainder often substituted for unavailable frigates, especially as convoy escorts and patrollers. These shallow-draft vessels proved invaluable on the blockade. They could go anywhere coasting traffic operated, investigating the shallow bays and river mouths denied to frigates, and were ideal for controlling the stretches of coast between major ports as well as for monitoring secondary harbors. As with frigates, no squadron commander had enough of the smaller vessels. Unrated vessels formed half of the initial U.S. Navy, and all completed construction or purchases during the war were of that class.

Unrated vessels also formed the bulk of American losses during the war, as they did for the British. The obvious strengths of these armed cockleshells—quick to build, small crews, shallow draft, mission flexibility—were offset by the fact that they were fragile and susceptible to defeat by even slightly superior warships. The fact that inexperienced officers, the exact officers most likely not to turn away from an engagement against a superior vessel as fame and promotion teetered in the balance, commanded these weakly timbered craft compounded the problem. Whether inexperience or size caused the large number of weather-related losses to British unrated vessels during the War of 1812 cannot be accurately determined.[4]

One final category of vessel used by the Royal Navy, though not included in the naval list, deserves at least a passing mention. Between 1793 and 1815, the Crown hired numerous merchant ships to serve as transports or as escorts for convoys. Variously referred to—depending upon their exact role—as hired merchantmen, hired ships, armed transports, or hired armed vessels, they moved British troops and supplies as well as freed valuable frigates for service on the blockades of France and the United States.[5]

Though the ships of 1812 held many similarities regardless of ownership, the owners differed tremendously. The relatively young U.S. Navy may have been short on traditions and often seemed short on government support, but it held some important advantages. Even the Navy's small size was a blessing of sorts, allowing all major units to be manned and commanded by experienced professionals upon the outbreak of war. The officer cadre had gained tremendous experience during the Quasi-War, campaigns against the Barbary pirates and piracy in home waters, antismuggling efforts under Jefferson's Restrictive Acts, and skirmishes against the British during the years leading to 1812. The Navy enlisted only volunteer crews, providing a level of seamanship, if not military discipline, unapproachable by newly fitted out British vessels and sometimes superior to British vessels long on station. Men and officers received good wages, supplemented by prize money during times of conflict, though promotion for officers was exceedingly slow during peace—not necessarily a negative in this case, as it provided a strong pool of junior leadership material to draw upon as the Navy expanded. The overall command structure for the Navy was compact, consisting of the president of the United States, who operated through the secretary of the navy, and a tiny support staff, while Congress carefully controlled the purse strings.

Each major port had naval facilities capable of at least restocking perishables and conducting minimal repairs, though all stations found themselves strained by the declaration of war (table 3.3 lists the yards—capable of building and repairing naval vessels—and stations of the U.S. Navy during the War of 1812).[6]

That a state of unreadiness should have existed within the navy of the nation that declared war may seem somewhat strange. As Leonard F. Guttridge and Jay D. Smith wrote, "There is an element of unreality

TABLE 3.3. *Yards and Stations of the U.S. Navy,*
Atlantic and Gulf Coasts

Location	Status
Portsmouth, N.H.	Yard
Charlestown (Boston)	Yard
New London, Conn.	Station
New York	Yard
Philadelphia	Yard
Washington, D.C.	Yard
Gosport (Norfolk, Va.)	Yard
Wilmington, N.C.	Station
Charleston, S.C.	Station
St. Marys, Ga.	Station
New Orleans	Station

Source: Dudley, *Naval War of 1812,* vol. 1.

about the refusal of James Madison's administration and the Eleventh Congress, while contemplating war against the greatest naval power, to bring the American Navy up to a confidant fighting strength."[7] The words of other historians—Theodore Roosevelt, Alfred T. Mahan, William M. Fowler Jr., and Harold and Margaret Sprout among them— have been less kind. In actuality, not upgrading the Navy made excellent sense to both president and legislature for four reasons: cost, enemy naval strength, operational objectives, and projected time line. The first two reasons held center place in a long-running political clash.

The navalist versus antinavalist debate that had raged within Congress since the early 1790s determined the form and function of the Navy in 1812. Navalists supported a large fleet with vessels capable of standing in a line of battle, securing proper recognition of the national flag, and protecting American mercantile interests abroad. Though handicapped by the expense of such an ambitious building program, it appeared that under the last Federalist president, John Adams, navalists had triumphed. In 1800, however, the election of Thomas Jefferson and his subsequent concentration on budget reductions allowed antinavalists to end the planned building of a battle fleet. Most antinavalists, including Jefferson, did not support complete abolition of maritime resources; rather, they felt that the fleet should be tied directly to defense of American waters.[8] Ideally, a small fleet not only cost less to operate and maintain, it avoided embroiling the United States in European wars while still envisioned by antinavalists as adequate to defend the nation's coasts. Antinavalists felt their position justified when, in April 1801, a British fleet entered the strongly fortified harbor of Copenhagen, capturing or destroying most of the (nominally neutral) Danish fleet. Seized by the imagery, they claimed with unabashed certainty that if the large Danish fleet could be disposed of so easily in a strong harbor, then any tiny American battle squadron built should just be signed over to the British to avoid damage to American ports. The engagement off Cape Trafalgar in 1805 appeared to provide the final nail in the navalist coffin: Nelson's victory affirmed a seemingly unchallengeable British naval dominance. The Copenhagen mentality had one final impact on the course of the war. The Republican government in Washington, as well as some naval officers, believed that American warships should be retained in port and sally in "penny-packets" instead of as a combined squadron, preventing their wholesale destruction while at anchor or at sea.[9] The limitations of such thinking will become apparent in discussion of the opening months of the war.

With a blue-water strategy abandoned, the small Navy became a component in a coastal defense plan centered upon flotillas of gunboats (small vessels usually mounting one large pivot gun and two to four smaller cannon)—or perhaps "should have become a component," as no one seems to have bothered to devise an operational plan meshing the rated naval vessels into a coherent coastal defense scheme before the war. Some 165 gunboats, out of over 200 contracts let since 1801, supplemented the larger naval vessels. Flotillas, often with many vessels still in ordinary, deployed at Portsmouth, Boston, Newport, New London, New York, Philadelphia, Baltimore, Norfolk, Wilmington, Charleston, St. Marys, and New Orleans.[10]

When checked in their storage sheds on the eve of the war, most of these vessels proved unusable because of neglect and rot (only sixty-two hulls could be floated at the declaration of war). The best of these suffered from top-heaviness, making them unseaworthy in all but moderate weather; nonetheless, they often performed well when properly deployed.

Fortresses, gun emplacements, mobile batteries, and floating batteries, all to be manned by militia, formed the final echelon of Thomas Jefferson's scheme for the defense of the American coast. Many of these had not been completed by 1812, and those that had been finished suffered from various states of disrepair and inadequate garrisons.[11] Most politicians seem to have viewed the Navy on the eve of war as, at best, one component in a coastal defense strategy. Since 1801, they had assumed its probable destruction if committed against the Royal Navy and its potential destruction even sitting in port. Thus Madison's government opted to quest for leverage against Great Britain's abuses upon the high seas in the fertile valleys of Canada rather than upon the Atlantic Ocean.

Why Canada? Most important, it formed the only practical objective for an American offensive against Great Britain. Its seizure would have offered a diplomatic bargaining chip other than the (failed) economic pressure of past years. Militarily, the waters of the Great Lakes, necessary for transport and logistics, thrust into the heart of Upper Canada; and from that base, once captured, a campaign downstream along the St. Lawrence River, a logistical route into Lower Canada, would finish the business. Also, the American Army expected to have the weight of numbers on its side, and the Royal Navy could do little about an inland war (that changed, of course, as the Great Lakes quickly emerged as an arena of intensive combat between American and British naval forces). The entire campaign should have lasted at most a few months, more likely a few weeks—a very short war.

Madison appears to have clung to the concept of exchanging a conquered Canada for British redress of the wrongs specified in his War Message. To have publicly stated differently, however, would have turned the spirit of the war from one of defense of American rights to one of territorial aggrandizement against a beleaguered Great Britain— contrary to the moral self-perception of the young Republic, and certainly objectionable to many of its inhabitants. Taking up arms for freedom was one thing, fighting for land when more than enough still lay untouched was something else entirely.[12] Nonetheless, five very good reasons existed for permanently annexing Canada to the United States: boundary problems would be eliminated, the British could no longer incite the northern Indian tribes, fishing rights would be secured, control of all North American lumber and masts would limit British shipbuilding while enhancing that of the United States, and those valleys were indeed fertile when compared to the "miasmic" plains apparently limiting American westward expansion.[13]

America's small regular Army and numerous militia (the Eleventh Congress voted for increased military, but not naval, appropriations in preparing for potential war in 1811) would have quickly conquered Canada, precluding a need or the lead-time required to expand the Navy. There was no "unreality" to the Republican administration's prewar decisions regarding the Navy, nor should those decisions be condemned with ease. Contemporary logic, founded in solid observation, led to a conscious decision to relegate the U.S. Navy to the sidelines, and relative safety, during what was anticipated to be a short war.

The Royal Navy, with traditions stretching across centuries, stood as Britain's bulwark during war. Because of the tremendous size of the fleet as well as recruiting, promotion criteria, and the demands of nearly twenty continuous years of conflict, the quality of ships, officers, and crews varied tremendously by 1812 (table 3.3 lists ship availability numbers and relevant locations at the onset of war).

The Royal Navy officer corps depended on a mix of merit and patronage (also termed *interest*) for promotion. To become a lieutenant required testing by a board of captains after several years of service, and was open to a very select group of warrant officers of sufficient rank as well as midshipmen. The efficiency of the testing varied, depending on name and patronage, so poorly prepared officers sometimes reached the rank of lieutenant. The next step, commander, relied on success in battle or "interest." The jump to post captain, from which promotion to admiral became a question of merely surviving those more senior on the list, depended exclusively on the Admiralty, though commanders of distant stations could temporarily promote officers to captain to fill vacancies. At this stage of an officer's career, success in battle often mattered less than powerful friends in high places.[14]

This system promoted men with greatly differing characters and abilities to the ranks of captain and admiral, and a highly variable performance resulted when these men operated independently. In Dean King and John Hattendorf's *Every Man Will Do His Duty: An Anthology of Firsthand Accounts from the Age of Nelson*, seaman William Richardson, writing of his time on board the frigate *Minerva*, described serving under an officer who "in the course of three or four years had got made a post captain when only nineteen years of age; he could work the ship very well, and that was all." The constant floggings substituted by the young captain for poorly developed leadership skills almost drove the men to mutiny. Other accounts, however, do speak well of their ships, mates, and officers.[15]

The life of the crew on board a British man-of-war varied from harsh to hellish, depending upon the vessel's officers. With the best-intentioned officers, possessed of an interest in their crew's welfare, life was simply harsh: a harshness dictated by the danger inherent to all ships at sea, the constantly deteriorating food supplies, the threat of any number of vitamin-deficiency diseases on long voyages, the monotony of cruising with little hope of action, and the knowledge that there could be no escape from their lot until the war came to an end. If, however, the captain or first lieutenant was a "flogee," life became hell at sea as punishments striped the backs of even the best of the crew for any real or imagined infraction. Most ship's companies fell between those two extremes.

N. A. M. Rodger, writing of the Royal Navy in the years immediately preceding the French revolutionary struggle, paints a much gentler picture of the lot of the common sailor in the Georgian Navy. He found their lifestyle to be equal or superior to that of most of Great Britain's commoners, almost, at times, to the exaggerated level of the typical naval recruiting broadside of the era: food aplenty, grog aflowing, music and dancing nightly, and all the prize money you can carry! As with those broadsides, Rodger seems to have overstated his case, perhaps because of his small sample size. Regardless, his views are too positive for the constantly expanding Royal Navy of 1793 through 1812, tempered as it was by the continuous pressure of almost two decades of Anglo-French conflict. The firsthand accounts presented by King and Hattendorf offer another picture—one of hardship, danger, and frustration occasionally leavened by the joy of victory or the simple pleasures of a sailor's life.[16]

By 1812, captains obtained an estimated 75 percent of their crewmen through impressment, while established crews often transferred from vessel to vessel over the course of years without setting foot on land or seeing loved ones ashore.[17] In any vessel, the resentment of the newly impressed mingled with the experience of the older hands, until eventually they merged into a ship's company united by their common bonds: the danger of life at sea, the repetitive formulas of day-to-day existence in a British man-of-war, the strict discipline of the Articles of War, and the daily rum ration.[18] All these factors taken together seem to indicate that Jack Tar was sometimes a less-than-content man, thus the infrequent mutiny and the more commonplace desertion.

Lord Wellington reputedly remarked to the captain of a British sloop-of-war, "Everything goes like clockwork; but, sir, I would not command an army on the same terms you do your ship, for the Crown of England. I have not seen a smile on the face of any individual since

I have been on board her."[19] And Wellington himself was no slouch as a disciplinarian! Perhaps the proper way to understand this statement is as a comparison of the strict discipline required to keep a crowded ship afloat and the looser state of discipline needed for a force with solid earth beneath its shoes. As for "smiles," Wellington's presence may have been intimidating to both crew and officers, to say the least.

Regardless of the level of discontent among British crews, mutinies were infrequent. The Nore and Spithead fit the mold of those unusual actions of collective indiscipline common to most wars, while, in 1797, the crew of the *Hermione* mutinied because of their captain's cruelty (the usual reason, historically, for mutinies in the Royal Navy).[20] Desertion, on the other hand, was typically an individual rather than a collective action, and thus occurred more frequently, plaguing the Royal Navy throughout the war. Initial high levels of desertion not only prompted the Admiralty to order shore leave suspended but also led directly to the decision to transfer crews between ships without allowing them ashore. Historian Daniel Baugh observed that individual captains protested this policy (in vain) as detrimental to morale.[21] Desertion would plague British operations along the North American coast and especially in the Chesapeake Bay.

Yet all these factors taken together fail to address some very important issues. If British tars were war-weary by 1812, they had reason. The Royal Navy had driven the fleets of France and its allies from the sea, while substantially reducing their furtive *guerre de course*. Thousands of merchantmen and warships had been destroyed or now sailed under British colors. Every colonial possession of France now supported the British war effort, having been seized directly by the officers and sailors of the Royal Navy or by the British soldiers whom they safely transported and landed. Hundreds of British naval vessels blockaded the length and breadth of the French European hegemony, while others escorted convoys across routes ranging from the Indian Ocean to the Baltic Sea to the Atlantic basin. Still others supplied the British Army directly confronting major French forces in Spain. The British sailor, whether volunteer or swept up by the unfeeling press, may have been tired of war, but experience had made him very, very good at his trade. Though he may have been willing to run if given the opportunity, there should be no doubt that collectively the seamen of the Royal Navy would fight for England, for their ship, and with great skill against the United States.

And there was the Royal Navy's incentive program. Like his officers, Jack loved prize money. By 1812, little enough existed as most enemy shipping had been driven from the seas. An American war offered to change that, returning the Navy to the days when riches appeared to officers and admirals in an instant, while some sailors secured enough to build a cozy tavern to support their old age.[22] Unfortunately, conflicts between the requirements of duty and the desire for prize money would develop during the blockade of 1812–15.

The orders defining that "duty" originated in the nerve center of the Royal Navy at Whitehall, home of the British Admiralty. A complex interweaving of king, prime minister, Parliament, Cabinet, and the Admiralty Board under the first lord of the Admiralty, the Whitehall hierarchy not only monitored almost two dozen diverse boards and functions but also handled thousands of decisions each month.[23] Those decisions ranged from strategic directives to the selection of officers for individual vessels. Thus the Admiralty held the responsibility for preparing for a potential war against the United States, for determining the proper strategy to follow once war began, and for allocating the ships and men to the theater as appropriate to secure its strategic goals. Obviously, it would play a major role in the efficiency of the blockade of the United States.

The belligerents' public navies did not struggle alone, though they often gave the appearance of not wanting their helpmates around. Both Great Britain and the United States commissioned privateers during the war, a very large private navy in the case of Mr. Madison. These navies consisted of privately owned and armed vessels operating under a government-issued "Letter of Marque and Reprisal" that legalized what would otherwise be termed piracy—the technical difference that of being tried and hanged as a pirate or incarcerated as a prisoner of war if captured.

In the United States, two types of privateers developed: the true privateers who preyed exclusively on enemy craft, and the letter of marque traders who moved cargo through the blockade, but were more than willing to take a weak or unprepared ship as prize. As could be expected from a privately equipped navy, vessels varied from one-gun pilot boats to converted merchantmen to custom-built ships equivalent to the smaller naval frigates, though the schooner (especially the Baltimore-built schooner) won the greatest accolades as a raider from Americans and British alike.

Regardless of origin, ship, or performance, privateers faced a certain amount of disdain from the public navies. In both countries, naval officers resented the competition for that scarcest of commodities, veteran seamen. The lure of easy money under easy discipline (no matter how false the advertisement) held an appeal to many seamen unequaled by calls to a patriotism which too often disguised a harsh lash. Two additional factors contributed to the detestation of privateers by officers of the Royal Navy. Privateers possessed no concept (or perhaps shackles) of duty—unfettered by any mission, they could pursue and take prizes that "rightfully" belonged to (better yet, in the purses of) dutiful navy officers. Just as important, the defeat of an enemy privateer, even if superior to the victorious vessel, seldom brought the recognition or promotion that accompanied victory over an enemy naval vessel. Yet duty dictated that the Royal Navy seek out and destroy these nuisances, while British privateers feasted on fat American merchantmen.[24] As the narrative of the blockade unfolds, the critical role of the American private navy and the equally important attitude of the Royal Navy will be revealed as integral to the efficiency of the blockade.

The first impact of any blockade fell upon merchant shipping. On the eve of war, Great Britain mustered 2,263,000 tons of shipping, or 20,637 vessels, of which an estimated 7,500 to as many as 9,000 engaged annually in distant trade. Numerous coasters and local traders comprised the remainder of the registry, while a large fishing industry increased the size of Britain's maritime fleet to around 2.5 million tons.[25] As much as 10 percent of the merchant fleet directly supported the Royal Navy, which thus became a stimulus to the fleet's growth.[26] Trade in the opening decade of the 1800s had waxed to such an extent that numerous port improvement projects were undertaken, such as the West Indies Docks on the Isle of Dogs (London) completed in 1802 and capable of handling 600 ships of 300 to 500 tons burthen per month. This increase, driven since 1793 by the tempo of war, had been at the expense not only of France and its allies but also of the neutrals caught between British orders in council and Napoleon's Continental System. The United States stood first among those neutrals, and hundreds of formerly American hulls now sailed for British merchants to ports far less frequented by Yankee traders.[27]

As opposed to the growing British merchant marine, the world's second largest merchant fleet, that of the United States, had exhibited tremendous variation in capacity since 1793 in response to the conflict in Europe. Its registries reflected almost 1.2 million tons of nonfisheries shipping on the eve of war. An examination of paid duties reveals that over 66 percent of American tonnage traveled to foreign markets in 1811, perhaps twenty-five hundred of the estimated eleven thousand vessels in service. The remainder of the tonnage constituted a large coasting trade, primarily along the Atlantic shore.[28]

Driven by the lucrative shipping needs of a war-torn Europe, the American merchant marine became the world's largest neutral carrier in the last years of the eighteenth century. Maritime profit depended in equal measure upon the vagaries of war and the policies enforced by Britain's Royal Navy. From 1806 to early 1812, American merchants suffered under a trying series of embargoes and nonimportation acts, all instituted by Thomas Jefferson, James Madison, and their supporters in Congress in attempts to force the British government to change its economic policies without recourse to war. The most damaging of these self-inflicted economic wounds was Jefferson's embargo of 1808–9. American exports had stood at $108 million in 1807 and dropped to only $22 million in 1808. The outcry against the embargo, especially from the merchants of New England, actually threatened disunion rather than endure such economic suicide.[29] When in April 1812 Madison issued a second order for embargo, he understood the potential political and economic price tags attached if the merchant marine of his nation remained too long confined to port. Similarly, the people of the United States knew that this very serious step was more than another attempt to apply economic coercion against Great Britain—it was meant to safeguard the merchant vessels of the United States during the soon-to-be-declared war.[30]

As the protection of friendly commerce and the interdiction of enemy commerce are central to blockade theory, the measurement of effectiveness in those areas is critical to evaluating overall blockade efficiency. Ship captures and disruption of trade form the key indicators, as reflected in prize lists and government records. Fluctuations in insurance rates are also a prime measurement of blockade effectiveness, with rates invariably increasing in areas threatened by enemy action. Lloyd's of London determined the premiums for British international and coasting trade, while various insurance companies operated in major American ports.[31] Whether directed at the stoppage of trade by blockade or its harassment by *guerre de course*, the outrage of merchants, as expressed to their respective governments, can also be examined. Finally, the ability of the blockaded merchant marine to resume activity at the end of the war should reflect the effectiveness of the blockade.

The United States' declaration of war failed to surprise the officers of the Royal Navy. They found it reason to cheer. America not only offered the second largest merchant marine in the world on a golden platter, but protected it with a tiny fleet that, perhaps, would fight well enough to provide glory and promotion for some. Britain's unde-featable Royal Navy would triumph—because it always triumphed. A British journal, the *Statesman,* posted only one week after the announcement of the war in England, offered a different, and as it developed a far more realistic, opinion: "The Americans will be found to be a different sort of enemy by sea than the French. They possess nautical knowledge, with equal enterprise to ourselves. They will be found attempting deeds which a Frenchman would never think of; and they will have all the ports of our enemy open, in which they can make good their retreat with their booty."[32]

The war against the United States would, indeed, prove different from the struggle against France. Britain's vast superiority in men-of-war mattered little if sufficient numbers could not be concentrated against the United States, while the impressive ships-of-the-line could not capture what they lacked the speed or draft to catch. Too often long at sea and undermanned, British ships faced American vessels carrying numerous and fresh crews, thus surrendering an edge in bat-tle. The attitude of British officers both reduced potential assistance from the privateers crewed by their countrymen and created a damag-ing disdain for the effectiveness of American privateers. Most impor-tant, the Royal Navy had to protect Britain's sprawling merchant marine.

In the U.S. Navy, experienced officers and crews fully manned its vessels. The fighting ability of the American heavy frigates provided a shock value which placed the Royal Navy in a reactive mode. The tiny U.S. Navy did not fight alone—a tremendous private navy also preyed upon the vulnerable British merchant marine. Finally, the Americans often operated in home waters, though to the far-ranging mariners of the United States, most waters apparently felt like home. Those waters, particularly their intersection with land, are the subject of chapter 4.

4

The Geography of the Blockade

For almost three years the conflict between the United States and Great Britain stretched across the world's sea-lanes. The blockade, however, existed only off the coast of the United States. The length, varying terrain, and climates of that coast offered a tremendous challenge to the Admiralty and its chosen commanders.

In June 1812, the United States possessed slightly over nineteen hundred miles of coastline bordering the Atlantic and the Gulf of Mexico (map 4.1). This extensive interface is best examined in four geographic theaters: northern, mid-Atlantic, southern, and Gulf. The northern theater (map 4.2) extended from the Canadian border to mid–New Jersey. The coastline ranged from dangerous rocks and shoals interspersed with small sand beaches to superb deep-water ports and anchorages—Portland, Portsmouth, Newburyport, Boston, Newport, Stonington, New London, and New York. Both Boston and New York had developed into major entrepots for the nation. Many small villages and towns served as outports or provided lesser docking facilities for local fishermen (and smugglers). The deep-water ports were not, however, always approachable without problems. A series of underwater sandbanks, virtually continuous, paralleled the length of the northern shores from New York to Labrador and eventually joined the Grand

Banks. Though not always immediate navigation hazards, the banks created strong local currents paralleling the shore. At some points, such as Cashoes Ledge, the sandbanks actually rose to within six feet of the surface, while Sandy Hook and the East Bank constricted the southern entrance to Long Island Sound. That passage allowed the transit of deep-laden vessels during only one hour of high tide. Depth, of course, varied almost minute by minute at any bar—thus the need for experienced local pilotage in approaching most ports.[1]

Climate proved a major concern for British officers in the northern theater. The prevailing westerlies made blockade station keeping difficult in stormy weather and favored escaping vessels, while the notorious "nor'easters" threatened a lee shore during the long winter season, from November to March. The cold itself was a bitter enemy to the crew and tended to freeze furled sails and rigging, hampering the response to any blockade runner. Temperature inversions produced day-long fogs, at their worst from April to June. Lt. Henry Edward Napier, on blockade off Boston during 1814 in HMS *Nymphe*, cast additional light on weather severity:

> In most climates we may expect fine weather after thunderstorms, but on this coast an almost constant fog, still and damp, reigns paramount throughout the months of April, May and June, with longer intervals of fine weather, as it approaches July, when its visits become less frequent and its continuance shorter. The only interruption to this detestable weather is storms and hard rain with now and then a gleam of sunshine, which seldom continues more than a few hours. I have been assured by several people that they have known these fogs to last three weeks, without the slightest intermission.[2]

The mid-Atlantic theater (map 4.2) stretched from southern New Jersey to the Virginia–North Carolina border. As a vessel traveled south, the shores of the area quickly switched from shingle to sand. As with the northern theater, sandbars existed close to shore, often blocking even shallow-draft vessels from crossing them at low tide. The critical aspect of this region was the presence of two major bays, the Delaware and the Chesapeake (maps 6.1 and 6.2 in chapter 6 address the Chesapeake, setting for two intensive British campaigns, in greater detail). Philadelphia, Pennsylvania's largest city and a deep-water port, stood on the banks of the Delaware River, which emptied into the bay of the same name. Baltimore, near the head of the Chesapeake Bay, was

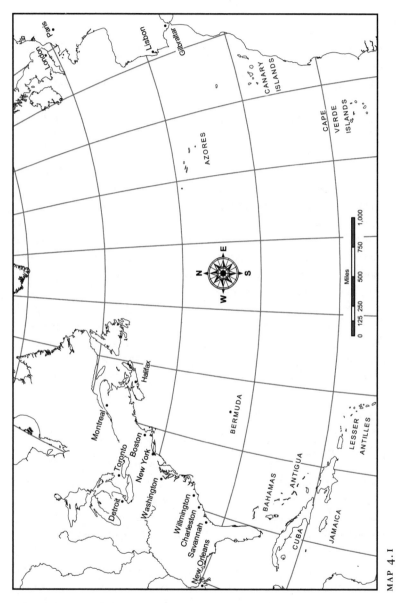

MAP 4.1
The Atlantic basin.

capable of serving deep-draft vessels and had assumed an importance for merchant shipping almost as great as that of New York and Boston. The closest export point for much of the United States' "bread basket" agricultural region, it shared the bay's shipping with the smaller ports of Norfolk (marginally deep water) and Portsmouth as well as numerous fishing villages and small towns along the bays. Several rivers and creeks of varying navigability entered both bays, their heads of navigation (for floats and rowed vessels) extending several miles inland. These waterways served as the region's highways, supporting large plantations, small agricultural homesteads, and fishing villages. They also made ideal access points for smugglers and final refuges for vessels endangered by nature or war.

Weather was less of a concern along this stretch of coast due to the ready shelter offered by the bays. Winters still presented extreme hazards due to ferocious onshore winds and freezing temperatures, but it was the late summer that held a threat present but less prevalent in the north: various forms of fever. The numerous marshes along the bays were breeding grounds for mosquitoes, and water, desperately needed by naval vessels, often lacked purity. The wealthier members of the local populace fled the yellow fever, malaria, and typhus epidemics during the late summer. Naval forces did not share that option.

The British Navy's fear of disease was based upon experience: one-third of a crew exposed to typhus in port invariably died, and 40,000 men died of yellow fever in the West Indies from 1809 to 1812. Compare those losses to the 1,417 British dead at Waterloo or the 1,690 dead and wounded at Trafalgar. Note that northern cities also suffered from various epidemics, commonplace in most urban environments, but the more southerly coasts of the United States were unhealthy even without crowded conditions.[3]

The southern theater (map 4.3) encompassed the shores from North Carolina to Spanish Florida. Shoals and shifting sandbanks had earned it a reputation as the most treacherous of North American waters, especially off Capes Hatteras and Lookout in North Carolina. A series of barrier islands extending from the Virginia border to Cape Lookout protected the sounds and coastal waters of that state. Ocracoke inlet, navigable by vessels of ten feet or less draft, constituted the only viable penetration of that barrier. North Carolinians had developed a sizable transshipment business at the village of Portsmouth on Ocracoke Island, transferring goods from deep-draft ships to shallow-draft coasters capable of sailing the local estuaries.

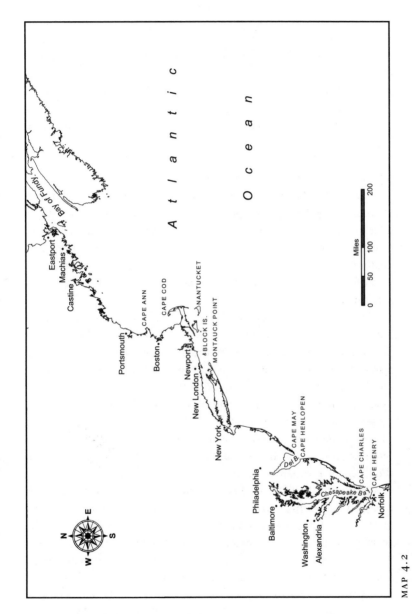

MAP 4.2
The northern and mid-Atlantic theaters.

A similar chain of barrier islands stretched from Charleston to Spain's Amelia Island, though they were more often broken by short stretches of open water. Between islands and sand bars there existed only one true deep-water port in the South: Beaufort, South Carolina. Wilmington, located on the Cape Fear River, could take only medium-draft or shallow-draft vessels. Charleston could accommodate deep-draft vessels (using local pilots) at high tide, and only shallow-draft vessels at low due to its bar, while St. Marys, Georgia, on the St. Marys River, could accommodate medium vessels on high tides and larger vessels only on an extreme tide. Savannah, on the Savannah River, could take deep-draft vessels, but careful pilotage was required. Many smaller ports and villages also existed in the southern theater, supporting the local fishing industry and the coasting trade.

Weather in the South was much milder than in the northerly regions, though freezing temperatures and snow occasionally occurred. The true dangers came from sudden wintry easterly winds capable of changing shorelines overnight and driving unwary captains to their deaths on the many shoals and sand bars of the region. As in the Chesapeake Bay, the fear of summer diseases existed as a valid concern for ship captains.

The most recently acquired and settled portion of the United States was the Gulf theater (map 4.3). Protected in places by large barrier islands at some distance from the mainland, the usually peaceful waters remained difficult to navigate without local pilotage due to sandbars and the ever-changing delta of the Mississippi River. New Orleans, outlet to the sea for almost all goods produced west of the Appalachians, was a deep-water port (with pilotage), while Mobile, soon to be acquired from the Spanish, offered similar capacity. Coastal settlements were few because of the difficulty of the local terrain and the recent acquisition of the area by the United States.

Weather in the Gulf of Mexico was usually excellent year around, though disease remained even more of a concern for seamen. The normal weather did have an exception, however, which also applied to the entire coast of the United States. From June to October tropical waves formed off the African coast, many gathering force as they moved across the Atlantic toward the Caribbean, and then to North America. It was not unusual for hurricanes to reach 125 mph, and winds of 200 mph sometimes existed near the eyes of the storms. Many ships caught in their full fury simply disappeared; those on the edge of such storms could do little except lower topmasts and run before the wind

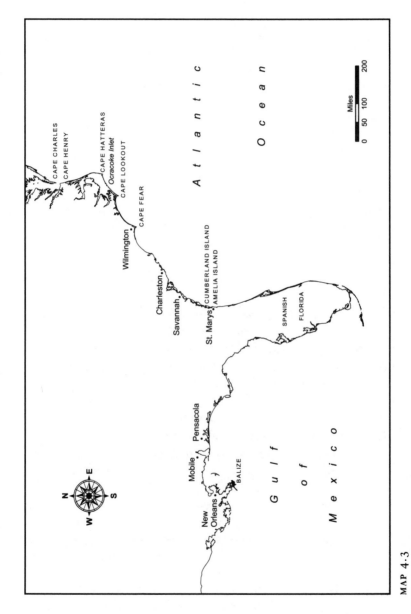

MAP 4·3
The southern and Gulf theaters.

TABLE 4.1. *Hurricanes during the War of 1812*

Date	Location	Notes
23 July 1812	Puerto Rico	—
14 Aug. 1812	Jamaica	19 Aug. to New Orleans
19 Aug. 1812	Puerto Rico	—
12 Oct. 1812	Jamaica	14 Oct. to Cuba
20 July 1813	Bermuda	—
22 July 1813	Dominica, Martinique	23 July to Puerto Rico
1813	Dominica	—
26 July 1813	Bahamas, Bermuda	—
31 July 1813	Jamaica	5–9 Aug. over Atlantic
19 Aug. 1813	Gulf Coast	—
25 Aug. 1813	Dominica	27 Aug. to Jamaica
27 Aug. 1813	Charleston, S.C.	—
7 Sept. 1813	Leeward Islands	—
19 Nov. 1813	Nova Scotia	Fleet at Halifax damaged
1813	Belize	—
1 July 1814	Charleston, S.C.	—
22 July 1814	Puerto Rico	—

Source: Tannehill, *Hurricanes,* 249–50.

on reefed sails. Nor were harbors always safe havens, as the tremendous storm surges ripped ships from anchor, while waterspouts and tornadic winds ravaged ships and port alike. These hurricanes had been known and feared since the times of Columbus, causing merchants to avoid the usual storm routes over the summer and autumn months. Such avoidance was another luxury unavailable to naval vessels, and table 4.1 illustrates vividly the number of hurricanes that they needed to avoid during the War of 1812.[4]

The internal transportation system of the United States held just as much importance to the story of the blockade as the length of its coast. Roads were few and often no more than dirt traces, especially in the South and West. Even in the more densely settled areas near urban centers, waterborne commerce was less expensive than land transportation—small boats not only cost less to maintain than wagons and draft animals, they could transport far more tonnage per trip than land conveyances.

Thus the economy relied upon the country's many inland waterways for moving goods and people. In the West the primary routes of the Ohio and Tennessee Rivers drained into the Mississippi, and virtually all goods funneled through New Orleans. In the South, river systems led to the ports of Savannah, Charleston, Beaufort, and St. Marys, while North Carolina was blocked behind its Outer Banks in the north, leaving Wilmington on the Cape Fear River as its only primary port. The rivers of the mid-Atlantic states emptied into the Chesapeake and Delaware Bays. The major ports of the north all stood at river mouths, depending upon those rivers to move goods to and from the hinterlands. Some efforts at internal transportation improvements had been made, notably the Great Dismal Swamp Canal (opened 1812), but the declaration of war found American commerce still funneled into relatively few ports, relying largely on the coasting trade instead of roads to move goods and travelers.[5]

A land-sea interface featuring barrier islands and offshore sandbars favored the continuance of coasting during the blockade. These sheltered waters created paths for shallow-draft merchantmen inviolable to the batteries, if not the boats, of British ships. Whether in southern or northern waters, however, a number of points of vulnerability existed. In the North, promontories such as Cape Ann and Cape Cod forced coasters into deeper water. To the south, the rough waters around the North Carolina capes forced coasters to use routes beyond their shoals, while navigable gaps pierced the barrier islands of Georgia and South Carolina at several points. The potential for continued coasting certainly existed during the war, as did the potential for the blockade to interrupt it.[6] But the war, of course, was not limited to American coastal waters.

Britain provided the major markets for American exports in the years leading to the War of 1812. British home markets, colonial markets, and the army in the Iberian Peninsula consumed tons of American wheat and provisions.[7] Intrepid American merchants and captains continually pushed for new markets; by 1812, the American flag flew over merchant shipping and whalers across all the world's seas. Still, as with British seamen, Americans found themselves at the beck and call of the winds and currents and followed the traditional routes for sail-driven vessels. The westerlies, blowing from North America to Great Britain, offered a quick passage, barring incident, of some three to four weeks. The return trip, either into the teeth of the stormy westerlies on the northern route, or with more favorable winds (though sometimes becalmed) and fewer storms on the southern route, routinely took five to twelve weeks.

The fact that geography limited sea-lanes to a trail following wind and current between set terminals enhanced the effectiveness of *guerre de course*. Without these watery highways, the chance of meeting a potential prize somewhere on the tremendous surface of the Atlantic would have been minimal. American raiders during the War of 1812 followed the established lanes but hunted near their terminal points. Thus the Bay of Fundy, the Caribbean, the western approaches to the British Isles, and the waters off Portugal became favorite stalking grounds for the public and private navies of the United States.

Aside from defining the potential arenas of combat, oceanic winds, currents, and weather visibly impacted British command and control. Orders that originated in Great Britain had a turnaround time of eight to twelve or more weeks; micromanagement of the war thus proved an impossibility (which is not to say that it was not attempted). The admiral on station or the captain of a solitary naval vessel therefore possessed tremendous discretionary power by default.[8] Both the government and the Admiralty expected him to be ambassador and warrior wherever he sailed, making the decisions best serving his nation (within, of course, the limitations of the Admiralty's orders). Success was mere duty—failure devastated careers. From that perspective, British and American navies had much in common.

As illustrated in table 3.3, the U.S. Navy benefited from easily accessible (at least distance-wise) yards and stations. British blockaders off France's Channel coast had enjoyed that same luxury—one they lacked in North American waters.[9] Halifax, one of two home stations for the North American Squadron, lay approximately 750 nautical miles northeast of New York, or four to six days' sail under favorable conditions. The peacetime winter base of the squadron at Bermuda lay almost the same distance southeast of the mouth of the Chesapeake Bay and required approximately the same transit times as noted above.[10] British Caribbean bases, Antigua and Jamaica, which dispatched vessels to the Gulf theater and as far north as Charleston, South Carolina, during 1812 and 1813 lay over 1,100 nautical miles from New Orleans and Charleston. Aside from transit time concerns, all sites shared other common problems.

Halifax, a deep-water harbor tucked into the rocky coast of Nova Scotia, had served as a major colonial dockyard and base for the Royal Navy for several decades before the War of 1812. Yet it had never been fully developed, lacking even the dry dock necessary to repair underwater damage to a ship's hull; and, as with all isolated bases, Halifax

suffered from a shortage of skilled naval artisans.[11] The dangers of bitter cold, an often frozen harbor, and vicious easterly gales dictated that
ships relocate to the warmer climes of Bermuda during winter. Unfortunately, the needs of war commanded in even stronger language that
the base be used year round. That necessity would eventually have a
high price tag in wrecked and damaged vessels.

Though an ideal site for a harbor during much of the year, Halifax
was less than ideal for a naval base because of its isolation, low agricultural productivity, and small population. The first two drawbacks
required the importation by sea of materials and foodstuffs, usually
from the United States in the years preceding June 1812. The declaration of war by its primary supplier created an obvious dilemma for the
station. The last flaw meant a shortage of labor in the base's critical
shipyards, and far more importantly in the long run, a shortage of
sailors for pressing into His Majesty's ships. Historian Barry J. Lohnes
astutely observes that some degree of isolation was a prerequisite for
British overseas naval bases, as it enhanced defensibility against land
forces. That requirement implied an ability to support such bases by
sea, a plan severely hampered by heavy British logistical demands in
European waters. The resulting shortages of material, provisions, and
manpower reenacted itself at all other North American and Caribbean
bases.[12] Though additional manpower trickled into the port throughout the war, only in July 1814 could the *Times* report significant reinforcement: "700 seamen and 300 artificers arrived in Halifax in June,"
with others to follow now that Napoleon had abdicated.[13]

Bermuda, winter station of the squadron, had long been a valuable
British anchorage even though development as a naval base began only
in 1807 (completed by late 1814). As a tiny Atlantic island, Bermuda
possessed an even smaller population and fewer material resources
than Halifax. Both the labor to build its facilities and the shipwrights
and laborers to staff those facilities had to be imported from Great
Britain. Despite the island's relatively good location for watching the
American coast south of the Chesapeake Bay, the small size and shal-
lowness of its harbor made it less than an ideal base. Nonetheless, it
received heavy usage during the War of 1812.

The Caribbean bases of Antigua and Jamaica are peripheral to the
narrative of the blockade, which, as the Admiralty dictated, remained
essentially the province of the North American Squadron, especially
after 1813. They experienced many of the same problems of isolation
suffered at Halifax and Bermuda, though tempered by the lengthy

British presence in the area, the tremendous economic interests present in the West Indies, and the intense campaigning in the Caribbean during the wars against France. From mid-1812 to early 1815, squadrons operating from these bases faced the unenviable task of countering numerous American raiders evading the British blockade—privateers and naval vessels loosed into a shipping-rich environment.[14]

The logistical support structure of the Royal Navy constituted only one portion of its geographic problems. Virtually all British captains and sailing masters of 1812 possessed the skill to navigate the Atlantic and make landfall off the American coast. Operating in that littoral environment, however, required more than skill; it called for experience. British officers possessed recent charts of the French coast with newly discovered navigation hazards, vagaries of currents, and locations of enemy batteries all marked from personal experience or contact with other experienced officers. Unfortunately, regular soundings along the coast of the United States ceased with the Revolutionary War; thus British vessels carried charts that were often thirty or more years out of date. A land-sea interface changes considerably in thirty years. Rivers dump tons of silt into harbors or directly into the ocean. The sea erodes unprotected shores or piles sand upon them. Between wind and wave, sandbars appear, disappear, or shift position. Undiscovered rocks and reefs still hide just beneath the water's surface. New wrecks lie in shallow water. Terrestrial landmarks recorded on old charts disappear. Even local weather patterns and currents may undergo extensive change. Add to these the hazard that cartographers sometimes transcribed hastily scribbled notes from charts of the 1780s incorrectly, and the difficulties of navigation for the British in American waters are readily appreciated.[15] Until knowledge of local waters could be gathered and disseminated, British vessels operated inshore—as required by a close blockade—with a considerable amount of risk. This situation greatly favored American captains and their intimate knowledge of their own coast, both in evading blockaders and in continuing coasting traffic along the verge of the interface.

Clearly, the blockade of the United States would differ from those against France. From its transatlantic nature and the corresponding lengthening of communications to the uncertainties of its land-sea interface, interdicting the maritime forces of the United States posed new challenges to the premier strategy of the Royal Navy. Still, from the most senior admiral to the greenest of lieutenants, all loudly concurred that victory against the upstart Americans would come quickly. One must wonder, however, just how many of those closest to the Admiralty—those who knew exactly how thinly war with France stretched the Royal Navy—silently questioned whether this new conflict could be ended without some great risk.

5

1812: Birth of a Blockade

The outbreak of war found Great Britain woefully unprepared for
hostilities. Operational initiative firmly in hand, the U.S. Navy
forced the British to delay a military blockade while responding to the
American opening moves. This allowed the majority of the United
States' merchant marine to return to safe ports for the duration of the
war. As British naval strength shifted from Europe, however, the U.S.
Navy found its operations restricted as its ports came under blockade.
Though the British missed the opportunity to cripple the American
merchant marine, by December the Royal Navy had established a
tentative military blockade—little more than a patrol—of New York
and Boston.

On 3 April 1812, Congress placed the coast of the United States
under embargo. Unlike its Jeffersonian predecessor, an offensive
measure aimed at Great Britain, this embargo was defensive in nature.
President Madison intended to remove the merchant marine from a
potential war zone, preserving it for use after the conclusion of a short,
victorious war against Great Britain.[1]

Preceding even that measure, the Admiralty had warned the North
American (based at Halifax, Nova Scotia) and Newfoundland stations
to be on the alert. A 9 May missive followed awareness of the embargo
and ordered captains "to attack, take or sink, burn or destroy, all ships

or vessels belonging to the United States or to the citizens there of" in the event of war. Nevertheless, hope for peace forced the Admiralty to include a warning to avoid action or incitement until an actual declaration of war occurred.[2] In response, Vice Adm. Herbert Sawyer at Halifax concentrated his frigates and waited.

The United States declared war on Great Britain on 18 June. Congress immediately ordered pilot boats dispatched to Europe to warn American merchantmen to take shelter in neutral ports for the duration of the war.[3] On the twenty-first, Commodore John Rodgers in the *President*, forty-four, sallied from New York in search of a homeward bound West Indies convoy. His squadron included the frigates *United States*, forty-four, and *Congress*, thirty-eight, sloop *Hornet*, eighteen, and brig *Argus*, sixteen. Rodgers sailed without formal orders, though his plan to sail as a squadron had been communicated to Secretary of the Navy Paul Hamilton in a letter written on 3 June. Hamilton's undelivered orders to Rodgers, dated 22 June, not only ordered the distribution of American vessels into two squadrons (the second under Commodore Stephen Decatur) but also limited their operations to near the coast.[4] Those orders, had Hamilton dispatched them earlier, might have proven disastrous. Rodgers would have sailed with only the *Hornet* in company, the frigates *Essex* and *John Adams*, as well as the brig *Nautilus*, not yet being ready for sea.[5] Hamilton had ordered Decatur's squadron—the *United States*, *Congress*, and *Argus*—to cover the approaches from Boston southward to the Chesapeake, while Rodgers covered the Chesapeake itself. Operating near the coast and divided, either force could have fallen prey to the small but concentrated British Halifax Squadron. By sailing with all available ships and operating in Atlantic shipping lanes instead of along the coast, Rodgers avoided a potential debacle.

On 23 June, the squadron gave chase to the British frigate *Belvidera*, thirty-six. Despite light damage, the *Belvidera* escaped, giving Sawyer his first warning of war upon its return to Halifax on the twenty-seventh. Sawyer immediately dispatched a vessel under a flag of truce to New York to verify the declaration of war, losing several valuable days in which interception and defeat of Rodgers could well have been possible.[6] Sawyer is sometimes maligned by historians for this decision. Barry J. Lohnes wrote as prelude to several paragraphs of Sawyer's sins, "If the competence of Admiral Herbert Sawyer is an indication, perhaps the more energetic naval officers remained in European waters."[7] Perhaps, but the *Gentlemen's Magazine and Historical Chronicle* reported a war scare as early as June 1794, years before the *Chesapeake-Leopard* affair of 1807 almost erupted into open conflict, while little more than a year earlier an American vessel had fired on a British warship without the nicety of a declaration of war.[8] Sawyer's orders were specific: do not initiate combat until certain that a state of war existed. The decision to verify that such a state indeed existed met the letter and spirit of those orders, making the delay in proceeding to American waters unavoidable. Once the existence of a state of war had been confirmed, Sawyer deployed his resources as best he could considering the shortage of hulls, materiel, and men—the supply of which was the ultimate responsibility of the Admiralty. William M. Fowler Jr. offers a much more reasonable assessment of Sawyer's situation: "Lord Nelson himself would have had trouble in the Halifax command, and Sawyer was certainly no Nelson."[9] Sawyer's actions reflected neither timidity nor incompetence; rather, they arose from the average British senior officer's experience of continually dealing with an Admiralty much quicker to place blame than to provide support. Verifying the existence of war, however, proved the least of Sawyer's quandaries.

His responsibilities included providing convoy escorts, patrolling the waters around Halifax, seeking out and destroying enemy cruisers and privateers along over one thousand miles of coastal United States and the extensive coastline of Canada, and capturing American merchantmen. He also had to establish a military blockade of the major American ports. Both logic and naval experience dictated that the best place to accomplish or abet these missions was off the enemy's ports—natural funnels for merchantmen, privateers, and warships alike. Ship availability lists, however, reflected Sawyer's dilemma. His command contained only one ship-of-the-line, six frigates, and sixteen unrated vessels.[10] A portion of his naval assets were needed to support convoys, and to commit the remainder piecemeal off American ports would risk their destruction by the superior squadron under Rodgers. By sailing at once, Rodgers dictated the tempo of the naval war for 1812. Sawyer could not implement a close blockade; he could only concentrate his heaviest vessels and react.

Across the Atlantic, far separated from the developing theater of war by wind and waves, the British government revoked the hated orders in council that initially had provoked the United States. The date was 23 June, the same day the *Belvidera* fled toward Halifax, pursued by Rodgers's squadron. But the government acted less from any desire to avoid an American imbroglio than to vent rapidly building internal economic pressures. In June 1812, many British mills and factories, especially in the cotton-dependent cloth sector, still stood idle as a result of Jefferson's embargo, the Non-Importation Acts, and the War Embargo. Earlier in the year, some forty thousand cotton-mill workers had struck for higher wages and increased work hours. The number of unemployed in London and Manchester alone had doubled between 1810 and 1812. These problems, coupled with the highest taxes in British history, forced merchants, industrialists, and shipowners to unite, petitioning the crown for removal of what they perceived as the major problem: those orders in council interfering with neutral trade.[11] A petition from the Frame Work Knitters of Leicester was typical in wording of the dozen petitions placed before the House of Commons between March and July 1812. It represented the desire of eleven thousand signatories, who were "praying for the Repeal of the Orders in Council, . . . praying that the final state might not by a war with America, be a ruin to manufactures." Similar petitions with 14,000 and 6,560 signatures originated in Birmingham and Liverpool, respectively.[12]

Repeal owed more to internal concerns than to ongoing negotiations with the United States, but both the government and the Admiralty seemed fixated on the change as a preventative for the half-expected war. Despite earlier warnings to the North American squadrons, the Admiralty took no measures to strengthen them, nor did it offer any realistic operational plans to the squadron commanders. It would be slightly over a month after the repeal before the grim notice of war officially arrived in London, far too late for an early blockade. And while the Admiralty waited, Americans continued to sail.

The *Essex*, thirty-two, Capt. David Porter, left New York on 3 July. Unable to sail with Rodgers as originally planned, Porter put to sea at a fortuitous time. Only two days later a British squadron under Capt. Phillip V. Broke (Sawyer remained in Halifax) appeared off Sandy Hook. Aside from Broke's *Shannon*, thirty-eight, it included the *Belvidera*, thirty-six, *Aeolus*, thirty-two, and *Africa*, sixty-four. The only American warship trapped in New York was the unfortunate brig *Nautilus*, fourteen. The *Guerriere*, thirty-eight, joined the British force on 14 July. Two days later the *Nautilus* attempted to run by the British squadron but surrendered after a six-hour chase—the first U.S. Navy vessel lost in the war.[13]

Unaware of Broke's force cruising off New York, Capt. Isaac Hull in the *Constitution*, forty-four, cleared the Virginia Capes on 12 July after leaving Annapolis on the fifth. His orders from the Navy Department, dated 18 June, read, "You will use the utmost dispatch to reach New York. . . . In your way from thence, you will not fail to notice the british flag, should it present itself . . . but you are not to understand me as impelling you to battle."[14] The last segment hints that Hamilton considered preserving a fleet in being far superior to expending ships in glorious battle—an important concept for the tiny American Navy of 1812.

On 16 July, Hull sighted a sail closing toward his ship off the coast south of New York; topsails of other vessels appeared in the distance. Despite light winds, Hull cleared for battle, determined to close the strange sail, which he did during the night. Dawn revealed the *Constitution* in imminent danger of capture by the entire British squadron. A two-day chase across a virtually windless sea followed, with both forces using oared boats to tow, and later kedge, their vessels forward until the wind returned. Hull escaped only through superb seamanship, the crew's hard effort, and luck. The *Constitution*, unable to reach New York because of the patrolling squadron, anchored at Boston on 27 July.[15] Meanwhile, Broke sailed for Jamaica with his squadron on 24 July to escort a large homeward bound convoy, an action necessitated by knowledge of the American squadron at sea. During the British squadron's time off New York, it had captured fourteen merchantmen and one warship, alarmed the local populace with a threat of invasion, and almost overwhelmed the *Constitution*.[16] All this in only nineteen days: there exists no better example of what an early blockade stood to accomplish.

Broke joined the convoy on the twenty-ninth, the same day that the official declaration of the war arrived in London. Unofficial notice, via dispatches from Sawyer, had reached the Admiralty on the twenty-fifth, but British leaders adopted a "wait and see (and hope this is wrong)" attitude.[17] When official notice made war a reality, four important decisions awaited the government and the Admiralty. First, since the United States was unaware that the orders in council had been rescinded, an immediate overture to restore peace offered hope for a quick settlement of the conflict. Second, the British government had to find a way to keep American grain flowing to Wellington's army, just then undertaking an invasion of Spain, at least until secondary grain sources could be developed. Third, American raiders, government and private, would wreak havoc on British shipping lanes unless a means could be found to contain or destroy them. Finally, in a navy stretched to the breaking point by the blockade of most of western Europe, where could the needed warships be found for whatever plan was eventually developed?

The delicate negotiations with the United States required a much more skilled touch than that of Sawyer, who, aside from being a rather junior admiral and personally inexperienced in diplomatic work, was due for rotation to another assignment. The Admiralty selected Adm. Sir John Borlase Warren for the role. A veteran of numerous sea engagements, the blockade of France, and successful anticoasting efforts, he had served as a cabinet member in 1802 and later as ambassador to Russia. At age fifty-nine, Warren seemed ideally suited to the job at hand, combining naval expertise with diplomatic experience.[18] Suitability became a moot point, however, beginning with contradictory orders requiring Warren to "attack, sink, burn or otherwise destroy" the commerce and navy of the United States while urging him to "exercise all possible forbearance" to facilitate negotiating peace.[19] These were to be only the first of several Admiralty decisions that eventually crushed Warren beneath a burden of impossible directives.

Strangely enough, the British government coupled its peace overture with the seizure of American vessels in British ports, the impoundment of American goods awaiting shipment from British docks, and the nullification of debts to American merchants. This included a sizable sum owed by the government for grain purchases.[20] Certainly this did not constitute a reconciliatory action. More important, American merchants, obviously unable to accept bills of credit drawn on London, would demand specie for grain shipped to the Iberian Peninsula under the soon-to-be-initiated licensed trade. This would develop into a severe drain upon Wellington's war chest.

Lord Wellington had written from Lisbon to his superior in London on 17 December 1811, "I recommend you to renew your measures in America, so far as to send there bills for 400,000 *l.*, to be laid out in purchase of corn."[21] A few months later, war with the United States now a reality, he penned, "All this part of the Peninsula has been long this year on American flour," and asked that alternative sources—Brazil, Egypt, even the Barbary states—be pursued.[22] Supplying the army on the Iberian Peninsula, particularly with Wellington engaged in a new offensive to drive the French across the Pyrenees, remained a major problem for both the government and Admiralty through 1814. Nor was that the only supply problem encountered, for American grain and provisions fed much of the Maritime Provinces of Canada as well as

British holdings in the Caribbean. The government's solution was to revive the successful licensing system once used to control trade under the now stricken orders in council. Initially, licenses, providing safe passage for ships possessing them as they traveled to designated ports with designated cargoes, were issued by the ambassador in Washington. Eventually, they came to be distributed by both diplomats (British and foreign) and admirals.[23]

As the war opened, several American captains seized ships engaging in licensed trade. On 6 July 1812, Congress passed legislation ordering government officials to take prize ships operating under license and assessing the owners a penalty of twice the value of vessel and cargo. Additionally, the law labeled the crime a misdemeanor, carrying up to twelve months in prison and a fine of one thousand dollars.[24] Unofficially, Thomas Jefferson best voiced the American stance a few weeks later: "If she [Britain] is to be fed at all events, why may we not have the benefit of it as well as others? . . . Besides, if we could, by starving the English armies, oblige them to withdraw from the peninsula, it would be to send them here; and I think we had better feed them for pay, than feed and fight them here for nothing. To keep the war popular, we must keep open the markets. As long as good prices can be had, the people will support the war cheerfully."[25] Avarice over integrity, or perhaps economic logic over military principles, apparently thrust the unofficial dogma to the fore in the early months of the war. The first successful condemnation of a licensed vessel did not occur until 31 December 1813.[26]

As the calendar edged toward that year, the licensing system served an additional British purpose. In an order dated 9 November 1812, the government directed the Admiralty, "Whatever importations are proposed to be made under [this] order from the United States of America should be by your licenses, confined to the ports in the Eastern States exclusively."[27] The term "Eastern States" referred to the section extending from New York City to the Canadian border. Well aware of the existing discontent in New England (thanks to public voting records, American newspapers, and British government representatives in every port), the new directive blatantly encouraged disunion by subsidizing wealth imbalance and creating British political-economic leverage. Such an assertion could be questioned—Britain had great need for the trade without subterfuge and hidden agendas—had not Admiral Warren been directed to make peace with the United States or "*any part thereof.*"[28]

The third and fourth parts of the Admiralty's dilemma were intertwined. A blockade had to be established to contain American cruisers, while additional naval elements were required for patrol and convoy duties against the few enemy vessels that would inevitably slip through any blockade. But despite its great size, the Royal Navy was stretched thin. Few vessels were available for North America and its eastern approaches, unless the Admiralty stripped convoy escorts in other waters or reassigned ships from the French blockade. The Admiralty considered both patently impossible with raiders already at sea and the French fleet still apparently strong within its fortified harbors. The option finally implemented was a half-measure. The Admiralty combined the stations in North America and the Caribbean under Warren's command while planning to reinforce his squadrons as ship availability increased. With slightly over one hundred ships in his command and a trickle of reinforcements, surely Warren could, if peace failed, sustain a close blockade.[29] The Admiralty also ordered that all merchant vessels sailing to or from North America proceed only in convoys. Vessels that sailed alone were subject to fine and were denied insurance.[30]

The fallacies of this realignment of commands are readily apparent. First, most ships in the new operational command had been committed to *existing* convoy and patrol lanes by 18 June 1812. Not only did war reinforce the continued need for those vessels, it created additional demands for patrollers and escorts. Even with reinforcements, direct protection of the merchant marine held priority, and extra vessels for blockade remained unavailable through the end of 1812. Second, Warren's squadrons were based as far apart as 1,700 miles. This distance required weeks of sailing simply to communicate with subordinates, while small dispatch vessels engaged in that task remained vulnerable to capture by privateers and American warships. At best, unity of command would have been difficult to achieve (and Warren never enjoyed the best of conditions). Finally, experience during the American Revolution strongly suggested that the quantity of ships allocated would be insufficient to blockade the United States, especially with Britain's underdeveloped regional naval bases. Adm. Hugh Palliser's calculations of July 1775 had specified fifty vessels at a time when that rebellion was confined to the New England area. This new war stretched far beyond that segment of coast. Considering Revolutionary War experience as well as the extension and development of the American coast by 1812, fifty vessels seemed an exceedingly optimistic estimate, though apparently not to the Admiralty.

Conflicting orders, coupled with the inadequate means available with which to implement them, resulted in a classic setup for failure. In the Admiralty's defense, however, time and time again since 1793 the Royal Navy achieved so much with so little that the mere thought of impossibility no longer found recognition in Whitehall, particularly in regards to the pathetically small U.S. Navy. By the second week of August, with plan in hand and Warren dispatched to Halifax, the Admiralty could only await developments. Along the shores of the United States, however, the conflict never slowed.

During the month of July, the sloop *Colibri*, sixteen, and three brigs appeared off the port of Charleston. They patrolled for two weeks, often so close to the bar that American officers suspected local pilots provided assistance to the British. Twelve merchantmen fell into their hands before they returned to Halifax, another example of the potential impact of even a limited blockade.[31]

On 2 August, the *Constitution*, now refitted and resupplied, sailed from Boston seeking Rodgers's squadron. Four days later, Broke left the *Africa* to escort the homeward bound convoy, taking the majority of his ships to New York, where he hoped to meet Rodgers returning to port. Broke decided to detach his remaining vessels one by one for resupply. The *Guerriere*, having been at sea the longest, departed for Halifax that same day. Less than two weeks later, on 19 August, it encountered Hull's *Constitution* in a chance meeting on the open sea. In a vicious action, superior American gunnery battered the *Guerriere* into submission. Hull scuttled the sinking hulk and sailed for port to repair, resupply, and announce his victory. He arrived in Boston on 30 August.[32] The American squadron under Commodore Rodgers joined Hull there the following day, having taken only seven prizes during its cruise. Rodgers's ships were worn, and his crews suffering from scurvy, including several deaths, after less than three months at sea.[33]

Nor were matters quiet in the southern areas of operation during August. Sailing out of Charleston and finding British patrols now withdrawn, the ex–revenue cutter *Gallatin* captured a British privateer on the sixth. American private naval vessels also frequently based out of Charleston, and several prizes arrived there in August, courtesy of those raiders.[34] In the Gulf of Mexico, a devastating hurricane sank, disabled, or grounded the American flotilla at New Orleans. It also completely dismasted the British sloop *Brazen*, eighteen, patrolling off the delta. Only the extensive damage to the American force prevented its capture, and the jury-masted *Brazen* limped home to Jamaica.[35]

On 7 September, the *Essex* anchored at Chester, Pennsylvania, near the mouth of the Delaware River. Its cruise had netted eight merchantmen and the first British warship to be captured by an American naval vessel, the *Alert*, sixteen, on 13 August.[36] In Boston, Rodgers received a letter from Hamilton ordering ships to sail in small groups of no more than two frigates and a smaller vessel from this point onward. Since the earlier mission of distracting the British while American merchantmen made safe havens had been accomplished, and possibly because the sailing of his large squadron had captured fewer prizes than the efforts of the *Essex* alone, Rodgers agreed.[37] Yet news of Broke's depleted squadron's arrival off New York on 10 September must have tempted Rodgers sorely. Apparently, Broke bypassed Boston on the continuing journey toward Halifax to replenish, so no confrontation ensued. Rodgers, however, had certainly not lost heart. In a letter to Hamilton in mid-September he communicated his most recent intelligence on British movements, notably the arrival of Warren and several British men-of-war at Halifax. He went on to write, counter to any philosophy of maintaining a "fleet-in-being," his thoughts on the future of the war: "They are determined, it appears, to have Ships enough on our Coast: comparitively *[sic]* small as our force may be. I hope that we shall still be able however, by judicious management, to annoy them: and indeed if we had half their number, of equal force, I am satisfied they would soon be made heartily sick of our Coast: At any rate, should they send their whole Navy on our Coast, I hope it never will be urged as a reason for the few vessels we have not going to Sea."[38]

For Admiral Warren, arriving at Halifax almost two full months after receiving his orders, "Ships enough" definitely roused concern. He relieved Sawyer on 27 September, with less than welcome news from most quarters. Reports from the Caribbean stations had not arrived, so he was ignorant of their status and could not form a coordinated plan dividing responsibilities among the various commands. Nor could Warren simply deal with the responsibilities of commander in chief, North America, as he also had to wear Sawyer's former hat as commander of the Halifax Squadron until the Admiralty provided a replacement. Sawyer's command seemed a shambles, with ships in disrepair from long periods at sea and crews far understrength because of desertions and disease.[39] He had been unable to destroy the tiny

U.S. Navy or even to confine it to its ports, and had only minimally disrupted American shipping. Worse, the western Atlantic swarmed with enemy privateers from the Bay of Fundy to the Caribbean. In the first eight weeks of war they had taken one hundred merchantmen and a single naval vessel, as opposed to the U.S. Navy's record of eight merchantmen, and the British captures of one naval vessel, thirteen small privateers, and forty merchantmen.[40] Yet all those concerns remained secondary to the attempt to negotiate peace. On 30 September, Warren dispatched a missive to Madison offering peace based on the repeal of the orders in council. The proposal called for an immediate return to normality as it existed before the declaration of war, with reparations and any indemnities to be determined later by commissioners.[41] Only after this offer did he begin to place his command in order.

On 8 October, Rodgers with the *President* and *Congress* and Decatur with the *United States* and the brig *Argus* sailed jointly from Boston. Three days later they separated, in accord with Hamilton's orders. The frigate *Essex* had been designated to take the place of the *Argus* but was unable to sail from Chester until 28 October. The American sloop *Wasp*, eighteen, passed the Capes of the Delaware on the thirteenth, en route to Atlantic raiding. After meeting with heavy weather, it engaged the Royal Navy's brig *Frolic*, eighteen, then serving as escort to a British convoy. Emerging the victors, the crew of the *Wasp* found their celebration to be short-lived: the British *Poictiers*, seventy-four, forced the damaged American warship and its prize to surrender later that same day.[42]

In England, patience had shortened by mid-October. Merchants were losing ships daily, the news of the loss of the *Guerriere* had arrived, and Warren had not yet updated the Admiralty on the status of the peace proposal. Though not without hope for peace, the government, under immediate pressure, issued an order specifying "general reprisals against the United States" on 13 October. With restrictions removed, British officers no longer had to worry about their actions possibly damaging British-American diplomatic efforts.[43]

Though no blockade existed in October, patrols sometimes appeared, as in the case of Charleston from 14 to 31 October. Three British brigs captured nine merchantmen over two weeks' time. Capt. John H. Dent, commanding the Charleston naval station, responded by purchasing small vessels for local defense. Dent's concern was the "inability" of the U.S. Navy to free the southern coasts of enemy warships.[44] In truth, his government's decision to use its Navy in *guerre de course* reflected not naval inability, but a conscious choice to concentrate on damaging the British economy rather than directly protecting American coasts. Those coasts, however, certainly benefited indirectly from each convoy escort strengthened or cruiser reassigned to the protection of British sea-lanes.

On 25 October, the *United States* captured the British frigate *Macedonian*, thirty-eight, in a brief action.[45] A day later, Hull's successor, William Bainbridge, led the *Constitution* and the *Hornet* to sea from Boston. In a month with little good news for Admiral Warren, both events proved unpleasant in the extreme, his efforts to control the American situation obviously failing. But a letter written by American secretary of state James Monroe on 27 October provided the worst news of all: there would be no peace without an end to Great Britain's impressment policies.[46] Britain would not and could not surrender impressment. To do so would have left its tremendous Navy without crews in short order. The final days of October marked the end of the "Phony War" of 1812; the clock would not turn back.

November found little action along the northern segment of the United States' Atlantic coast. Though Warren had received substantial reinforcements in the form of three ships-of-the-line, ten frigates, and four sloops, most needed immediate repair due to storm damage. As welcome as the ships, Sir George Cockburn arrived as second-in-command.[47] Cockburn's reputation as a fire-eater and cutting-out specialist proved to be well deserved.

In the South, vessel purchases in Charleston continued with the schooner *Leila Ann*, renamed *Ferret* and placed in operation at Beaufort. The U.S. Navy also bought the schooner *Carolina* for use in Charleston.[48] The first American naval loss in the southern theater occurred on 22 November, when the brig *Vixen*, twelve, on its third fruitless cruise for prizes, fell victim to Capt. James Yeo in the frigate *Southampton*, thirty-two. The British enjoyed their prize for only five days. En route to Jamaica, both vessels wrecked on an uncharted reef.[49]

By the end of November both the government and the Admiralty knew that there could be no peaceful resolution to the war. On 27 November, the government issued an order directing Warren to implement immediately a "rigorous commercial blockade" of the Delaware and Chesapeake Bays. These orders excluded even licensed ships from entering the named waters. One day earlier, the Admiralty had dispatched messages to European neutrals warning of the impending blockade. But Warren, plagued with communication delays and the onset of winter, had too few vessels to begin the blockade any earlier than February 1813.[50]

December began on a positive note for Americans as the *United States* returned home with its prize, the British thirty-eight-gun frigate *Macedonian*. On 17 December, Captain Evans's *Chesapeake* sailed from Boston, intent on finding prizes.[51] Twelve days later the *Constitution* bagged the real prize, capturing and scuttling the British frigate *Java*, thirty-eight. This proved to be the last American frigate-to-frigate victory of the war.[52] The final American ships to return from cruises during the year—*President, Congress*, and *Argus*—had captured only a dozen vessels during their weeks at sea. Rodgers was understandably bitter, an officer who did everything correctly except find an enemy to fight. Though he had earned the rank of captain and the title of commodore, Rodgers was not a lucky sailor.[53]

The various legislative and command hierarchies were as busy as their ships during December. The Admiralty renewed its blockade warning to neutrals and dispatched another message to Warren, making him aware that no one less than the prince regent desired the blockade enforced immediately.[54] On the other side of the Atlantic, Congress voted a major increase in naval appropriations on 23 December. The $3.5 million expenditure for four ships-of-the-line, six frigates, and six sloops occurred far too late to substantially aid the war effort, however. Though some of the sloops would see action, the remaining vessels, or at least those not canceled, sailed only after the war's end. Finally, an oft-inebriated Paul Hamilton resigned his post as secretary of the navy on the last day of the year. William Jones, appointed in his place, reaped the benefits of the early successes of the U.S. Navy but soon faced the whirlwind those successes had sown: an ever-tightening blockade.[55]

The U.S. Navy accomplished its primary mission for 1812 in grand style. The vast majority of the American merchant marine on distant cruises made home ports—250 ships returned to Boston alone, with similar numbers verified as arriving safely in New York and Baltimore.[56] By sailing in squadron, the U.S. Navy had forced the British to concentrate their forces instead of stationing individual ships off American ports. Along the way, the Americans had captured six vessels of the Royal Navy, three of them frigates, while surrendering only two brigs and a sloop. As for the seizure of enemy merchantmen, the U.S.

Navy proved less successful, capturing only twenty-eight vessels.[57] Fortunately for the United States, Mr. Madison's private navy took up much of the slack.

Around three hundred privateers sailed from American ports during 1812. Most were true privateers, hoping to seize enemy shipping for profit, instead of letter of marque traders, seeking to move goods first and capture enemies only if a golden opportunity arose. Their total number of captures the first year of war remains uncertain, though slightly over three hundred seems conservative. Higher estimates tend toward five hundred vessels.[58]

Unfortunately, naval operations constituted the minor portion of the American plan for a short, victorious war. The seizure of Canada, whether as a bargaining chip or as an extension of the American union, formed the hub of all strategic planning (such as it was). On 6 August 1812, the first prong of a three-tined attack not only failed but also resulted in a debacle. Gen. William Hull surrendered his entire army and the town of Detroit to an inferior British force. The two columns remaining did not achieve success, though they at least did not lose significant ground.[59] Failures on land revealed the absolute necessity of controlling the Great Lakes, and naval officers, ratings, building materials, ordnance, and munitions soon began to flow in that direction.[60] This effort resulted in shortages of those same resources along the Atlantic coast. Shortfalls continued throughout the war, which proved to be neither short nor victorious.

On the British side, Halifax experienced the same drain. For Warren, as 1812 came to an end, larger problems existed. In particular, he continued to experience a shortage of warships. Since June, aside from the six vessels lost to enemy action, two vessels had fallen to French ships and ten to wreck or storm. Because only twenty-seven reinforcing vessels reached the North American command in 1812, and those of Cockburn needed immediate and extensive repairs, Warren's position had actually weakened since August.[61] Ships under repair, however, often resulted in a usable manpower pool. Even there, he was stymied by an admiralty court in Halifax which proved slow in adjudicating prize cases. Of the 144 vessels taken as prizes during 1812, several could have been bought into the service immediately and crewed with available manpower, providing immense relief on the convoy routes. Eventually, the Navy did purchase several vessels for that purpose, but only when the court finally adjudicated the 1812 prizes— in 1813.[62]

In addition to the American situation, Warren and the Admiralty shared a common concern that a French squadron escaping from Europe would join the Americans and ravage the West Indian trade, or perhaps, even reestablish the French colonial empire. On the surface the fear seemed valid, but Wellington, astute as always, placed it in perspective: "If Bonaparte is wise, and has money, he will send out a large fleet. He has no money, however, and he must have found before now that a fleet cannot be equipped and maintained, as he maintains his armies, by requisitions on the unfortunate country which is made the seat of war."[63]

Warren was concerned with the French, burdened with convoys, and under pressure to institute a full blockade of the Chesapeake and Delaware Bays. It is little wonder that his final message of the year to the Admiralty, aside from offering suggestions for defeating the large American frigates, begged for additional ships to combat "the Swarms of Privateers and Letters of Marque, their numbers now amounting to 600," throughout his command. Without reinforcement, Warren feared that "the Trade must inevitably suffer, if not be utterly ruined and destroyed."[64] With too few ships and too many problems, Warren's composure began to crumble under the Admiralty's demands for results. There had been little blockade in 1812, and little more followed in 1813.

1813: The Grip Tightens

By spring of 1813, the Admiralty had provided Admiral Warren with enough ships to (barely) maintain a military blockade from the Chesapeake north to Boston, to patrol along the New England coast, and to enforce an economic blockade of the Delaware and Chesapeake Bays. At the same time, his superiors pressured Warren to destroy the tiny U.S. Navy whose victories were becoming intolerable. Warren responded by staging a major raid into the Chesapeake Bay, hoping to destroy one of the two American warships trapped therein. He accomplished little except the weakening of his military blockade. Meanwhile, the Admiralty ordered the economic blockade extended to include most of the United States outside of New England. It was, and remained, a paper blockade.

On 3 January, Cockburn sailed from Bermuda, winter headquarters of the North American Station. Leading his squadron from the *Marlborough*, seventy-four, he had orders to check on the blockaders off New York before detaching vessels to the Delaware Bay and then sailing to blockade the Chesapeake, where the summer campaign would ultimately begin. He arrived off New London on 29 January, but contrary winter winds prevented his squadron from reaching Lynnhaven Bay, just inside the mouth of the Chesapeake Bay, until 23 February.[1]

As American naval vessels made repairs in port, prepared to sail, or headed home after extended cruises, the schooner *Enterprise*, twelve, and the brig *Viper*, twelve, sortied from New Orleans. The former returned with minimal results, but the *Viper* fell prey to the British frigate *Narcissus*, forty, after several weeks of fruitless cruising off Havana.[2]

The chill of winter may have slowed action in the theaters of war, but it did not stop it. American naval vessels remained at sea, privateers continued to capture British merchantmen, and Warren prepared to at last undertake a full military blockade as well as the economic blockade of the Delaware and Chesapeake Bays. Trained naval officer that he was, Warren initially attempted to follow orders to the letter, though he privately and publicly questioned their ultimate feasibility, leading to an extended correspondence with the Admiralty—and his eventual relief. Both British strategy for 1813 and Warren's continuing dilemma become apparent in examining those letters.

On 9 January, the Admiralty advised Warren of its displeasure that "the great force placed at your disposal" had not established an effective blockade and contained or destroyed the American Navy. Reluctantly, their lordships proposed to increase his strength to ten ships-of-the-line, thirty frigates, and fifty sloops (other unrated vessels were not mentioned), sharing with Warren their expectation that the majority of the vessels, especially the ships-of-the-line, would be returned quickly—as soon as his forces captured or destroyed the large American frigates. By this time the Admiralty had realized that the American heavy frigates resembled third rates more than existing British frigates, thus the proposed increase in ships-of-the-line. As suggested in Warren's letter of 29 December, they also razeed—removed the upper deck—from four seventy-four-gun ships, hoping to emulate the capabilities of the American vessels. The first of the forty-four-gun razees appeared off the coast of the United States in late 1813. The Admiralty clearly defined how these new warships should be used: "It is of the highest importance to the character and interests of the country that the naval force of the enemy should be quickly and completely disposed of."[3] At least the razees did appear on the American coast in 1813, something that cannot be said for many of the remaining ninety warships promised to Warren.

The Admiralty also dispatched Henry Hotham to serve as captain of the fleet, relieving Warren of much administrative worry, though it expected Hotham to return with the ships-of-the-line once those resources had been used to eliminate the American frigates in the summer campaign of 1813. Usually a commander in chief nominated his own fleet captain; the Admiralty denied Warren that option. Reading only slightly between the lines suggests that Melville assigned Henry Hotham a twofold mission: encouraging Warren to destroy the American Navy while privately informing the Admiralty of the "real" situation in the North American command. Later correspondence from Hotham to the Admiralty—a stream of private reports from the summer of 1813 through the opening months of 1814—provide seeming confirmation of the captain's planned role in the blockade of the United States.[4]

In addition to this promised wealth of vessels and a captain of the fleet, the Admiralty committed two battalions of Royal Marines and a battery of artillery, plus transports, to the 1813 campaign. Finally, from their chairs in distant London, the Admiralty criticized Warren because the frigate *Spartan* had been observed sailing alone on 28 November 1812, a time when the large American frigates were known to be at sea.[5]

A second communication followed on 10 February, in part responding to Warren's letter of 29 December 1812, received at Whitehall in mid-January. Warren could not have enjoyed reading it. The Admiralty criticized Warren for failure to communicate intelligence on British and American naval strength. It estimated that those strengths stood at ninety-seven and fourteen pendants, respectively. Their lordships questioned why the outnumbered American fleet still existed, and asked why, since it still existed, Warren had not blockaded the vessels inside their ports. The Admiralty stated flatly that because Warren had failed to accomplish either of those objectives, they had been forced to assign a large number of additional ships to convoy duty, as well as a force of fourteen ships-of-the-line and frigates to patrols in the eastern Atlantic. The letter warned:

> Under these circumstances their Lordships are not only not prepared to enter into your opinion that the force on your station was not adequate to the duties to be executed, but they feel that, consistently with what other branches and objects of the public Service require, it may not be possible to maintain on the Coast of America for any length of time a force so disproportionate to the Enemy as that which, with a view of enabling you to strike some decisive blow, they have now placed under your orders.

As for privateers, the only practical answers were "blockading their Ports, and of not permitting our Trade to proceed without protection."

Of course, their lordships hoped that the number of privateers at sea were "in a great degree exaggerated; as they cannot suppose that you have left the principal ports of the American Coast so unguarded as to permit such multitudes of Privateers to escape." To end a thoroughly angry letter, the Admiralty advised Warren of the dispatch of a sloop for the use of the admiral commanding the Leeward Islands Station, rather than assigning it to Warren for use in his command as needed.[6]

Several very important observations can be inferred from these letters. Contemporary British naval strategists tended to concentrate on the enemy fleet and major enemy ports where those fleets were based. The blockade of France had reinforced that strategic outlook, and by 1812 that blockade had been successful overall. The Admiralty viewed privateers as a nuisance—though a dangerous one—controllable by reliance on a combination of blockade, patrol, and convoy system. Since privateers used the same ports as the enemy navy, the military blockade served to contain both. The switch to the American theater, however, called for a shift in viewpoint that the Admiralty seemed unable or unwilling to make. Geographically, blockading the coasts of the United States posed problems different from blockading Europe. The lack of nearby bases, especially when winter virtually closed Halifax, was less important than the longer length of coastline and the numerous bays, inlets, and river mouths to shelter enemy vessels. Unless all these, as well as the numerous minor ports and recognized major ports, could be at least closely patrolled, then privateering, the sailing of small naval vessels, and the return of prizes could not be stopped.

American privateers proved themselves far different from their French brethren. Most French private raiders operated by dashing from a port, securing a prize or two, and quickly returning home, often all on the same day. Even raiders out of the French Caribbean islands generally used the same procedure.[7] Most American privateers, schooled to the transoceanic trade throughout their careers, engaged in long voyages, especially to the rich sea-lanes off England, Scotland, and Ireland. Nor did they fear for refuge initially, as Napoleon and his allies—as well as neutrals such as Norway—gladly opened their ports to these vessels and their prizes (though obviously the raiders did have to contend with running the blockade of those ports).[8] Despite such operational differences, the Admiralty continued to place less emphasis on the control of American privateers than on the destruction of the American Navy.

As with privateers, the navies of France and the United States differed in size and ability. The French Navy was the second largest in the world and was still building vessels on the day of Napoleon's abdication in 1814. Many of its most experienced officers, however, had fled France or died under the guillotines of the Revolution, and France's merchant fleet never supplied the number of experienced seamen required to operate its warships effectively. Perhaps more important, the British blockades prevented both the revolutionary Navy and its imperial successor from honing their seamanship and combat skills. Inexperience, as much as any intrinsic superiority of the Royal Navy, doomed French naval endeavors. As early as 1805, Napoleon instituted the Equipage de Marine, turning sailors by the thousands into second-class infantry battalions, several of which were assigned to various armies. The losses of 1812 forced an even greater draft from the fleet; at least eight thousand went to the Iberian Peninsula in the last two years of war, while a minimum of ten thousand struggled at Leipzig.[9] By 1814, the majority of French sailors were fighting ashore, and the British blockade held at bay wooden hulls manned by ghost crews. In early 1813, the strong British military blockade of French ports continued for fear of what could happen, rather than through an accurate assessment of enemy capabilities.[10] And that blockade consumed the bulk of the Admiralty's resources.

The American Navy was tiny in comparison to the French Navy, but possessed, at least initially, highly experienced sailors and a skilled officer corps. Just those differences dictated that a change in tactics, if not in strategy, should have been introduced by Britain into the North American theater; yet the Admiralty proved inflexible, treating the American Navy as if strong squadrons might erupt from port at any minute. The five U.S. Navy single-ship victories of 1812 certainly served to channel Admiralty actions, acting as a gauntlet thrown at its feet. Only destruction of the insulting enemy remained an option, and that enemy was no longer the United States, but the U.S. Navy as symbolized by the frigates *United States*, *President*, and *Constitution*.

The Admiralty's views on British force availability proved as interesting as its focus on American naval forces. Two related themes constantly appeared in communications with Warren: the numerical superiority of British vessels in the theater of war and the qualitative superiority provided by the ships-of-the-line.[11] The Admiralty's letter of 10 February noted that ninety-seven vessels were available to Warren but failed to mention, as all missives following failed to acknowledge, that over half of those ships were in the Caribbean and many of the remainder were dedicated to convoy duties. The latter task required virtually all the lighter class of vessels so valuable in inshore work. In fact, Warren, as of 28 March, mustered only twenty-eight ships and two tenders for blockade and patrol duty. When Warren submitted his plan for blockade based on these numbers, the Admiralty offered no comment on the paucity of vessels. It did suggest that he include a ship-of-the-line (from the reinforcing vessels) with each squadron and maintain a tight blockade of Boston even in winter.[12]

Amazingly, the mathematics of thirty British vessels opposing fourteen American warships and dozens of privateers along almost two thousand miles of coastline seems to have been overlooked by the Admiralty, and the much criticized Warren no longer dared complain nor plead for extensive reinforcements. Admittedly, the Admiralty's urging that Warren "strike some decisive blow" in the letter of 10 February disappeared from later communications, but only because Warren had offered a decisive blow of his own: an advance into the Chesapeake Bay with the ultimate aims of destroying commerce, ending the use of the bay as a haven for privateers, and capturing the *Constellation*, then completing its fitting out at Norfolk. With the American heavy frigates, at that time bottled in northern ports, refusing to run the blockade on less than the most favorable of terms, Warren's plan appeared to be the only viable offensive option (barring major reinforcements of regular infantry and a direct assault on Boston or New York). In the same letter in which the Admiralty approved Warren's plan of blockade, it also blessed his offensive into the Chesapeake, stressing the point that "in the choice of objects of attack, it will naturally occur to you that in every account any attempt which should have the effect of crippling the enemy's naval force should have a preference."[13] Oddly enough, neither Warren nor the Admiralty acknowledged the fact that the concentration of naval assets for a summer campaign would immediately invalidate Warren's proposed (and approved) plan of blockade which already called for the use of all available warships.

A final concern of the Admiralty related to Warren's request that his station commanders in Jamaica and the Leeward Islands be given increased local autonomy, with Warren taking overall control only in the case of a French breakout. Though Warren did not specify his reasons, those stations provided more headaches than assistance to his blockade. As fleet commander, all administrative details for the stations fell to him, and with no captain of the fleet to assist (Hotham arrived after this series of letters) that workload landed atop the administrative details of Warren's own station and squadron paperwork (though Sir George Cockburn took over the latter after his arrival). It was Warren's responsibility as fleet commander to distribute supplies, ships, and men to his scattered squadrons, as well as to integrate those squadrons into his own operational plans. Yet when he tried to exercise command of his forces by shifting ships north from the Caribbean, he received direct negative feedback from Melville. The first lord discouraged his admiral from weakening the Caribbean stations through reassignment of warships, as the British merchants raised a hue and cry at the mere rumor of such a move. This letter, in essence if not officially, effectively removed the warships from Warren's control.[14] If the beleaguered admiral had considered that shifting those vessels would drive home the true weakness of his blockade, perhaps forcing the release of the reinforcements which he desperately needed to maintain it, protect commerce, and pursue limited offensives, then his bit of subterfuge failed. The Admiralty eventually agreed to officially split the stations, but it would be Warren's replacement in 1814 who would reap the benefits of that largesse.

On 4 February, Capt. Charles Stewart of the *Constellation* breathed a sigh of relief as his vessel at last headed for the capes of the Chesapeake after weeks of delays in sailing. Imagine his horror at finding two British ships-of-the-line, three frigates, and two smaller vessels just entering the bay. Stewart quickly fled to Norfolk and began preparations to defend the harbor. The next day, the *Emily*, a licensed merchantman out of Baltimore, was turned back by the squadron, first victim of the economic blockade of the Chesapeake. The first captures appear to have followed one week later with the seizure of two large schooners.[15] Only on 6 February did Warren officially proclaim the commercial blockade of the Delaware and Chesapeake Bays, ordered 27 November 1812, as implemented.[16]

On 22 February, Secretary of the Navy Jones issued an order requiring all vessels to sail individually (after leaving harbor in groups, where possible) to increase the damage to British commerce. He felt the order necessary due to the expected increase of ships on blockade duty.[17] Seemingly making a lie of the circular's basis, one vessel arrived home without seeing a blockader. The *Constitution*, with news of the victory over the *Java*, at last returned to Boston on 27 February. Its small consort, the *Hornet*, had already begun its journey home and three days earlier had scored its own victory, destroying the British

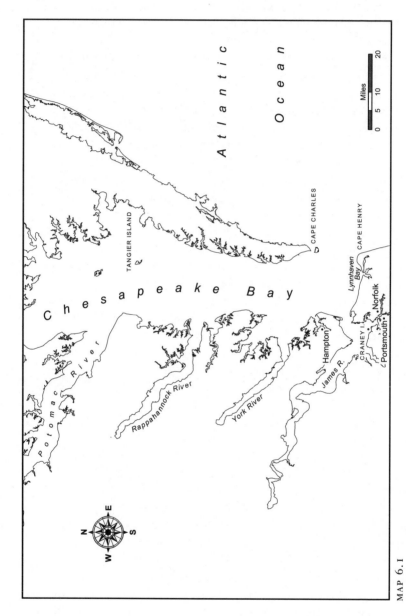

MAP 6.1
The lower Chesapeake.

brig *Peacock* off the coast of Guyana.[18] Boston celebrated the news of the *Java*'s demise, while Lloyd's of London released statistics near the end of February that evoked a different reaction in England. In the words of the *London Times*, "Five Hundred Merchantmen and 3 Frigates [captured or sunk]! Can these statements be true? And can the English people hear them unmoved? Any one who had predicted such a result of an American War this time last year would have been treated as a madman or a traitor."[19]

Cockburn at last arrived at Lynnhaven Bay on 3 March. Warren, in the *San Domingo*, seventy-four, joined him off Hampton Roads ten days later. This union brought total British forces in the bay to four ships-of-the-line, five frigates, two sloops, two brigs, and three tenders, or approximately half of the total vessels available for the blockade of the United States.[20] Such a concentration of force certainly appeared overwhelming.

Cockburn had used the days before Warren's arrival to observe American defensive positions around the *Constellation*, to sound and buoy channels, and to institute the commercial blockade of the Chesapeake. He determined that only a boat attack could succeed against the American frigate and, upon Warren's arrival, Cockburn attempted three such assaults, each meeting with failure. This course of action proved profitless, and the British commanders spent the remainder of the month planning and implementing action against American vessels hiding in the numerous waterways of the Chesapeake.

As the plans of Warren and Cockburn developed, the war continued around them. On 13 March, Congress confirmed appropriations for building six sloops for the Atlantic and authorized four others for the Great Lakes.[21] Two days earlier, it had nominated two representatives as peace commissioners, possibly because of the knowledge of the impending arrival in the United States of a representative of Tsar Alexander of Russia, who had offered his services in the negotiation of peace. The tsar's emissary arrived on 18 March, bringing with him the first details of the severe losses experienced by Napoleon in his 1812 campaign.[22]

In late March, Cockburn learned from American sources of the arrival of the Russian mediator. He forwarded the information to Warren, who discussed and delayed while advising Croker of the opportunity. Croker's answer, dispatched 17 May, settled the question of diplomacy: "I have their Lordships Commands to repeat to you their approbation that neither you or Rear Admiral Cockburn should have

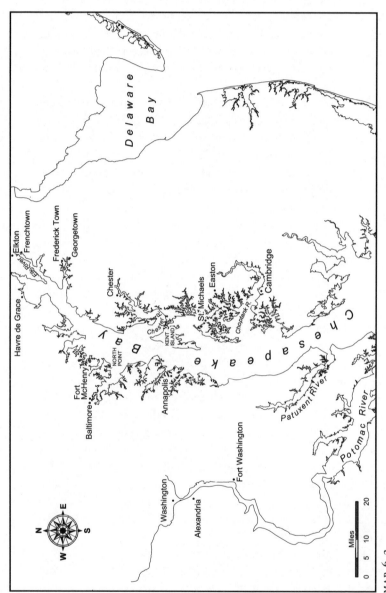

MAP 6.2
The upper Chesapeake.

thought yourselves authorized to enter into any Negotiation, or to defer or relax your measures of hostility on the proposition from the Russian Minister, or from the American Government."[23]

Warren's indignation at receiving this critical response can well be imagined as his original charge, to negotiate peace between the two countries, had been the chief reason for his appointment in the first place! But the British government refused to accept the offer of mediation; a peaceful ending to a useless little war was no longer the real objective. In a public declaration on 9 January 1813, the prince regent described the unwarranted American reasons for declaring war and the failure of the initial British peace initiatives. He then took the first step toward an increasingly hard-line stance, writing that "his Royal Highness confidently looks forward to a *successful issue* to the contest in which he has thus been compelled most reluctantly to engage." Apparently, the obsession with regaining the face lost to the tiny, despised enemy navy had blossomed to overwhelming proportions for the prince regent and his Cabinet, as well as the Admiralty. Needless to say, the appointment of two negotiators by the American Congress had been premature.[24]

Two additional British communications in March are of interest, one illustrating that problem solving was occurring, the second revealing that the war was approaching a new level of intensity. Both recognized that the struggle with the United States had assumed grim proportions. On 6 March, Warren issued a new standing order to the North American Station:

> Their Lordships trust that all the Officers of His Majestys Naval
> Service must be convinced that upon the good discipline and
> the proper training of their Ships Companies to the expert
> management of the Guns, the preservation of the high character
> of the British Navy most essentially depends, and that other
> works on which it is not unusual to employ the Men are of very
> trifiling *[sic]* importance, when Compared with a due preparation
> (by instruction and practice) for the effectual Services on the day
> of Battle.[25]

Recognizing that deterioration in gunnery skills may have contributed to the loss of vessels on the station, Warren ordered all possible practice with great guns and small arms, though he included a subtle reminder to record everything in the logs as the Admiralty was watching. Neither showpiece ships nor niggling concerns about gunpowder expenditure in training had a place in the increasingly dangerous and significant American theater.

On 25 March, the British government decided to extend the economic blockade from Rhode Island to New Orleans, encompassing all the major American ports and supplemented by patrols along the intervening coastline. Lord Melville, hoping to avoid any misunderstandings, addressed a private communication to Warren on the following day:

> We do not intend this as a mere *paper* blockade, but as a complete stop to all trade & intercourse by Sea with those Ports, as far as the wind & weather, & the continual presence of a sufficient armed Force, will permit & ensure. If you find that this cannot be done without abandoning for a time the interruption which you appear to be giving to the internal navigation of the Chesapeake, the latter object must be given up, & you must be content with blockading its entrance & sending in occasionally your cruisers for the purpose of harrassing & annoyance. I do not advert to enterprizes which you may propose to undertake with the aid of the Troops, as these will of course be directed with an adequate force to special objects. I apprehend also that it is scarcely necessary for me to request your most particular attention to the leaving an adequate force on the Jamaica & Leeward Islands. . . . The providing of sufficient convoys between Quebec & Halifax & the West Indies will not escape your attention, nor the husbanding & refitting your Force by having a certain number only engaged in cruising, so that the whole may be kept as effective as possible, & your blockading vessels be occasionally relieved.[26]

A memo from Croker followed on 28 April—somewhat more than a reminder concerning the expanded commercial blockade, as it stressed control of the privateering menace and of American trade by maintaining a blockade "of every port to which your force may be adequate and which shall afford any facilities either to the Privateers or Merchant Ships of the Enemy." Croker added that the Admiralty "considered that for these purposes your Force will be always adequate," not necessarily an accurate assessment.[27] Warren received Melville's correspondence sometime between 17 and 26 May (the receipt of Croker's note cannot be verified). He forwarded the declaration of the new blockade to the North American Station on the latter date. He should then have redirected his forces to meet its requirements. As the following pages detail, however, Warren did not attempt to implement the augmented commercial blockade until much later in the year. The admiral still had his eyes fixed on destroying a portion of the U.S. Navy: the *Constellation*.

On 1 April, Cockburn received promotion to the rank of rear admiral. Almost as if to celebrate, he and Warren opened a devastating littoral campaign in the Chesapeake Bay. The next day a successful cutting-out expedition on the Rappahannock River netted a privateer, three letter of marque traders, and two merchantmen. By 5 April, the Royal Navy had captured thirty-six additional sail and driven several others ashore. The devious Cockburn used the American vessels taken on 2 April to enter shallow waterways and approach their unwary former compatriots, resulting in easy victories. By 22 April, the fleet stood off the Patapsco, and while Warren cruised and harassed the area with boat attacks, Cockburn formed a light squadron of two frigates and six unrated vessels, raiding in the shallow northern end of the bay and along the Elk River. One week later, he briefly captured Frenchtown, burning or destroying five schooners, an artillery battery, munitions, and flour. He also confiscated all the available cattle, though he left British Treasury Bills equivalent to their market value. The third of May found the squadron at Havre de Grace, where it destroyed another battery and a foundry. Unfortunately for the local inhabitants, the militia decided to make a forlorn stand. After scattering them, Cockburn burned much of the village, beginning a policy that he would use throughout the war. If resistance was not offered, Cockburn only destroyed contraband. Resistance, whether militia or individual, prompted Cockburn to burn local homes in an attempt to discourage repetition of such actions. This policy made Cockburn the most hated Briton in the eyes of most Americans, who learned to pronounced his name "cock-*burn*" and ridiculed him in their press. Yet the British sailors he saved through such harsh measures seem to have idolized him. Georgetown and Fredericktown received the same treatment on 4 May, and three days later, having given Americans a taste of real war, Cockburn rejoined the fleet.[28]

Outside the Chesapeake, United States military forces remained active. The *Hornet* had arrived at Holmes' Hole, Massachusetts, on 19 March, loaded with prisoners of war and unchallenged by any blockaders.[29] On 9 April, the *Chesapeake* entered Boston, having taken only three prizes on its cruise. No British vessels blocked its entry. Six days later, American forces in the Gulf theater seized Spanish Mobile, quickly occupying and improving the fort guarding it and stationing several gunboats in Mobile Bay. This coup left Pensacola as the only port in the upper Gulf of Mexico friendly to Britain. Finally, in another of the continual blows to Warren's blockading efforts, the *President* and the smaller frigate *Congress* escaped from Boston on 30 April, taking advantage of a favorable wind.[30] Though a ship-of-the-line, three frigates, and a sloop blockaded that port and nearby waters, they proved too few for the weather conditions. Only the sloop spotted the American frigates, and it dared not give chase.[31]

On 13 May, Warren and Cockburn took the Chesapeake Squadron back to Hampton Roads and the ever-strengthening defenses surrounding the *Constellation.* Four days later Warren departed for Halifax with forty prizes. He intended to meet the promised marines and escort their troopships to the bay. At the same time, Capt. Robert Barrie in the *Dragon* escorted thirty prizes to Bermuda. While there, he refitted and replenished before returning to the Chesapeake Bay and command of the winter blockading squadron. Cockburn maintained command at Hampton Roads, intercepting shipping and surveying the area in preparation for the final assault on the *Constellation.*[32]

Remaining in the Chesapeake presented Cockburn with two major problems (the same problems existed throughout the blockade). First, his vessels needed provisions, fresh produce, and fresh water in great quantity to maintain the health of his crews. Second, his crewmen often deserted to the Americans. The need created a debilitative cycle. The region held abundant supplies, but to procure them men had to be sent ashore. Inevitably some deserted. Occasionally, entire boatloads fled, and once in the country they usually found immediate safety. Throughout the Napoleonic Wars, the Royal Navy averaged five hundred deserters per month—unsurprising in a navy based on impressment and the "cat." Men often served years without pay and, transferred from vessel to vessel, spent years without touching land or seeing loved ones. The closeness of the American coast seemed a siren call that many could not ignore.[33] Some died trying to reach it, as Stewart wrote to Jones on 21 May: "Their loss in prisoners and deserters has been very considerable; the latter are coming up to Norfolk almost daily, and their naked bodies are frequently fished up on the bay shore, where they must have been drowned on attempting to swim."[34]

Desertion was not a new problem for the British—it had plagued them in those same waters during the American Revolution. The

HMS Shannon Commencing the Battle with the American Frigate Chesapeake.
By June 1813, the Royal Navy badly needed a victory against the U.S.
Navy's frigates. Capt. Philip Broke of the *Shannon* provided that victory—
but only by disobeying the British Admiralty's standing orders!
©*The Mariner's Museum, Newport News, Virginia*

Nore, Spithead, and two mutinous crews who attempted to take their
ships into French ports had increased the fear of frustrated desertion
turning to mutiny during the Napoleonic wars. Even without the fear
of mutiny, British captains could never afford to see their hard-to-
replace crews decimated by desertion made easy. Along the coasts of
the United States, the problem extended far beyond the Chesapeake
and throughout the conflict. Warren's Port Standing Orders for Nova
Scotia, issued 1 October 1813, directed that "all fishing Boats and
Coasters are to be strictly examined for Deserters," while a circular
read to all crews near the end of 1814 pleaded with them to recall their
patriotic duties to England and reminded them of the penalties should
they run.[35]

A different type of "running" remained firmly in the minds of

American sailors. Stephen Decatur's *United States* with the *Macedonian* and the *Hornet* sailed to Fisher's Island, above New London, on 24 May, the first stage of "running" the blockade. On 1 June, Decatur attempted to escape into the Atlantic, but found the way barred by two British warships. Moving too quickly for the entire enemy squadron of two ships-of-the-line, two frigates, and a sloop to unite and trounce him, Decatur fled to a strong defensive position several miles above New London on the North River.[36]

The first of June proved to be a very bad day for the U.S. Navy. The *Chesapeake*, under Capt. James Lawrence, attempted to leave Boston, having orders to sail as soon as possible. Waiting, alone on blockade, Capt. Philip Broke in the *Shannon* had been preparing for the encounter for weeks. Heavy gunnery practice, interrupted only by burning captured vessels—Broke refused to weaken his crew by assigning men to prizes—had produced a quality apparently absent from most British vessels on the American station. Broke sought battle so eagerly that he had dispatched his consort, the *Tenedos*, and their tender to water. *La Hogue*, seventy-four, had been on station off Boston, but sailed in late May for Halifax, short of provisions. Broke even sent a message to Lawrence, offering single battle. It arrived after the *Chesapeake* sailed. Nevertheless, Lawrence made directly for the *Shannon*, his own death, and the first American frigate loss of the war.[37]

The victory made Broke a hero—one who never completely recovered from wounds received during the engagement. The *Shannon* and its prize sailed the following day for Halifax, leaving Boston uncovered and allowing the brig *Siren* to complete a cruise from New Orleans untouched. In winning his victory, Broke not only weakened his own patrol area in an effort to provoke a single-ship action but also ignored Admiralty orders and allowed Boston to remain unblockaded for over two weeks after the battle.

In a letter dated 9 July, the Admiralty castigated Griffith, immediate commander of the region's blockaders, for not maintaining a minimal blockading force of two frigates and one ship-of-the-line off American ports under his watch. They also demanded the captain of *La Hogue* (Broke's immediate superior) as a scapegoat for vessels escaping from Boston after the *Chesapeake-Shannon* engagement, ordered the avoidance of single-ship frigate engagements with the large American frigates, and stressed the need to intercept ships returning to American ports.[38] On the other hand, Broke's victory made him an instant hero and it is doubtful whether most of the government or the public cared about the local military ramifications—the victory provided a tremendous (and much needed) morale boost throughout Great Britain. Still, the Admiralty recognized that a victory such as that of Broke severely compromised the efficiency of the blockade, and within that parameter Broke clearly erred by deliberately weakening the cordon in an effort to lure Lawrence to battle.

Available records do not detail how many privateers and letter of marque traders escaped from Boston in those weeks, nor how many merchantmen, privateers, and their prizes brought needed goods into the port. If those records did exist, the true price of Broke's battle for glory, pride, and personal redemption could be measured. Nor was Lawrence without fault. His engagement with the *Shannon*, which might have been easily avoided during the early maneuvering of the two ships, defied Jones's circular of 22 February, which stressed the war on commerce. Even victory would have sent the *Chesapeake* limping back to port for additional months of refitting. Lawrence paid with his life for ignoring his orders; had he emerged victorious, however, death would have been Broke's only alternative to being condemned by court martial.

With the Boston squadron dispersed and the New York squadron off New London searching for a way to get at Decatur's ships, the *Argus* sailed from New York on 8 June, not seeing enemy sails until seventy miles off the coast, where it narrowly avoided British reinforcements bound for the Chesapeake. Again, a British squadron had failed to keep the blockade in mind, distracted by the chance to capture an American frigate or to recapture the *Macedonian*. This error definitely had a price. Lt. William Henry Allen's orders required that he deliver a new ambassador for France to L'Orient, then raid shipping on the coast of England, burning prizes instead of sending them into port. By taking the war to England, the secretary of the navy hoped to distract major elements of the Royal Navy while increasing the already loud cries against the war being voiced by British merchants. Allen followed his orders to the letter, and as columns of smoke began to rise within view of the English coast, the Admiralty thickened its local patrols. On 12 August, the British brig *Pelican* defeated the *Argus*, Allen dying four days later of a wound received in the battle. The final price of the neglected blockade included a diplomatic mission completed, nineteen merchantmen destroyed in British home waters, and a large public outcry, bringing exactly the results that Jones had sought in commerce raiding.[39]

Or almost exactly the results Jones sought—he would have preferred the *Argus* safely home, just as his preference would have been to have the *Chesapeake* cruising in prize-filled waters rather than captured in some unproductive quest for glory. Future operational orders reflected exactly that:

> You are also strictly prohibited from giving or receiving a Challenge, to, or from, an Enemy's Vessel. —The Character of the American Navy does not require those feats of Chivalry and your own reputation is too well established, to need factitious support. Whenever you meet an equal Enemy, under fair Circumstances, I am sure, you will beat him; but it is not even good policy to meet an equal, unless, under special circumstances, where a great object is to be gained, without a great sacrifice. —His Commerce is our true Game, for there he is indeed vulnerable.[40]

Though the success of the *Argus* served as a focal point of British public concern, it is difficult to give that raider all the credit for the increase in patrols in British coastal waters during 1813–14.[41] The increasing number of American privateers operating therein strongly contributed to the Admiralty's decision to increase local patrols. Regardless of the strength of those patrols, they never managed to reduce American depredations upon the British merchant marine in its home waters, depredations allowed by the flimsy cordon off the coasts of the United States.

June brought additional pressure to the Chesapeake. Cockburn continued raiding and blockading, the *Narcissus* capturing the revenue cutter *Surveyor* at anchor in the York River on 12 June. Warren rejoined him on the nineteenth, bringing total forces in the bay to eight ships-of-the-line, twelve frigates, eight unrated ships, several tenders, and six transports carrying 2,650 troops.[42] This concentration of shipping accounted for nearly 70 percent of forces available to meet the North American Station's responsibilities, including the blockade.

The frigate *Junon* made a last attempt to engage the *Constellation* ship-to-ship on 21 June, but fifteen American gunboats and shallow water combined to halt the effort. The next day a direct amphibious landing sought to capture the Craney Island fortifications. Success would have placed the *Constellation* in an untenable position, but American gunnery repulsed the assault. Substantial British casualties resulted from the action (between light and heavy, depending on whether American or British reports are read, though both agree that the British lost two barges).[43]

Despite the failure to capture the American frigate, Warren continued operations in the Chesapeake rather than withdraw and reinforce
the greatly stressed coastal blockade. Feeling that he needed a success
to justify the presence of the marines, Warren ordered a landing and
assault on Hampton, Virginia, for 1 June, even though the village was
operationally worthless. The British forces achieved a striking victory
over militia forces, capturing three stands of colors and seven guns.
Unfortunately, two companies of troops variously identified as Canadian irregulars or French chasseurs (French prisoners serving as skirmishers in exchange for their freedom) began raping, murdering, and
pillaging. The incident served to increase the tendency toward barbarity in a war where, as Henry Edward Napier wrote, even Quakers were
forced to be less-than-neutral bystanders. After bringing the troops
under control, Warren allowed them to engage in professional pillage
for nine days, partially resupplying the fleet by that process. While
land operations progressed, shallow-draft vessels harried shipping for
ten miles up the James River and a heavier force used boat actions to
disrupt commerce on the Elizabeth River.[44]

On 2 July, Warren ordered Cockburn to switch his flag to the *Sceptre*,
seventy-four, and lead a small squadron composed of an additional
ship-of-the-line, a frigate, and a troopship with 250 marines to raid
Ocracoke Inlet. Warren himself, after leaving ten sail in Lynnhaven
Bay to blockade the mouth of the Chesapeake, proceeded to the
Potomac River. Still intent on destroying American warships, he hoped
to reach the corvette *Adams*, refitting below Washington. His vessels
entered the Potomac on 13 July and advanced thirty miles upstream
before shallow water spared the *Adams*. Warren did manage to surprise
the American naval schooners *Scorpion* and *Asp* at anchor in the Yeo-
comico, a tributary of the Potomac. The *Asp* fell to British boarders; its
consort escaped.[45]

Cockburn's force arrived at Ocracoke Island on 12 July, discovering
an absence of other blockading forces. He quickly seized the village of
Portsmouth, which owed its existence and continued survival to a
thriving transshipment business, transferring goods from deep-draft
Atlantic traders to shallow-draft vessels of the Carolina sounds. Boats
quickly rowed to capture a privateer and a letter of marque trader
anchored just across the bar. Following that success, Cockburn directed
his small craft to raid into the sound, gathering supplies for the fleet.
Four days later, the squadron sailed to rejoin Warren, but only after
Cockburn paid the citizens of Portsmouth for the supplies taken by his
men. The small force reported to Warren off the Potomac on 19 July.

Nymphe's Cutter & the Paragon, August 15, 1813.
The all-too-few British warships in American waters during 1813 often used
their ship's boats to extend their patrol radius. This led to the occasional
mismatch, as a lone cutter or longboat attempted to inspect a well-armed
American privateer posing as a "harmless" merchantman.
©The Mariner's Museum, Newport News, Virginia

Despite the capture of two vessels of the private navy, Cockburn's raid
had accomplished little except perhaps invoking fear in some North
Carolinians and anger in others. His recommendation to Warren that a
small force of light warships be permanently stationed off Ocracoke
apparently went unheeded.[46]

For the remainder of July and August, Warren and Cockburn roved
the Chesapeake Bay at will, one day sounding the Severn River and
examining Fort Washington, another day cutting out vessels on the
Patapsco or rowing up the Miles River to destroy an American battery.
They actually took possession of Kent Island for a month, using it as a
watering station and a place for sick crewmen to recover, away from
the mainland, and thus the lure of desertion.[47]

On 6 September, unwilling to face the region's autumnal "fever
season" and continued desertion, Warren split his fleet into three

parts. Cockburn in the *Sceptre* along with several vessels requiring long-term repairs and the transports sailed for Bermuda. The bulk of the fleet, under Warren, escorted all prizes to Halifax, checking on other blockading squadrons in passing. These ships also sorely needed refit, and their crews required rest. Barrie in the *Dragon*, commanding a force of two frigates, two brigs, and three schooners, remained at Lynnhaven Bay to handle the winter blockade and occasionally venture into the Chesapeake proper to discourage local commerce.[48]

Through late June the northeastern coasts had been unblockaded if not unharassed. A 14 June letter to Jones from Capt. Isaac Hull, commanding Portsmouth Naval Yard, stated, "The coasting trade here is immense. Not less than fifty sail last night anchored in this harbor."[49] To combat British patrollers and privateers, Hull planned to use the brigs *Siren* and *Enterprise* as convoy escorts. By 24 June, the situation had changed. A frigate, sloop, and two brigs had trapped the tiny *Enterprise* in port. Hull now proposed using his brigs on short cruises, as coasting appeared completely stopped by this new British squadron.[50] His proposal, however, was premature. With the concentration of British vessels in the Chesapeake and the demands of convoys to and from Canada, the blockaders soon sailed away. Coastal traffic resumed, as did escort duty. In August, Hull used gunboats to escort shipping around exposed Cape Ann, and on 14 August his convoy efforts paid dividends when the *Enterprise* and a gunboat teamed to capture a Canadian privateer which had been interfering with coastal traffic.[51]

On 5 September, the *Enterprise* cruised the Maine coast, searching for privateers and British patrols. Hearing gunfire off the harbor of Portland, Lt. William Burrows investigated, discovering the brig *Boxer,* fourteen, under Cdr. Samuel Blyth. After a brief, spirited action, the *Boxer* surrendered. Both captains died early in the engagement. Rumor circulated that the captain of the British brig had been paid by the merchants of Portland to escort a Swedish merchantman into port. Supposedly, he fired several shots while unsuccessfully "chasing" the vessel into port (for the sake of appearance, just in case other British vessels happened to be nearby). These reportedly attracted the attention of the *Enterprise*, though no mention of the shots appeared in the official report.[52]

On 27 September, the *President* returned to Narragansett Bay. It had taken twelve prizes and encountered no difficulty making an anchorage, actually capturing the blockading squadron's tender, the

Highflyer, as the large frigate passed through the weak cordon. On that date, many of Warren's ships from the Chesapeake campaign were anchored at Halifax or Bermuda for refit and resupply. Only twenty-four ships remained committed to the coastal blockade and patrols.[53]

Stung by the loss of the *Boxer* and the victorious return of the *President,* Warren strengthened the blockade and increased patrols along the northeastern coast as ships became available. Though an American revenue cutter captured the Canadian privateer *Dart,* five, on 13 October, the American brig *Rattlesnake* found itself and its convoy driven into port by a British frigate on 1 November and trapped there for several days.[54]

At last getting back to the business of blockading, Warren extended the Admiralty's economic blockade to include Long Island Sound and Montauk to Block Point. His official justification—"finding that the Enemy by withdrawing his Naval force from the Port of New-York, and establishing at the Port of New-London a Naval Station, to cover the Trade to and from the Port of New-York"—is questionable, as the American ships had fled to New London in an attempt to survive against a superior force, the frigates being trapped there for the duration of the war.[55] Rather, Warren was probably driven by the large licensed trade being conducted from the port of New York (often dozens of vessels each day) and the privateers and letter of marque traders escaping under that cover, even as prizes of the Americans safely returned to harbor. Capt. Jonathan Hayes had complained in October to his admiral of the neutral flags "by hundreds, and Licenced Vessels out of number" passing his station each day bound for Boston and New York.[56]

Warren advised his captains of the blockade on 16 November and wrote the Admiralty on the twentieth. Considering communication lag, the earliest that the British government could have advised neutrals of the blockade would have been near the end of December. Capt. Robert Dudley Oliver, senior officer off New York at that time, requested that the Swedish consul at New York, Henry Gahn, "communicate this intelligence to the other Neutral Consuls" on 2 December. He warned Gahn that "after the sixth of December no vessels whatever will be permitted to sail from any Port in Long Island Sound."[57] It should be noted that a snap blockade announcement generated the potential for rich prizes until word spread and ships stopped using the newly blockaded stretch of coast. Regardless of purpose, Warren's orders proved too little and too late—too little because the

HMS Moselle in Charleston Bay, 1813.
Before late 1814, British admirals wasted few of their warships on the
blockade of America's southern ports. When even one raiding vessel, such
as the *Moselle,* could send the large flocks of merchantmen fleeing for safety,
it is difficult to understand why British commanders often ignored the
economic importance of the region.
©*The Mariner's Museum, Newport News, Virginia*

coast of New England was not included, and too late because the winter season had arrived to hamper blockaders.

As if in mockery of Warren's proclamation, the *Congress* entered
Portsmouth, New Hampshire, on 14 December, albeit having taken
only four prizes during its cruise. Finding its timbers rotten, the Navy
placed the *Congress* in ordinary and shipped its guns to the Great
Lakes. Finally, the *Constitution,* now commanded by Capt. Charles
Stewart, exited Boston on the last day of the year; as usual in successful escapes, it sighted no blockaders.[58]

A British presence along the southern and Gulf coasts during 1813
remained virtually nonexistent, though the blockade communicated by
Warren to the various stations on 26 March as well as the actual plans he
later submitted to the Admiralty should have kept light units off those
coasts at all times. The British frigate *Herald* and its tender attempted

to force Mobile Bay, recently occupied by American forces, on 3 June. Three gunboats forced the abandonment of the attack. The two vessels returned to Mobile in October, with the same results.[59] In August, the British sloop *Colibri* and brig *Moselle* landed men on Dewe's Island, South Carolina, apparently for watering and provisions. They moved to Hilton Head on 22 August, two days after completion of watering. After only three days of patrol they attempted to flee before a hurricane that savaged Charleston on 26 August; trapped on a lee shore, *Colibri* ran aground and was destroyed.[60] A second storm lashed St. Marys on 16 and 17 September, sinking three American gunboats, beaching four others, and leaving a final gunboat stranded five hundred yards inland. Quickly repairing this damage, the base commander was capable of instituting a convoy system between St. Marys and Savannah in early December.[61] The only other British activity in southern waters involved a reported cutting-out expedition at New Inlet, North Carolina, during October and two brigs, *Recruit* and *Dotterel*, briefly off the South Carolina coast the first week of November.[62]

The hurricane season that plagued the South had not left the British unscathed. A storm of tremendous proportions cut a swathe through the Caribbean in late July. It pounded the major British bases there between 23 and 26 August. Though devastating to the population and merchant vessels, the Royal Navy experienced no outright losses, only varying degrees of damage to every vessel on the stations.[63] At the end of a long supply line for masts, spars, cordage, and canvas, refitting was slow. Halifax experienced a similar disaster on 12 November. The remnants of a late season hurricane drove almost every warship in the harbor aground, over thirty receiving damage that required major repairs before sailing. Those repairs would still be under way in March of the following year.[64]

Hurricanes and the sailing of the *Constitution* brought a fitting end to the 1813 campaign. For both the Admiralty and Warren, little had gone as planned. Warren failed to activate the initial stage of the Admiralty's 1812 economic blockade until 21 February 1813. His plan for the blockade, shared with the Admiralty in March, called for the available twenty-eight vessels to be deployed as follows: Chesapeake Bay, six (plus tender); Delaware Bay, three; New York, one; Block Island to Montauk Point, two; Bay of Fundy, five; Nova Scotia, three; Ocracoke to Beaufort, South Carolina, two; Savannah to St. Augustine, Spanish Florida, one; and cruising and relief, five (plus tender).[65] The Admiralty accepted the plan with little comment, despite glaring weaknesses. Not only did the South receive too little and the Gulf no cover-age, but the uncommitted ships were too few to patrol and relieve, indicating that portions of the coast, notably New England, would be unpatrolled. It should also be noted that Boston, base of numerous public and private naval vessels, received no direct coverage under this deployment.

Given the meager resources allotted to his command by the Admiralty, this was the best plan that Warren could devise, with extra ships to be slotted in as they arrived. Unfortunately, the Admiralty also con-tinually stressed that the tiny American Navy should be destroyed so that the ships-of-the-line could be returned to England. With those American vessels either snug in port or safe at sea, Warren acted to meet that challenge in the only manner available. His extended foray into the Chesapeake sought destruction of commerce only as a sec-ondary goal, the primary effort appearing to have been the capture or destruction of the *Constellation* and, possibly, the *Adams*. In the midst of the operation, one approved and encouraged by the Admiralty, War-ren received word that the economic blockade of the Delaware and Chesapeake Bays must be immediately extended to include the entire coast from Long Island southward to New Orleans.[66] With his entire relief and cruising force as well as every newly arrived vessel in the Chesapeake, Warren chose to give the commercial blockade lip service only. He even ignored a personal missive from Melville, dated 26 March, requesting that he abandon the bay in favor of the blockade if he had not yet captured the *Constellation*.[67] In doing so, Warren not only left gaps in his existing blockade when ships sailed for provisions or water, he placed his small vessels and frigates at risk, in part prompting a second order from his superiors on 10 July, prohibiting British frigates from singly engaging the *Constitution*, *President*, or *United States*, as well as the Admiralty's issuance of several reminders to keep a ship-of-the-line with each blockading squadron.[68]

Why did Warren maintain that expedition, so apparently crippling to the effectiveness of the blockade? First, fault must be placed with the Admiralty's focus on the destruction of the U.S. Navy. Warren felt forced into some aggressive action regardless of available warships. Second, he was aware that he lacked the assets to implement the demanded blockade of the majority of the American coast, with or without the forces committed to the Chesapeake Bay campaign. Real-izing that attempting to institute the extended blockade could only result in failure, modest or otherwise, he opted for a potential victory against American naval forces in the Chesapeake. Even the two British successes of the year outside the bay, the capture of the *Chesapeake* and the trapping of Decatur's squadron, reflected the same focus on the destruction of the U.S. Navy, and each success left holes in the blockade that, militarily, more than offset the victories gained.

It is easy to imagine Warren as a beaten man after the Chesapeake offensive and months of effort wasted on American warships that would probably run the blockade over the winter. His extension of the blockade—closing the last entrance to Long Island Sound and adjacent ports—sounded grand on paper, but he could not redeploy to strengthen it with his worn vessels, exhausted crews, and the dangers posed by winter weather to blockaders. The twin hurricanes, striking all of Warren's major bases except Bermuda, must have felt like some holy vengeance, leaving a strengthened blockade to wait until 1814. Even Henry Hotham, a man carefully selected by the Admiralty to assist Warren in bringing the North American situation under control, felt the weight of failure upon his shoulders. In a private letter to Melville dated 6 November, he wrote,

> I accepted [the position of captain of the fleet] as a duty to your Lordship, and I have held it till this time for the same reason; Such as your Lordship's intentions and my expectations have been disappointed, and I feel the ends for which I was sent to it have not been answered, I cannot longer continue in it with a conscientious discharge of duty to the service, or to myself, without requesting you will be pleased to relieve me as soon as arrangements for that purpose can be made. As the operations of the summer are concluded and the Commander in Chief is about to return to Bermuda for the winter, the present appears to me the most proper period for making this communication that the object of it may be effected before he embarks again; and it is with his permission I submit it to your Lordship.[69]

While the Royal Navy could not establish an effective command of the coast, the United States government needed little help to blockade itself. President James Madison, at last concerned about the amount of American commerce going to Britain or its possessions, asked Congress for an embargo on 20 July. The Senate, feeling any commerce superior to no commerce, rejected the bill.[70] Madison then asked Jones to use the Navy to stop all intercourse with the enemy (he later made the same request of the army), and Jones issued a formal order to that effect on 30 July.[71] Despite some military success to this end, Madison again requested an embargo, and finally received approval on 17 December. It decreed that all sailings from and entries into American harbors by domestic and international vessels, including coasters, cease. Only public and private naval vessels and prizes were exempt. Appeals for additional exemptions (to relieve the hardship of isolated settlements, for example) could be made directly to the president.[72] With the ease of a pen stroke, the British had their economic blockade, courtesy of "Little Jimmy."

If some American civilians showed an interest in helping the British, just as many took a more loyal wartime approach and attempted to visit mayhem upon the enemy. One of the most popular ways seemed to be with explosives. This mode of warfare should have been of little surprise to the Admiralty. American Robert Fulton had attempted to sell several of his naval inventions—mines, submarines and spar-torpedoes, and steam-powered warships—to both the French and British governments between 1797 and 1805. Both countries rebuffed his "barbarous" approach to war. Fulton returned to the United States in 1805 and offered his talents to support the American struggle against Great Britain during the War of 1812. Aside from the use of floating mines, often termed "Fultons" as well as "infernal devices," Fulton built and launched the first steam warship, the underpowered *Demologus*, at New York in late 1814.[73]

Many Americans apparently did not share the European reluctance to take advantage of new naval technology. On 5 June, the crew of the *Victorious* found a "Fulton" floating toward their ship on the tide. A July attempt to destroy the *Plantagenet* off Cape Henry ended in a premature explosion. Several of these floating mines were also anchored at the narrows of Portsmouth (New Hampshire) Harbor to protect it against attack.[74]

A group of New York merchants made the only successful attack of the year. They used the schooner *Eagle* to attempt to destroy Capt. Thomas Hardy's *Ramillies*. The merchants loaded the *Eagle* with black powder hidden beneath provisions, an item always needed by blockaders. The owners hoped it would be moored adjacent to Hardy's flagship when it exploded; instead, only a few crewmen and an officer were unloading the craft into launches—eleven seamen and the lieutenant died. Their deaths in the explosion angered British officers and crewmen, and forced Warren to issue an order to search all captures before bringing them alongside a warship.[75]

On 23 August, a courageous American in a submersible attempted to attach a torpedo to the *Ramillies*. Afterward, Hardy ordered that his vessel be kept in constant motion and had its bottom swept with a cable every two hours. He also warned the local inhabitants by broadside that he would take harsh measures if one more such "cowardly" act occurred. According to the *Gentleman's Magazine*, Hardy *did* take harsh steps, keeping American prisoners on board his vessel to share his fate if *Ramillies* fell prey to such dishonorable devices and holding American crews on board their captured vessels to discourage a repeat of the *Eagle* episode. Apparently the region's inhabitants took the captain as a man of his word, and the *Ramillies* experienced no further close calls with "infernal devices."[76]

The war along the Canadian border remained stalemated in 1813, despite Perry's victory at Lake Erie on 6 September. Nevertheless, that theater continued to have its impact on both American and British navies. Aside from the recruitment drain on eastern ports, Jones transferred the entire crew of the *Macedonian*, as well as its guns, from the hopeless situation at New London to the Great Lakes. Likewise, the crews of the *John Adams* and *Alert* as well as large detachments from the *Argus* and the *Constitution* trekked into the hinterlands. In December, the Admiralty required Warren to lay up four badly needed vessels, dispatching their crews and guns westward to the lakes.[77]

While both Atlantic navies suffered this internal attrition, the first steps toward peace were underway. Stimulated primarily by the American victory on Lake Erie (promising no immediate end to the war) and the need to concentrate British resources for the deathblow against Napoleon, Viscount Robert Castlereagh, British secretary of state for foreign affairs, dispatched a letter to Madison in November requesting direct peace negotiations. The American president quickly accepted this overture, largely because of the continued stalemate along the Canadian frontier.[78] The news of Napoleon's defeat at Leipzig, arriving in Washington on 31 December, probably helped push the decision to accept peace talks, though Madison firmly instructed his delegates that no conditions of the declaration of war should be negotiated away.[79] Even with stalemate on the border and Napoleon near collapse in Europe, Madison could insist on such terms—in some small part due to the relative ineffectiveness of the blockade during the first two years of war.

As some people played with explosives and others prepared to talk, the private navy continued to make inroads into British shipping. With open ports plentiful, privateers ranged the Atlantic. The *True-Blooded Yankee* made its own ports, taking command of an Irish island for six days, then a Scottish harbor, where it burned seven vessels after provisioning and watering. The Portuguese and Spanish coasts proved a gold mine (more literally, a specie mine) for privateers. In January 1813, the *Dolphin* opened the year with two captures. By midyear multiple privateers, occasionally working together, captured as many as forty-five vessels in a month. The *Lion* alone seized fifteen to twenty vessels in November, as well as $400,000 in specie destined for Wellington's coffers, but soon in American hands.[80]

This successful privateering occasioned a sharp series of letters directed to Melville by Wellington. "Surely the British navy cannot be so hard run as not to be able to keep up the communication with Lisbon for this army!" he wrote, followed by, "I have the honor to enclose a letter containing the report of the capture and ransom of the *Canada*, horse transport, by an American privateer," and "If they only take the ship with our shoes, we must halt for six weeks." At last, Wellington wrote in disgust, "I am certain that it will not be denied, that since Great Britain has been a naval power, a British army has never been left in such a situation."[81] When Melville responded in mid-August with a letter hinting at his own frustration and assigning blame thither and yon, Wellington lashed out:

> What I have written has been founded upon my own sense of want of naval assistance on this coast . . . and I assure you that I neither know nor care what has passed, or may pass, in Parliament or in the newspapers on the subject.
>
> I complain of an actual want of naval assistance and co-operation with the army. I know nothing about the cause of the evil, I state the fact, which nobody will deny; and leave it to government to apply a remedy or not as they think proper.[82]

Wellington had developed a low opinion of the Admiralty by the end of 1813, and he certainly knew the cause of his problem: an unblockaded United States and the horde of privateers harrying his supply line.

For Warren, Cockburn, and the captains responsible for stopping those privateers, 1813 had been a year of misdirection and miscues, capped by natural catastrophe. As winter extended its icy grip, privateers ran pass Barrie's Chesapeake blockade on every north wind. In a single day, eight to ten vessels escaped Barrie's squadron during a snow storm on 20 December 1813, though three others wrecked in the same attempt. As early as November, Barrie had readily admitted that "In spite of our utmost endeavours the Enemy's Clippers continue to pass us every Northerly Wind."[83] Boston and New York simply could not be closely covered without losing vessels in the breakers. The northeast coast was pitiless to patrollers, and the South and Gulf remained unblockaded and virtually unpatrolled. With only twenty-five to thirty seaworthy vessels out of Halifax, and similarly reduced squadrons in the Caribbean, is it any wonder that Warren's last letter of the year to Croker reeked of doom, gloom, and near hopelessness?

> Sir
>   . . . having sent the *Barossa* to Jamaica to carry home specie, and every other Ship that could be spared without raising the Blockaded ports of America, I lament to find that both the Leeward Islands and Jamaica are still very deficient of a Force adequate to their protection, or to perform the various extensive Convoy Service required to be done in those places—
>   The Hurricanes in the West Indies & at Halifax, have unfortunately increased the difficulty of carrying forward the Service, and very considerably crippled and diminished the disposeable part of the [North American] Squadron, I have already Stated these circumstances to you in my letters from Halifax, but am compelled to repeat the same, in order to entreat their Lordships atten[tion] to the state of my Ships, and extreme necessity of encreasing the Force in every part of the West Indies.
>   . . . Every exertion is making at New York, Philadelphia, and Baltimore to prepare Vessels of War, the rapidity with which the Americans, build and fit out their Ships, is scarcely credible, and I am apprehensive of the mischief their Cruizers will do to our Trade—
>   Several large Clipper Schooners of from two to three hundred Tons, strongly manned and armed have run thro' the Blockade in the Chesapeak, in spite of every endeavour and of the most vigilant attention of our Ships to prevent their getting out, nor can any thing stop these Vessels escaping to Sea in dark Nights and Strong Winds, their Lordships will be pleased to observe by Captn. Barrie's letter which is herewith enclosed, an instance of Several of these Schooners passing out in a Squadron and outsailing every Ship in Chace.

Two Ships of the Line each to be called 76 guns are to be finished and launched in March, one at Portsmouth the other at Charlestown near Boston.

The Southern Coast about Charlestown [South Carolina] is a retreat for the Enemys Privateers and Letters of Marque, I am anxious to Send Small Cruizers thither to destroy and intercept them, the large Class of our fast sailing Brigs are the best adapted and I should be very happy if their Lordships w[ould] cause some to be Selected and ordered to join me.

I take the liberty likewise to represent that as all the American Men of War, Privateers and even Traders, are particularly good Sailing Vessels such of his Majesty's Ships as are appropriated to my Command, should be of the same description—I have the honour to be Sir Your most obedient humble Servant

John Borlase Warren[84]

After only a little over a year of too few ships, too many contradictory directives, and the resulting failures, Warren was finished. It only remained for the Admiralty to select their new champion, hand him his orders, and put him on a fast ship for Bermuda. Even there, it dithered.

7

1814–1815:
The Wooden Wall Complete?

The abdication of Napoleon in April 1814 allowed potentially massive land and naval reinforcements to reach North America by August. The extension of the commercial blockade to New England in April, coupled with the new warships, at last afforded the Admiralty an opportunity to interdict all the coastal regions of the United States. Instead, a policy of aggressive raiding developed as a diversion for the main British effort from Canada, and the Royal Navy again concentrated its assets in the Chesapeake Bay, followed by an abortive invasion at New Orleans. In the Chesapeake, a successful raid on Washington, D.C., left its government buildings in flames, but an assault on Baltimore suffered firm repulse. In the final analysis, the raiding in the Chesapeake did more harm than good for the blockade, and the British cause in general, by removing ships from the blockade itself while diverting men and supplies from the vital Canadian frontier. Along that frontier, British forces managed to secure portions of Maine but found an invasion via Lake Champlain throttled by American naval forces, unweakened by any response to the Royal Navy's raids along the Atlantic coast.[1] At the end of December, the peace commissioners meeting in Ghent reached an accord and the blockade dissolved in March 1815, though numerous American vessels already at sea continued preying on British merchantmen for several months.

As in the previous year, Cockburn sailed from Bermuda on 3 January for the blockade off Boston and New York. The *Sceptre* found the going difficult and almost foundered before reaching New London. American sources reported that the ship had hogged, an assertion supported by the transfer of Cockburn and most of his officers to the *Albion*, seventy-four. While off New London, Cockburn advised Hardy to cover his furled sails in painted canvas until needed to prevent their freezing in the rain that usually fell before a severe drop in temperature. Cockburn then sailed for the Chesapeake Bay, stopping briefly to inspect the Delaware Squadron.[2]

American vessels also sailed, or attempted to sail, that winter. The schooner *Alligator*, patrolling the coast between Charleston and Savannah, found itself briefly trapped by a British frigate and two smaller vessels near Charleston in late January. But the schooner defeated their cutting-out expedition, and the Royal Navy vessels cruised away. In early January, the American brigs *Enterprise* and *Rattlesnake* ran the blockade from Portsmouth, New Hampshire, beginning a cruise that ended in March at Wilmington. They captured only four prizes, but none of the vessels had problems entering the unguarded port. On the eighteenth of that same month, the *Adams* used the cover of a gale to exit the Chesapeake. It sailed by Barrie's blockading squadron in the same manner that privateers had sailed by it throughout the winter. After taking a few prizes, the *Adams* found haven in an unblockaded Savannah on 29 April.[3] The *Constellation* made two attempts to run the blockade in February, but Barrie's squadron successfully blocked both. The sloop *Frolic* enjoyed more success in sallying from Boston on 18 February, though its luck expired 20 April, overmatched by the British frigate *Orpheus* off Cuba. The *Frolic* had taken only one prize. The *Peacock* escaped New York the first week of March, tasked with delivering military supplies to St. Marys. Touching only long enough to unload and resupply, the sloop began a cruise that netted fifteen prizes, including one of His Majesty's brigs.[4] In the Pacific, the epic cruise of Capt. David Porter and the *Essex* ended under the guns of the British frigate *Phoebe* and sloop *Cherub* on 28 March. Since 1812, Porter had taken over forty prizes and virtually destroyed the British whaling industry in the Pacific.[5]

The military blockade seemed virtually nonexistent in the opening months of the year. A continued lack of ships, the wear of the Chesapeake campaign, and damage from hurricanes in late 1813 forced Warren to leave most of the coast either weakly patrolled or not patrolled at all. British trade suffered for it, as ship after ship vanished to foreign and American ports, sailed home on promise of ransom, or was burned by American captors.

The commercial blockade, as well as the economic interdiction inherent to the military blockade, was another matter. It certainly gave the appearance of success in the opening months of 1814—unarmed merchantmen no longer ran the blockade, coastal trade had virtually ended, and neutrals no longer legally entered American ports. Such success, however, had little to do with the Royal Navy's close blockade. Instead, President Madison and Congress had embargoed their nation in the name of ending illegal trade with Great Britain and stopping American assistance to the Royal Navy. The embargo succeeded in neither. Smuggling via the Canadian border continued. The water-dependent traffic with Amelia Island simply diminished slightly in quantity, despite the naval forces based at St. Marys, and increasing numbers of Spanish vessels entered New Orleans. Many British officers probably still received their newspapers, though they had to send forces ashore to fetch them instead of having them delivered. Most important, the embargo crippled American internal trade and stopped the duties that provided most of the income of the United States government.[6] President of a nation already heavily in debt, Madison severely erred in prohibiting that commerce.

After some six weeks of the embargo, Madison apparently realized his mistake in stopping all coastal trade. Local customs officials bonded a number of vessels traversing the sheltered waters of the Chesapeake Bay, Long Island Sound, and the South Carolina–Georgia coast—significantly, waters less frequented by the Royal Navy or heavily patrolled by American forces. At Baltimore, bonds ranged from $1,500 for a 15-ton craft to a staggering $54,900 for the 198-ton steamship *Chesapeake*. If vessels deviated from their assigned route, their owners forfeited the bonds to the national government. Between February and March 1814, seventy-two coasters averaging slightly over 51 tons each were bonded to sail from Baltimore. At least thirty-eight vessels operated from New York and eighty-five along the southern coast.[7]

By the new year, changing circumstances had made the long-existing nonimportation laws as well as the embargo untenable. Great Britain now had access to the ports and markets of northern Europe, so attempts to injure Britain via economic coercion were no longer viable. At home, Madison's embargo angered those who depended on the coasting trade for livelihood and markets. It increased smuggling without diminishing interactions with British buyers. An editorial in the *Niles' Weekly Register* of 22 January 1814 lamented that "it is truly distressing to observe the prevalence of treasonable practices in the United States."[8] British lieutenant Henry Edward Napier wrote, "Self, the great ruling principle, more powerful with Yankees than any people I ever saw. Begin with a dollar and proceed to any amount, you may always buy a Yankee in almost any rank and station!"[9] The embargo had failed, and on 31 March the president requested its repeal. Congress met his request on 4 April, by which date almost four months of opportunity for trade in the face of a British blockade that would never be weaker had been lost.[10]

In truth, the blockading officers seemed happier to see the end of the embargo than many Americans. Capt. C. Upton, charged by his admiral to gather intelligence on the disposition and status of the U.S. Navy in New England, concluded his 6 April response with, "The Embargo has been so rigid, I have not met a single vessel out-ward-bound, or seen a News-paper later than the 11th March, nor have I observed thro' any other channel, any species of Intelligence worthy [of] communicating."[11] Yet the loss of intelligence sources was less the issue than the loss of prize money. Lieutenant Napier, fresh to Boston Bay on board the frigate *Nymphe* in early April, enthusiastically noted in his journal, "At daylight on the seventh spoke an American fisherman, who informed us that the Embargo had been taken off twelve days ago. . . . The prospect of making money is a pleasing one to most people, at least it is so to a poor devil like myself. Therefore the repeal of the Embargo Act gave us all great pleasure, as the coasting trade is very considerable and like a spout it rushes with double force when the impediment which stopped it is removed."[12]

And so it seemed to be. The *Nymphe* stopped numerous coasters and fishing vessels from April to July, a few under license, some to be taken as prizes, but most to be ransomed. For the captains on station the latter course made sound fiscal sense. Most captured vessels were so small as to bring nothing in a prize court, yet the populace needed the vessels, especially the fishing smacks, to survive. If a little money could be made by not burning such vessels, and burning brought nothing at all, then leaving Americans with their harmless fishing boats, for a price, was sound business. For page after page, Napier noted in his journal ransoms that totaled thousands of dollars. Eventually, disturbed by what in a time of peace would be labeled extortion, the young lieutenant wrote, "Making prize money resembles killing a sheep; one likes to eat it but cannot bear the distress of the animal's death."[13] Notations in the newspapers of the period suggest that Napier's compassion was felt by a minority of British officers; and even he failed to note that ransom was illegal in the Royal Navy.

Along with taking or ransoming prizes during the day, the *Nymphe* often engaged in boat work at night. The boats crept into the local harbors and bays, cutting out any likely coasters and burning the remaining vessels. Day or night, however, the words of Napier reveal a strong concentration on coastal traffic—a concentration perhaps more accurately described as tunnel vision. The frigate encountered four American vessels bound to or from the Atlantic during Napier's stay, a merchantman (possibly an American prize), a letter of marque trader, and two privateers. Three of the ships safely entered harbor, while one of the privateers escaped to plunder British shipping.[14] Three reasons existed for such focus toward the land: observation of American warships, distraction by the ready wealth of coasting traffic, and, after 1 April, the orders of Vice Adm. Sir Alexander Cochrane, who replaced Warren as commander of the North American Station.

The coming of spring brought two changes to the blockade, aside from the lifting of the embargo. In Europe, Napoleon failed to find a strategy to defeat the larger allied armies. Short of men and almost totally lacking in support from the French populace, he could only delay the date of his abdication. Paris capitulated on 30 March, and Napoleon abdicated on 4 April. During the winter and spring, British reinforcements to North America increased slightly and, with the French surrender, the potential for massive reinforcements existed. Instead, a British government now deeply cognizant of the steadily mounting national debt chose to reduce its costs by immediately placing as many vessels as possible in ordinary. The number of warships available to the North American command increased to approximately eighty-five, enough to barely meet the needs of blockade without convoy duties.[15]

The North American command itself had changed in structure on 25 January, though final implementation occurred only in the spring. The Admiralty advised Warren that the command was to be separated into its component stations, as he had initially sought in the spring of 1813. Since the North American Station required only a vice admiral, *Admiral* Warren would be relieved as soon as feasible. Intentionally or not, it was the best way to ease into retirement a man who had given years of his life to the defense of his country.

The Admiralty selected Vice Adm. Sir Alexander Forrester Inglis Cochrane as the new commander at Halifax. Cochrane had served against the Americans during the Revolutionary War, gaining post rank in the West Indies. During the long war with France, he had endured the misery of blockade duty in the Channel (serving briefly under Warren) followed by a wealth of small boat experience in the Mediterranean. From 1805 to 1814, Cochrane served as commander in chief of the Leeward Islands Station (again under Warren for part of that time). He was knighted for his efforts in the Battle of Santo Domingo in 1806. At age fifty-six, Cochrane appeared relatively young, energetic, and successful. He also possessed another quality that made him, in the eyes of the Admiralty, the best choice for the role: Sir Alexander Cochrane openly hated America and Americans. In 1781, while a young Alexander made post in the Leeward Islands, his brother had died at Yorktown. He never forgave the United States.[16]

Cochrane arrived in Bermuda the first week of March, though the exchange of command did not occur until 1 April. Cochrane used the intervening time to study the situation and make plans. He dispatched a letter outlining his scheme of blockade, ship status, and needs in vessels and men to the Admiralty on 8 March (table 7.1). Cochrane noted that this blockade, which included the coast of New England, would require a total of 30 frigates, 40 sloops, and 20 additional unrated vessels, as well as the listed razees and ships-of-the-line, for a total of 102 hulls. These figures did not include convoy escorts. At the time of his letter, the North American Station had an effective strength of 15 ships-of-the-line, 4 razees, 15 frigates, 17 sloops, and 7 unrateds, or a total strength of 58 vessels to blockade the coast *and* cover convoys.

Cochrane also requested additional men, both to replace the shortages on the station and to activate several suitable ships among prizes at Halifax and Bermuda. This request was very similar to those made by Warren in late 1812 and early 1813, except for two differences: Cochrane knew the ships could be made available if the Admiralty so wished, and his words reflected the positive attitude of a man not yet thrown into the crucible of North American service.[17] As with Warren, however, the new commander in chief did not receive everything for which he asked, though he did select his own captain of the fleet to replace Henry Hotham, who shifted his pendant to command of the squadron off New York in late July 1814.[18]

The Admiralty had issued Cochrane orders upon his selection for

TABLE 7.1. *Cochrane's Proposed Blockade of 8 March 1814*

Patrol Area	Line	Razee	Frigate	Sloop	Unrated
Gulf of St. Lawrence	—	—	1	2	1
Nova Scotia to Cape Breton	—	—	2	3	2
Bay of Fundy to Boston Bay	—	1	2	3	2
Boston Bay to Nantucket	2	—	3	3	2
Rhode Island and Long Island Sound	1	1	2	3	1
New York	2	1	2	2	1
Delaware	1	—	3	2	1
Chesapeake Bay	1	1	4	4	4
Coast of North Carolina to Charleston	—	—	2	2	—
Charleston to Tybee	—	1	2	3	1
Tybee to St. Augustine, Fla.	—	—	2	3	1
New Providence	—	—	2	4	2
Gulf of Mexico	—	—	1	4	2
TOTAL	7	5	28	38	20

Source: Vice Admiral Sir Alexander Cochrane to Secretary of the Admiralty John W. Croker, 8 March 1814, UkLPR, Adm. 1/505, 633, Public Record Office, London.

command. The primary responsibility remained the military blockade of the United States, while the secondary responsibility continued to be the economic blockade of all areas except New England. Finally, the Admiralty ordered Cochrane to create a diversion in the Chesapeake and along the coast that would tie down local troops and militia, preventing their transfer to the critical Great Lakes theater. To accomplish the latter, a brigade of troops from Wellington's forces would be transferred to Bermuda as soon as the European situation allowed.[19]

Cochrane took his orders to heart. The 7 April raid on Pettipau, eight miles up the Connecticut River, was the first of an increasing series of boat attacks in areas previously untouched by the Royal Navy.[20] Other raids followed, ranging from the Chesapeake Bay through the New England coast, with the *Niles' Weekly Register* exclaiming on 9 July, "The eastern coast of the United States is much vexed by the enemy. Having destroyed a great portion of the coasting craft whose owners were hardy enough to put to sea, they seem determined to enter the little out ports and villages and burn every thing that floats."[21]

Even more revealing was an 24 April communication from Cochrane to Cockburn:

You are at perfect liberty as soon as you can muster a sufficient force, to act with the utmost hostility against the shores of the United States. Their government authorize and direct a most destructive war to be carried on against our commerce and we have no means of retaliating but on shore where they must be made to feel in their property what our merchants do in having their ships destroyed, and thereby be taught to know that they are now at the mercy of an invading foe. This is now the more necessary in order to draw off their attention from Canada where, I am told, they are sending their whole military force. Their sea port towns laid in ashes and the country invaded will be some sort of retaliation for their savage conduct in Canada, where they have destroyed our towns. . . . It is therefore but just that retaliation be made near to the seat of government from whence these orders are enacted.[22]

Having made his intentions toward the American coast clear to his subordinates, Cochrane turned his attention to the economic blockade. Understanding the folly of leaving a large stretch of the coastline unblockaded, he issued a proclamation extending the economic blockade to New England.[23] Despite reinforcements, however, length of coast and shortage of ships resulted in a paper blockade. The obvious nature of Cochrane's proclamation forced Madison to respond publicly, condemning the illegality of Great Britain's actions. Addressing the international community, he promised neutrals that the U.S. Navy would not interfere with their entry into or exit from American ports.[24] Madison gained little with his rhetoric; it was not the U.S. Navy that neutrals feared.

He had a point, though: enforcing the blockade differed greatly from proclaiming it. The *Constitution* proved that once again when it spent two days unmolested outside the Charleston, South Carolina, bar in March, then made port at Marblehead, Massachusetts, on 3 April, though closely chased by two British frigates. Two weeks later, the *Constitution* sailed unmolested to Boston for a refit, taking four prizes and running a small man-of-war aground along the way.[25] On 29 April, the *Peacock* captured the British brig *Epervier* off Cuba. The American sloop returned to an unblockaded Savannah on 4 May, its prize having arrived three days earlier. The sloop *Wasp* escaped Portsmouth, New Hampshire, with no enemy in sight on 1 May. At least thirteen vessels, including two Royal Navy brigs (the *Reindeer* and *Avon*), struck to the *Wasp* before it disappeared in the Atlantic in October. Like other cruisers, the *Adams* found no British ships off Savannah on 5 May, when it began a journey to the African coast, and the *Peacock* sailed unmolested from the same port on 4 June for a cruise in Irish waters.[26]

Nor had coasting stopped: the New York Gunboat Flotilla (after rescuing an inbound brig on 19 May) escorted forty coasters from Saybrook, Connecticut, to New London on 23 May. Despite a running battle with three British warships, all vessels made port safely. On 14 July, a gunboat operating from Portsmouth captured a British tender and freed the coaster it had taken prize. These American successes should not be construed to mean that coasting continued unhindered. In a letter to Secretary Jones dated 24 June, Hull stressed the difficulty of completing the ship-of-the-line building at Portsmouth, local roads being so poor that coastal carriage of materials was a necessity. The interference of blockaders placed tremendous constraints upon acquiring materials needed to complete the vessel.[27] In the South, coasting trade plied back and forth from Charleston to St. Marys virtually undisturbed through early August.

Consistently, Cochrane's blockade failed to stop the sailing, or returning, of American warships, privateers, prizes, and coasters. One reason, as often stressed, was a simple lack of vessels. Yet Americans reported only three sightings of British patrol groups on the southern coast between January and early August—those attacking the *Alligator* in January, a group of three small warships off Charleston in March, and the razee *Majestic* and a sloop at St. Marys in May. None of the ships lingered, though the last force briefly engaged two gunboats while sounding the bar.[28] Where were the British vessels? Apparently the damage from the 1813 storm at Halifax kept a number of them in port as late as May 1814.[29] The opening convoys of the year also required extra coverage. Cochrane concentrated the remaining vessels on the Chesapeake and northward, especially along the previously unblockaded New England coast.

Such dispositions account for the unblockaded ports in the South, but how could American warships and privateers continually run the blockade into northern ports without losing at least one vessel? Weather provides part of the answer. The cold and storms of the 1813–14 winter continued into May, while persistent fogs lingered into the summer. Perhaps more important, Cochrane's urge to strike American ports, to carry the war home to the American populace, took ships off station for raids. Crews and captains focused on burning, prize taking, and ransom, instead of on the military blockade.[30]

Meanwhile Cochrane's operational planning assumed proportions beyond the blockade of the United States. As outlined in a letter to Earl Bathurst on 14 July, it included an attack on Washington or Baltimore, followed by the capture, apparently with intent to hold, of the Gulf Coast from Pensacola to New Orleans. The latter effort would be supported by massive slave uprisings and Indians operating as native auxiliaries. The ravaging of coastal towns would continue. In this, as in other letters, Cochrane never mentioned bringing peace; his goal was to take destruction to America.[31]

From Cochrane's perspective, Indian aid and slave uprisings appeared very feasible. Part of his original orders of 25 January had been to investigate the possibility of aid from the Creek and Choctaw nations on the Gulf Coast. He had dispatched the frigate *Orpheus*, Capt. Hugh Pigot, to negotiate with the tribes in early April. Pigot's report proved positive, and Cochrane dispatched weapons, as well as a cadre of Royal Marines, to the gulf in late July. Both Pigot's report and a letter of 10 May from Cockburn were optimistic as to prospects for a slave uprising. Cockburn, who had been freeing slaves since the previous year and resettling them in Bermuda or Jamaica, wrote that Americans tried desperately to keep their slaves from his squadron, while the four-hundred-strong "Colonial Corps" organized over the winter performed well as skirmishers.[32] As it happened, the Creek and Choctaw refused to march without the British army at their side, while slaves simply failed to respond to the call for rebellion. The expected aid did not materialize when the campaign in the gulf finally began.

The Admiralty accepted Cochrane's plan wholeheartedly. Their letter of 10 August detailed the New Orleans effort, which would have to wait until later in the year pending the availability of additional reinforcements from Wellington's army. Meanwhile, Cochrane was free to use the first battalions from the Peninsular Army in other endeavors. Those units, eventually reinforced to forty-five hundred men, arrived at Bermuda on 25 July, under the command of Brig. Gen. Robert Ross, one of Wellington's best officers.[33]

President Madison, unaware of what the immediate future held for his capital city, asked James Monroe to draft the most pivotal communication since the coming of war. Addressed to the peace commissioners on 27 June, it read, "On mature consideration . . . you may omit any stipulation on the subject of impressment, if found indispensably necessary to terminate it [the war]. You will of course not recur to this expedient until all your efforts to adjust the controversy in a more satisfactory manner have failed."[34] Madison never recorded his reasons for choosing this moment to drop the single most vexing issue in Anglo-American relations since 1793, but they can be extrapolated with some certainty.

The Canadian border remained stable, with the American Navy dominant on Lake Erie. The army had gained strength—though nowhere near the strength planned—and experience, but little hope remained of conquering Canada, a critical part of initial military goals. On the coast, the South and gulf had not been blockaded, though depredations against northern coastlines continued to increase. Vessels of the U.S. Navy and the private navy continued to sail, disrupting Britain's shipping, usually returning home, and often getting prizes into port. The country, as a whole, seemed more willing to fight than on the day that war was declared. Though the nation was self-sufficient—no one starved, and the implements of war continued to be produced—its government had little money, thanks to the tremendous expenses associated with warfare, Madison's embargo, and the blockade.

The single most influential event occurring immediately before 27 June seems to have been the arrival in New York, on 9 June, of the news that Napoleon had abdicated.[35] The American declaration of war against Great Britain had occurred at the apogee of Napoleon's powers, with British resources stretched to their utmost. His abdication did not mean the end of impressment as an issue; another war in a month or a year could quickly return it to the fore. Instead, Napoleon's end meant the release of hundreds of ships and thousands of the best soldiers in the world for service against the United States. Madison's nightmares no longer centered on the blue cloth of the Royal Navy, cruising off the American coast, but on the red coats of Wellington's fusiliers marching through American grain fields. Both comparative evaluation and timing point to the end of the Anglo-French conflict as Madison's reason for dropping the demand that impressment be the pivotal issue of the peace talks.

Cochrane's thoughts in July did not dwell on peace but upon destruction. After receiving a letter from Lt. Gen. Sir George Prevost, commander of army forces in the Great Lakes theater, which described the willful destruction of private property by American forces, Cochrane notified the Admiralty that he would visit the same upon the American coast.[36] He proceeded to issue orders on 18 July requesting that his captains burn all villages, towns, and private property that they could reach. Secret orders accompanied the public orders, requiring the captains to refrain from damage to the property of sympathizers, or in areas that British forces might occupy.[37] President Madison responded to this proclamation with outrage, calling upon the people to unite against such barbarity and upon Cochrane to rescind his order. Cochrane answered that he could rescind the order only with the permission of the Admiralty, and that permission would not be forthcoming.[38] Fortunately for all concerned, his officers seem to have disregarded the missive.

Ross and his forces reached the Chesapeake on 15 August, joining Cochrane. The fleet numbered some fifty-one sail, including twenty transports. The admiral implemented the first portion of his grand plan immediately. He ignored Norfolk, where the *Constellation* still anchored, though it would have fallen easily to an attack from landward. Of Baltimore, economic entrepot, ship building center, and home port for numerous privateers, and Washington, governmental center and naval facility, he chose the latter for his first assault.

A small American gunboat flotilla commanded by Commodore Joshua Barney defended the water approaches to Washington. Faced with overwhelming British force, Barney could do little except retreat before the enemy advance. Rather than bypass the flotilla, Cockburn aggressively pursued Barney into St. Leonard's Creek. After a series of sharp defensive actions during which Barney retreated up the Patuxent River, the American commodore finally surrendered to the inevitable and scuttled his vessels. His men joined the force defending Washington as artillerists, and acquitted themselves with great gallantry at Bladensburg.[39] Cockburn's determined pursuit of the American force can be traced to his unpleasant experiences with the Chesapeake gunboat flotilla in 1813, when even frigates risked destruction if aground or becalmed. The thought of Barney's sweep-driven flotilla stealing past a windless fleet to reach the transports constituted a risk better not taken.[40]

With the American naval defenders eliminated, British forces under the command of General Ross and accompanied by Admiral Cockburn landed at Benedict on the Patuxent River on 19 August and roundly defeated the American forces at Bladensburg five days later, opening the way to Washington. So thorough was the demoralization of the Americans that the retreat became known as the "Bladensburg Races." After receiving word from James Monroe that Ross would reach the city in a few hours, Commodore Thomas Tingey burned the buildings of the navy yard and those vessels and stores which could not be rapidly relocated. Ross, Cockburn, and their raiders arrived in Washington shortly thereafter. Soon the capitol building and the White House flamed brightly, though not before Cockburn and his officers enjoyed a dinner abandoned in haste by the Madisons and a spot of souvenir hunting in the presidential mansion. Cockburn restrained himself in the taking of trophies, retaining only the pillow from Dolly Madison's chair as a souvenir of the occasion. Throughout the night, British soldiers worked to destroy Washington's public buildings (and the office of a newspaper, the *National Register,* which had been highly critical of Cockburn's operations in the Chesapeake Bay; for good measure, he ordered his men to destroy all the *C*'s in the print boxes). Overall, however, both arsonists and looters seem to have been closely leashed by Ross and Cockburn, sparing the private citizens of Washington in person and property. After a long day and night of battle and burning, the British abandoned the city. By 26 August, British forces had rejoined the fleet after penetrating fifty miles into hostile territory, defeating an enemy blocking force, and leaving the American capital in flames.[41]

On 19 August, a small British force began working up the Potomac River toward Alexandria, Virginia. Fort Washington, barring their way, was voluntarily destroyed on sighting the British forces. The squadron stayed at Alexandria for three days, then fought its way back to the bay on 9 September, bringing twenty-two richly laden prizes with it. Despite its success, the raid delayed the concentration of the fleet after the Washington attack: Cochrane had decided to burn Baltimore as well. He needed the bomb vessels that had sailed with the Alexandria Squadron, and he apparently feared losing that entire force to some disaster on the Potomac.[42]

His delays allowed the strengthening of Baltimore's defenses, especially the militia needed to hold the city against a British landing force. Cochrane did not begin the assault until 12 September. Ross, leading from the front, promptly met his demise at the hands of an American rifleman; his successor proved unable to carry the city from the landward side. During that night and into the next day, Cochrane attempted to destroy Fort McHenry by naval bombardment. He failed.[43]

Alfred T. Mahan ignores the Fort McHenry failure in his study of the War of 1812, concentrating instead upon the land action.[44] To have stressed it would have denigrated the capabilities of a strong fleet operating against land fortifications. It is difficult to imagine anyone being misled by this, thanks to the quickly scribbled words of American Francis Scott Key, temporarily detained on board the bombarding fleet. Once set to the tune of a popular Irish drinking song, those words became the American national anthem, and "the rockets' red glare, the bombs bursting in air, gave proof thro' the night that our flag was still there." Those stirring words give proof, as well, to the limitations of a blockading fleet when faced with strong land fortifications.

Cochrane's own defense of the attack upon Baltimore may well have been written with the fear of a court-martial in mind. His dispatch of 17 September to the Admiralty declared the attack a "demonstration on the city of Baltimore, which might be converted into a real attack should circumstances appear to justify it." He claimed that (the honorably deceased) Ross concocted the plan, since the new moon, causing low tides, trapped his vessels in the bay for several days anyway. The former was convenient—the heroic Ross would share any blame for failure—and the latter an outright falsehood: exit to the sea remained open regardless of tides.[45]

Unable to gain clear access to Baltimore's harbor, Cochrane sailed for the mouth of the bay. At that point, he split his force, detaching a small squadron to interdict and harass the bay, and ordering Cockburn to Bermuda for a quick refit before assuming responsibility for the blockade of St. Marys, Savannah, and Charleston. Cochrane took the remainder of the fleet to Halifax, checking his blockading detachments en route.

What exactly had Cochrane accomplished? In support of the blockade, he had removed twenty-two small vessels that probably would not have voluntarily left the shelter of the Potomac basin. Cochrane had prompted the scuttling of a gunboat flotilla which could never have affected the blockade of the mouth of the Chesapeake Bay, and he had forced the burning of the Washington Navy Yard. He had also tied down thirty-one British warships that could have been used to place the American coasts under tighter blockade.

Politically, he had burned the capital and some government records. If it had been the capital of *The* United States instead of the capital of *These* United States (a situation which, regrettably and arguably, did not arise until the second half of the nineteenth century), there might have been some effect. Unfortunately for Cochrane, the young nation depended far less upon its capital than did most European countries. The government was functioning as well as ever within days. More important, the abortive assault on Baltimore potentially strengthened the American will to resist: they saw firsthand that neither Wellington's veterans nor the massed Royal Navy were invincible. As for the populace of Great Britain and Europe, another unwelcome picture unfolded. James Madison captured it in his message to Congress on 20 September 1814:

> In the events of the present Campaign, the Enemy, with all his augmented means, and wanton use of them, has little ground for exultation, unless he can feel it in the success of his recent Enterprises against this Metropolis, and the neighboring Town of Alexandria, from both of which his retreats were as precipitate as his attempts were bold and fortunate. In his other incursions on our Atlantic Frontier, his progress, often checked and chastised by the martial spirit of the neighboring Citizens, has had more effect in distressing Individuals, and in dishonouring his Arms, than in promoting any object of legitimate warfare. And in the 2 instances mentioned, however deeply to be regretted on our part, he will find in his transient success, which interrupted for a moment only the ordinary public business at the Seat of Government, no compensation for the loss of character with the World, by his violations of private property, and by his destruction of public edifices, protected, as monuments of the arts, by the laws of civilized warfare.[46]

Despite the barbarity sometimes accompanying sieges and the generally harsh conditions of incarceration for prisoners of war, most nations of the early nineteenth century expected a measure of restraint in the pursuit of military victory. The burning of government buildings, a precedent set by Americans along the Canadian border but certainly extended by the Royal Navy, looked as if it could grow to rival the worst outrages of Napoleon, and Europe understood such outrages from firsthand experience.[47] If the strongest arm of the world's most powerful nation engaged in such destruction today, what hope for tomorrow? Even members of Parliament spoke against the burning of Washington's public buildings, one objecting that he "reprobated the manner in which the war was pursued in America. At Washington we had destroyed buildings not connected with military purposes, though in Europe they had always been spared in the last 20 years."[48] Great Britain, struggling to restore equilibrium in post-Napoleonic Europe, did not need to engage in any actions engendering fear and distrust in that quarter.

There can be little doubt that the Admiralty, the War Office, and Cochrane had made major errors in strategic planning and operational implementation. This time it was not just the ineptitude of the blockade and economic misery for British trade that resulted, for the American commissioners at the peace talks achieved diplomatic parity, if not the swing of some small initiative to them, after the failure at Baltimore.[49] No significant event occurred to cause its relinquishment during the few remaining weeks of negotiation.

The Chesapeake Bay offensive was one of three initiated by the British in 1814. Governor Sir John Sherbrooke of Nova Scotia received a directive from his government to occupy enough of the District of Maine and nearby islands to guarantee communications between Halifax and Quebec. Supported by a fleet under Rear Admiral Griffith, Sherbrooke seized Eastport, Maine, on 11 July.[50] On 14 August, the *Adams,* bound for Boston after a successful cruise, damaged its bottom off Castine, and decided to anchor at Hampden, twenty-seven miles up the Penobscot River, until repairs could be made.[51] Unfortunately for the vessel, the British seized Castine and Machias, sealing the river's mouth. The captain of the *Adams* ordered it burned to avoid capture by the British. The conquering Sherbrooke gave the inhabitants of the area the option to stay if they swore allegiance to the crown. Many would not do so, and 25 percent of the population departed southward, leaving all their possessions behind.[52]

British strategists had designated both the raids within the Chesapeake and the occupation along the Canadian border as secondary efforts to the real invasion. They calculated that those operations would draw men and materiel away from the main thrust in the Great Lakes theater. There, on 11 August, Governor General Sir George Prevost, advanced along the west bank of Lake Champlain with eleven thousand men including many Peninsular veterans. His advance was stopped cold, not by a victorious American army but by the naval victory at Plattsburgh on 11 September. Without the British Navy to protect and provide his logistical support, Prevost had little option but to retreat. Like the British failure at Baltimore, Plattsburgh held significance in Ghent, especially in the minds of British commissioners who had hoped for so much and received so little.[53]

The southern coast finally received attention in August. Blockaders appeared off Charleston, Savannah, and St. Marys with distressing regularity. Local papers recorded that a ship-of-the-line, frigate, sloop, and two brigs made up the squadron that patrolled their coast.[54] By late August the squadron's depredations upon the coasting trade forced the commander at St. Marys again to institute convoys for its protection. The largest such convoy contained eighty-eight sail, giving some idea of the volume of coasting overlooked by the British before late 1814. Capt. Hugh G. Campbell estimated that his gunboats safely escorted $6 million in trade over the St. Marys River–to–Savannah route between late August and mid-October. The running battles behind the barrier islands of Georgia continued through the remainder of the year—two plucky gunboats actually sallied across the bar to capture the British privateer *Fortune of War* on 12 September.[55]

Neutrals continued to sail unmolested to and from Spanish Amelia Island, entering with European goods and departing with American cotton. Campbell wrote to Jones on 11 November 1814: "The trade to Amelia Island is immense. Upwards of fifty square-rigged vessels are now in that port under Russian, Swedish, and Spanish colors."[56] Cochrane finally acknowledged the importance of the southern coast in an early January 1815 missive, advising his subordinates that "the greatest pressure of the blockade may be carried to those parts of the coast where the privateering system is most encouraged and where the greatest possibility is then demonstratively proved to be most prevalent."[57]

On 12 January 1815, forces under Cockburn seized Cumberland and St. Simons Islands off the Georgia coast as a combination winter quarters and base for disrupting the coasting trade. Cockburn next raided St. Marys, penetrating nearly fifty miles upriver as his forces destroyed vessels and military stores. The British then withdrew, and American naval forces reoccupied the station. Trade quickly resumed, with a final British boat attack beaten off on 22 February.[58]

On the remainder of the southern coast, Ocracoke Inlet received only occasional visits from British patrollers, while Wilmington appears to have been left completely undisturbed during the last months of the war. It remained a base for privateers and their captures. Just one of the exploits of the *Kemp* illustrates the error in leaving any port open. The privateer sailed from Wilmington on 29 November 1814. It sighted a scattered convoy shortly after leaving. On 4 December, the *Kemp* anchored again in Wilmington, accompanied by its prizes—two ships and two brigs. No British patroller had disturbed the privateer's entry or exit.[59]

The Gulf theater remained quiet until December, though a small force had attacked the American fort at Mobile in September, losing a frigate for its trouble.[60] Cochrane concentrated his fleet at Ship Island on 8 December and captured the small flotilla blocking access to Lake Borgne six days later.[61] The Navy's portion of the attempt to capture New Orleans should have been complete at this point, but on 15 January 1815, it was needed to transport the remnants of the forces defeated by Andrew Jackson seven days earlier back to Bermuda. On the way to Bermuda, the Royal Navy pounded into submission the tiny but defiant fort guarding Mobile Bay.[62]

The battle of New Orleans assisted Andrew Jackson to the White House and fostered an American perception of victory at the end of the war—a war theoretically over some two weeks earlier. Even if the victor at New Orleans had been British, the vessels allocated to the blockade would not have noticeably changed before the practical (and time lag driven) end of the conflict. The key impact upon the blockade was the diversion of warships, October through December, to support the invasion rather than the invasion itself.

On the northeastern coast, the *Peacock*, having taken fifteen prizes, entered the port of New York on 29 October 1814, without sighting any British warships. On 28 December, with no British in sight, the *Constitution* sailed from Boston, pursued by the frigates of the local squadron only after the escape became known. The pursuit continued for over nine hundred miles—never catching sight of the *Constitution*, but certainly weakening the blockade.[63] The *President*, accompanied by the brig *Macedonian* carrying reserve supplies, sortied from New York on the evening of 15 January 1815. A British squadron cornered the large frigate, engaging in a running battle for several hours before the *President* surrendered. The American brig escaped, hardly noticed in the scramble to capture one of the largest American warships then afloat.[64] The *President* had the misfortune to be the first cruising American warship captured while trying to enter or leave an American port since the brig *Nautilus* fell to Broke's squadron in the first weeks of the war (the ill-fated *Chesapeake* never attempted to leave port for its cruise; it had intentionally engaged the *Shannon*). The *President* was also the last ship so captured. Even then, it served a duty to other vessels. With some blockaders chasing after the *Constitution* and others in disarray due to the fight with the *President*, the sloops *Hornet*, *Peacock*, and the supply brig *Tom Bowline* slipped out of New York on 20 January. They were the last vessels of the U.S. Navy to sortie during the war.

Across the Atlantic, the last four months of 1814 had been less than pleasant for the Admiralty as heavy losses to American government

President & Endymion, War of 1812, January 16, 1815.
The British squadron blockading Long Island Sound managed to capture
one of the American "super-frigates," *President*, in the waning weeks of the
war. Unfortunately, the entire squadron joined the initial pursuit of the ship,
leaving the sound without a blockade for several critical days. This allowed
several American raiders to escape into the Atlantic. Their depredations
against British warships and shipping would continue for three months
beyond the official end of the war.
©The Mariner's Museum, Newport News, Virginia

and private raiders continued in the shipping lanes. On 9 September,
Liverpool merchants and shipowners united to censure the Admiralty,
claiming eight hundred vessels lost in the past two years from their
city alone. They requested that the Regent intervene. On 30 September, Lloyd's of London reported that two U.S. cruisers and several privateers had captured 108 prizes during the month. When the Prussian
government commissioned a statue of the late Queen Louise of Prussia, the British agreed to transport it from the stoneworks in Italy to
France. The American privateer *Leo* interfered, capturing the ship and
the statue, and creating a diplomatic incident.[65]

Harried at sea by the Americans and at home by merchants and
shipowners, the Admiralty and the government became increasingly

The Constitution & the Cyane, February 20, 1815.
As with other vessels of Madison's public and private navies, broadsides from
the frigate *Constitution* punctuated the weakness of the British blockade even
after the war had officially ended. In late February, the *Constitution* engaged a
convoy protected by two British sloops-of-war, *Cyane* and *Levant.* After a short
but sharp action (allowing the convoy to escape), both vessels surrendered.
©*The Mariner's Museum, Newport News, Virginia*

receptive to a negotiated peace. The cost of the war was excessive,
and the heavy taxes levied to support military operations increased the
general resentment among the populace.[66] Britain's erstwhile allies
seemed to snicker at its inability to stop the Americans: the Bourbon
monarchy (which Britain had restored) and several European nations
regularly allowed Americans the use of their ports. Far worse, the dis-
ordered European political situation threatened another round of war,
this time between Britain's former allies.[67] The failure of the 1814
campaign along the Canadian border actually amounted to little in the
mountain of British problems, but it was enough. Representatives of
Great Britain and the United States signed the Treaty of Ghent on
24 December 1814. A copy arrived in New York on 11 February 1815

and was approved unaltered by the American Senate six days later, officially ending the war.

Notice traveled quickly to the blockading squadron, and the last great wooden wall fell apart, its constituent pieces sailing to new duties or to be placed in ordinary. Yet the "Wooden Wall Complete" had never existed. Even at its strongest, it had failed to keep American vessels from the seas, and the legacy of that failure, measured in death and destruction, lasted months longer than the blockade.

The American privateers sailed home first, usually discovering the return of peace after taking a final British merchantman. The *Constitution* captured the British sloops *Cyane* and *Levant* in a bloody action on 20 February, picking up other prizes before discovering the news of war's end.[68] The *Hornet* savaged the Royal Navy brig *Penguin* on 23 March, some seventeen days after the last British blockader received notification of peace. It then, after dropping its armament overboard while being chased by a ship-of-the-line, returned to the United States, arriving shortly after the brig *Macedonian*.[69] The *Tom Bowline* served as a cartel for the *Hornet*'s numerous prisoners, then sailed for home. The sloop *Peacock*, last of the vessels that had run through that splintered wooden wall with such ease, sailed a route that led all the way to the coast of Java. There, on 30 June 1815, it punctuated the inefficiency of the British blockade with one final broadside. Ironically, the last victim of the war carried the name of *Nautilus*.[70]

8

Challenging the Efficiency of the Blockade

The preceding chapters addressed the reasons necessitating the blockade and examined the British progress toward completing their wooden wall. Within the framework of those facts, in stark contrast to the words of Alfred T. Mahan, a number of weaknesses within the blockade become obvious. Central to those weaknesses lay the varying recourse to risk taking at all command levels of the Royal Navy. In evaluating this military tossing of the dice, three types of risk present themselves: good, bad, and unrecognized.[1]

The first important instance of British risk taking occurred before the beginning of the struggle. Despite indicators of an American declaration of war, the Admiralty opted to maintain few ships, and those without the support of a battle squadron, in North American waters. Resupply of Halifax and Bermuda also received a low priority as the Admiralty detailed replacement ships, men, and stores to the Royal Navy's struggles against Napoleon. It also ordered Sawyer to abstain from further aggravating the Americans. To the Admiralty, these actions constituted a good risk, one well supported by recent events. The United States had stood at the gates of war against Great Britain several times since 1794, in each instance refusing to enter despite immediate catalysts (and none existed in 1812) such as the *Chesapeake-Leopard* affair. Unfortunately, the Admiralty failed to consider three important points: the pacifist Thomas Jefferson no longer held sway in Washington, a new breed of southern and western politicians had gained control in Congress, and James Madison recognized the pressure the European conflict placed upon the Royal Navy.

Upon the declaration of war, the British government almost immediately followed its potentially good risk with an obvious misstep. Rather than weaken the European blockade, it dispatched Warren to North America without substantial reinforcements and offered Madison peace *on British terms*, without addressing the most critical aspect of American discontent—impressment. Meanwhile, the United States managed to get its merchant fleet safely into sheltered harbors as its private and public navies scored notable successes at sea. True, the Canadian offensive had not progressed as hoped, but since a strong blockade failed to materialize along the coast, time remained to finish the job in Canada rather than bow to British terms. In this case, Great Britain also had a precedent to call upon—the tenacity of the American colonists in clinging to their hope for freedom after 1776. The attempt to restore peace through unilateral diplomacy without removing vessels from the European blockade to back the effort militarily constituted a bad risk.

The U.S. Navy scored several notable single-ship victories against the Royal Navy in the early months of the war. In every case, the Americans held at least slight superiority over the British in one or more of four categories: overall size, weight of metal, size of crew, or seaworthiness of vessel. Naval historians often stress these factors in their analysis of the engagements and fail to consider the more critical relationship of ship captain and risk. An excerpt in the *Gentlemen's Magazine and Historical Chronicle*, from a book published in February 1813 by a Captain Layman (an obvious pseudonym), illustrates that contemporaries recognized the material problems presented by the heavy American frigates, but, as with historians, they failed to question why the engagements occurred at all.[2] In all instances, including that of the overmatched *Alert*, the British captain closed immediately, forgoing evasion despite knowledge of the enemy's weight of metal and poor conditions of his own ship, and in the case of the *Java*, despite a deck crowded by supernumeraries.[3] Only two vessels had convoy protection to legitimize aggressive action, and in all meetings the wind was favorable for an attempted disengagement. In every case, single combat was an apparent bad risk knowingly accepted by British captains because a far worse risk threatened any who avoided an enemy: the taint of cowardice, if not actual court-martial. As Lt. Henry Edward Napier recognized, fighting a superior foe meant acclaim even in failure, a legacy of the Navy's successes in the long war with France. Thus the threat of losing a vessel to a superior enemy actually constituted a no-risk situation for British captains, while failure to engage threatened unacceptable risk, especially in the initial months of the war when they felt the U.S. Navy to be somewhat contemptible. The resulting losses not only boosted American morale, they removed precious ships from the early blockade.

Perhaps the most important risk taking of the blockade occurred in the summers of 1813 and 1814: the decisions to concentrate available forces for offensives. Warren's plan to enter the Chesapeake in force is almost indefensible, something even the Admiralty recognized by midsummer. Yet his determination to take the risk of stripping his blockade in an attempt to capture American naval vessels in the bay is understandable, considering the Admiralty's repeated demands to destroy the U.S. Navy and quickly return the station's ships-of-the-line to Europe. As the situation developed, much of what Warren accomplished in ship captures and disruption of coasting traffic could have been handled by a much smaller raiding force under Cockburn, the remainder of his ships reinforcing the weak blockade and even extending it to major southern ports.

The offensives of 1814, in Maine and at New Orleans, coupled with the diversionary raid into the Chesapeake, required so many warships that a solid blockade could not develop until their conclusion. The plan, however, considering especially the potential for a successful invasion from Canada, seemed a good risk to both Cochrane and the Admiralty. A few more American ships evading the blockade appeared unimportant in light of an offensive that offered to end this lingering remnant of twenty years of war within a few months—and end it in favor of Great Britain. They were partially correct, as it certainly contributed to ending the war.

Perhaps the most significant unrecognized risk of the war for the Admiralty concerned American naval capability in 1812, and unsurprisingly so, as even the government of the United States had little conception of its own maritime abilities. For a country which had, since 1800, embraced coastal defense in lieu of a blue-water strategy, the United States accounted for a goodly number of British merchantmen and warships during the conflict. Though the bulk of this credit goes to the large self-mobilization of the private sector, the U.S. Navy (even the detested gunboats) deserves more recognition than indicated by its percentage of prizes, while the British themselves deserve the most credit for their own failure. When American maritime capability revealed itself, the Admiralty settled for half measures rather than risk weakening the blockade in Europe, and *without some risk* being taken, Great Britain paid a subsequent heavy price in losses when it could not establish a tight blockade of the United States. Analysis of several key factors further reveals the weakness of that incomplete blockade.

Table 8.1 tabulates successes and failures of attempted sorties by U.S. warships during each quarter of the war. A sortie is defined as one vessel attempting to leave port for the purpose of engaging British merchant shipping. The statistics for the first two quarters of 1812 illustrate an American Navy rested, generally prepared for war, and completely unblockaded. The last quarter of that year found most of those ships either undergoing refits, or, in the case of unrated vessels, diverted to convoy duty. With the notable exception of Decatur's squadron, trapped at New London, ships sailed as refitted during the following year. The final quarter of 1813 found unrated vessels, released from convoy duty by the embargo, swelling the ranks of raiders, while three of the four failed sorties belonged to the *Constellation* and its futile attempts to escape the Chesapeake. The U.S. Navy did not attempt sorties in the summer of 1814—the large number of raiders from the previous winter and spring quarters were undergoing refit, while some smaller vessels had again been diverted to convoy duties. Of the ships available for *guerre de course* after 1812—A number ranging by quarter from a low of 7 to a high of 12 vessels—the Navy averaged 37.8 percent at sea per quarter in 1813, dropping to 17.4 percent the following year. The average for the unblockaded forces available in 1812 had stood at 58.9 percent.[4] Obviously, the Royal Navy placed increasing emphasis on containing the American public navy, and just as obviously, their cordon occasionally failed.

The Admiralty never envisioned a military blockade promising total containment, thus the multilayered defensive system which included pursuit of enemy squadrons, strong convoy defenses, and roving patrols. Weather had usually proved the culprit whenever French vessels escaped from their interdicted European harbors, and such was expected in the blockade of the United States. What had not been expected by the Admiralty were the sailings during relatively good weather and the ports consistently open to returning vessels

TABLE 8.1 *U.S. Navy Sorties, 1812–1815*

	Summer 1812	Fall 1812	Winter 1812	Spring 1813	Summer 1813	Fall 1813
Attempts	11	11	3	6	2	2
Failures	1	0	1	3	0	0

	W 1813	S 1814	S 1814	F 1814	W 1814
Attempts	11	3	0	1	5
Failures	4	0	0	0	1

Sources: Compiled from various primary and secondary sources listed in bibliography.
Note: Exact dates of attempted sorties are noted in the text of chapters 4, 5, and 6.

(British blockaders failed to intercept and capture any of the thirty-six American warships returning to port during the war). Weather had less to do with the ability of the U.S. Navy to sortie and to return than did British strategic and operational warship allocations, conflicting objectives, and even the actions of individual captains, such as Broke.

Taken alone, table 8.1 certainly does not indicate that the British blockade was ineffective. To the contrary, the *Constellation* never reached the open sea, while the frigate *Macedonian* and other vessels found their crews and armaments diverted to the Great Lakes theater because of the pressure of the British blockade. In fact, the number of successful American sorties decreased each year, as did the percentage of American vessels at sea. What the table does reflect is the concentration of British blockaders on containing the American public navy—at considerable expense in Royal Navy hulls and in depredations upon the British merchant marine by the often ignored American private navy.

Naval officers on both sides of the blockade thought of the year as having three seasons, the relatively good weather for campaigning lasting from mid-March into July, the hurricane season of August to October, and the winter months of November through February. These seasons, however, were neither absolutes nor firm constraints upon the duties of blockading. The British active campaigning during 1814 actually extended well into the other seasons, while the remnants of a hurricane smashed the British fleet at Halifax in November 1813. Table 8.2 seems to hint that perhaps greater attention should have been paid to the seasons by British officers. The British-American loss ratio to natural causes of 32 to 1 appears extraordinary, but several mitigating factors existed.

TABLE 8.2. *Losses to British and American Naval Forces by Season*

	British Losses			American Losses		
Season	Enemy	Natural	Total	Enemy	Natural	Total
Campaign	7	5	12	7	0	7
Hurricane	9	12	21	6	1	7
Winter	9	15	24	6	0	6
TOTAL	25	32	57	19	1	20

Sources: Gossett, *The Lost Ships of the Royal Navy*, 86–95; Emmons, *Navy of the United States*, 56–200.
Note: Gunboats and losses on the Great Lakes are not included. Otherwise, the table reflects all known naval losses directly related to the War of 1812.

The Royal Navy often operated in unfamiliar waters using out of date and inaccurate charts. Its primary bases, Halifax and Bermuda and those in the Caribbean, were at the end of a long logistical chain. They lacked the infrastructure to quickly refit warships and the population base necessary to support the manning needs of the ships operating in those waters. Perhaps more important, the Royal Navy's relatively few vessels available for the gargantuan tasks called for in support of the blockade appear to have been forced to operate beyond their capabilities (table 8.15 reveals the extent of the shortage of warships). A portion of British losses can be attributed to inexperienced officers on board the many unrated vessels wrecked, and surely the undermanning endemic to the Royal Navy played its part. In the end, however, one important truth remained after all considerations by British commanders: the blockade, and naval operations in general, continued regardless of season, regardless of losses, and regardless of the impact of those losses upon the blockade's efficiency.

The U.S. Navy enjoyed advantages in direct proportion to the problems of the Royal Navy. American vessels were generally well manned, often above the naval guidelines, and every man a volunteer serving a limited tour of duty. The Navy Department listed the complement of an American heavy frigate as 450 crew and officers. The muster roll of the *Constitution* named 456, 475, and 461 souls at the time of engaging, respectively, the *Guerriere, Java,* and *Cyane* and *Levant*. The *United States* mustered 478 men against the *Macedonian*. The trend continued in actions involving American brigs (140 men), ship-sloops (160 men), and the smaller frigates (300 men), the exceptions being the defeat of the *Essex*, understrength after its long cruise, and the *Wasp* against the *Avon*, the second naval action of the voyage for the American vessel.[5]

TABLE 8.3. *Losses to British and American Naval Forces by Year*

Year	British Losses			American Losses		
	Enemy	Natural	Total	Enemy	Natural	Total
1812	9	10	19	5	0	5
1813	6	10	16	5	0	5
1814	6	10	16	8	1	9
1815	4	2	6	1	0	1
TOTAL	25	32	57	19	1	20

Sources: Gossett, *Lost Ships of the Royal Navy,* 86–95; Emmons, *Navy of the United States,* 56–200.
Note: Gunboats and losses on the Great Lakes are not included. Otherwise, the table reflects all known naval losses directly related to the War of 1812.

Additionally, naval officers knew the local sea-land interface intimately and avoided unfamiliar interfaces when at sea. Perhaps most important, U.S. Navy vessels had time to carefully refit after each voyage, picked their time to sortie, and enjoyed freedom of movement once through the British cordon. They were not tied to the apron strings of blockades and patrol zones; thus they could avoid losses associated with beating back and forth off a lee shore regardless of the season.

Table 8.3 examines losses by year. As expected, the Royal Navy experienced its worst yearly losses during the initial six months of the war, though the heavy attrition in 1813 and 1814 continued into the first three months of 1815. Rather obviously, the Royal Navy did not have the blockade well in hand at any point during the war; if so, American forces would have been contained and the Royal Navy's losses, at least to combat at sea, would have been reduced to virtually nil. The Admiralty began the war with 607 active combat vessels at its disposal. Over the course of thirty-three months, 57 became casualties of war (and 25 of these were combat losses). This loss constituted 9.4 percent of the Royal Navy's initial hulls. According to the vessels sunk or captured, as chronicled by W. P. Gossett, a similar loss percentage did not exist for any thirty-three-consecutive-month period during Britain's blockades of France. The highest loss for any thirty-three-month period was 2.8 percent of active ships (based upon the peak strength of the Royal Navy over those months), including naval transports. Moreover, their loss percentage constantly decreased over the course of the European blockades.[6] As a final emphasis, note where the losses occurred: 27 off the North American coast, 17 in the Caribbean, 10 scattered across the Atlantic, and 3 in the English Channel. The haphazard blockade, stepchild of the Admiralty's no-risk-in-Europe policy, never denied the Atlantic basin to American naval forces.

American warships represented only a fraction of the potential danger to British shipping. Any evaluation of the military blockade must address its success in containing the private navy of the United States. As Congress authorized over five hundred letters of marque during the war, and as over 250 vessels sailed at least once as privateers, it is impossible to collect sortie data with the accuracy reflected in table 8.1.[7] Instead, analysis must rely on British losses. Even there, the skein of evidence is tremendously tangled.

Privateers did not report all prizes. Poor record keeping and loss of ships' logs to enemy action or natural causes further reduced the accuracy of accounting. In both the United States and England, no government agency collected the data as a whole, though insurance companies and newspapers kept their own tallies. The usual sources for British ships captured are *Niles' Weekly Register* and the official post-cruise reports of American naval officers. Niles claimed that American public and private navies took 2,500 prizes during the war, of which 750 suffered recapture by the British. Lloyd's of London reported to Parliament the loss of 1,200 insured vessels, a number not incompatible with American sources once uninsured coasting vessels and convoy-dodgers are considered.[8] Working primarily from the mentioned sources, George F. Emmons collected and tabulated prize lists in 1853. Listing 257 captures by the U.S. Navy and 1,410 prizes taken by privateers, Emmons's work remains a standard statistical reference for period scholars.[9]

With an average loss of over one vessel per day to privateers, it is obvious that the blockade did not stop the private navy from leaving port, and if the estimate of only 750 recaptures was accurate, British blockaders also failed to keep prize vessels as well as privateers from returning to safe havens.[10] Table 8.4 provides data on the disposition of prizes taken by American public and private ships during the war.

Each of the 1,444 prizes listed either sailed under a prize master to a port in one of the designated areas, was identified as having been recaptured, or was burned or otherwise deliberately destroyed. The final category in the table contains cartels, ransomed vessels, or vessels stripped of valuables and allowed to continue. Note that some vessels not listed as recaptured probably suffered that fate, though records providing verification are unavailable.[11]

The manner in which Americans disposed of prizes offers impor-

TABLE 8.4. *American Prize Disposition, 1812–1815*

	1812	1813	1814	1815	Total
New England	161	86	39	50	336
New York	23	7	5	5	40
Delaware	7	2	2	3	14
Chesapeake	22	0	0	0	22
Southern	32	40	52	28	152
Gulf	5	1	1	0	7
Any port	29	56	37	63	185
Foreign	3	36	37	2	78
Recaptured	3	6	1	8	18
Burned	40	141	150	82	413
Other	39	60	55	25	179
TOTAL	364	435	379	266	1444

Sources: Emmons, *Navy of the United States*, 56–200; Coggeshall, *History of the American Privateers*.
Note: Emmons's prize list forms the basis for this table. Dispositions missing from Emmons (many of them) were collected by a thorough search of primary and secondary sources, of which Coggeshall proved the most helpful. Listed prizes that lacked at least some indication of eventual disposition were excluded from the table. This accounts for the variance from Emmons's total of 1,667 prizes taken by the U.S. Navy and privateers.

The 1815 totals represent a partial year due to the cessation of hostilities after February. It must also be emphasized that these numbers do not include all prizes; they include only those for which a disposition or planned disposition was documented. As many as 1,100 to 1,500 captures may not have been accounted for in available sources.

tant clues as to the effectiveness and ineffectiveness of the blockade. New England and the South remained important receiving centers for prizes throughout the war. The former was not blockaded until mid-1814, and the latter received attention from the British only as warships could be spared through late August 1814. Even then, the port of Wilmington apparently remained open. The sailing orders of prizes also indicate where privateers based. Logically, the captors wanted to send prizes to a port where their investors could monitor sales and share proceeds.

After 1812, foreign ports assumed importance in prize disposition, as well as in refit and resupply of the private navy. With Napoleon's abdication in mid-1814 statistics indicate that American privateers received support from neutrals and former English allies, as well as from the new French government and Napoleon's old allies.[12] Most important, these ports could not be denied to the United States' vessels by blockade unless that blockade stopped privateers from leaving home waters.

The increase in enemy vessels burned after 1812 was primarily due to the U.S. Navy. In 1813, recognizing that detailing prize crews weak-

The American Privateer "General Armstrong."
President Madison's private navy plagued British trade throughout the
war—and the successes enjoyed by American privateers showed no sign
of diminishing by the end of the conflict. Driven to desperate measures
by popular opinion and an irate Admiralty, British officers used any means
available to capture the swift vessels. This included, in the case of the
General Armstrong, violating international law by attacking the ship while
at anchor in the neutral port of Fayal on 26 October 1814.
©*The Mariner's Museum, Newport News, Virginia*

ened cruisers and subjected those crews to capture while returning
home, Secretary of the Navy Jones issued orders forbidding the practice. Instead, he mandated the destruction of all prizes.[13] Privateers
also burned prizes—after stripping them of valuables—but less frequently than the regular Navy. There was simply no profit in burning,
and profit financed the cruises even when it was not the total motivation for captain and crew. Privateers preferred to ransom a vessel, getting at least the promise of cash at a later date. The U.S. Navy even
used ransom in 1812, though the illegal practice appears to have been
quickly squashed by Hamilton, since no additional ransoming appears
in records.[14] Illegal or not, privateers continued to let British vessels
sail for cash, or promised cash, throughout the war.

TABLE 8.5. *Estimates of British Merchant Marine Tonnage Losses, 1812–1815, Based on Estimates of Prize Numbers and Estimates of Average Tonnage Loss per Prize*

Prize Number Estimates	Emmons (220 Tons per Prize)	Coggeshall (258 Tons per Prize)	Mitchell (110 Tons per Prize)
1,444 (Table 8.4)	317,680 (12.7%)	372,552 (14.9%)	158,840 (6.3%)
1,667 (Emmons)	366,740 (14.7%)	430,086 (17.2%)	183,370 (7.3%)
2,000 (Coggeshall)	440,000 (17.6%)	516,000 (20.6%)	220,000 (8.8%)
2,500 (Niles)	550,000 (22.0%)	645,000 (25.8%)	275,000 (11.0%)

Sources: Emmons, *Navy of the United States,* 56–200; Coggeshall, *History of the American Privateers; Niles' Weekly Register,* 6 January 1816; Mitchell, *European Historical Statistics,* 613.
Note: Percentages accompanying tonnage losses show estimates of the proportional loss of Great Britain's initial merchant tonnage of 2.5 million tons during the years 1812 to 1815.

The 1815 tallies represent the first quarter of the year. The large number of ships burned testifies to the effect of five U.S. Navy vessels at sea, while the number of ships dispatched to ports as prizes indicates an even greater number of privateers at large, perhaps as many as two to three dozen. The Royal Navy off North American shores, at its peak strength of the war, failed to maintain a military blockade capable of keeping American cruisers in port. There should be little wonder that its efforts had proven less efficient before early 1815.

Though American captains did not log the tonnage for most of the vessels taken prize during the War of 1812, enough records exist to estimate the total tonnage captured, both as a raw number and as a percentage of initial British merchant shipping. Emmons provided sizes for 2.7 percent of 1,667 prizes, with a range of 64 to 800 tons and an average of 220 tons burthen. Coggeshall cited tonnage for 7.3 percent of 1,800 listed captures, with a range of 50 to 700 and an average of 258 tons burthen. Additionally, an average of 110 tons per registered British vessel can be derived from B. R. Mitchell's *European Historical Statistics, 1750–1970.* Table 8.5 uses the average tons derived from Emmons, Coggeshall, and Mitchell to convert the three most common prize estimates and the verified prizes from table 8.4 into total tonnage estimates, and hence to a percentage of loss for the British merchant fleet as of 1812, including fishing vessels (2.5 million tons).

The result, a loss range of 6.3 to 25.8 percent, indicates a fairly devastating *guerre de course,* even at the lower estimate. Nor did the losses decrease appreciably over the course of the conflict, 25.2 percent occurring in 1812, 30.1 percent in 1813, 26.2 percent in 1814, and 18.5 percent in 1815 (estimated per table 8.4). Or rather, 18.5 percent in the first three months of 1815, a pace which could have statistically added

798 vessels to the American tally for that year if the war had continued (an additional 3.5 to 8.2 percent of initial British tonnage).

Though Royal Navy prizes and newly built vessels rapidly replaced British losses, the damage was done.[15] Failure to contain American raiders resulted in the loss of over $45 million in vessels and cargoes, captured or destroyed in British commerce lanes, and incalculable losses due to economic disruption (perishables rotted, additional labor costs, and market fluctuations—all while awaiting convoy—as well as disrupted coastal shipping). Insurance rates soared to their highest levels in twenty years of war. Premiums on Atlantic trade lanes during peace hovered at 2 percent. By late 1814, rates on the Newfoundland-to-London route averaged 10 percent, those on the Newfoundland to Caribbean lane approached 25 percent, and domestic trade in the Irish Sea purchased insurance at rates as high as 9 percent.[16] Those results seem to indicate that the Royal Navy's military blockade operated less effectively, even at the end of the war, than historians have assumed.

The success of British efforts in interdicting American merchant shipping, privateers, and warships is exceedingly difficult to measure because of the loss of admiralty court records.[17] Halifax and Bermuda, followed by the courts in the Caribbean, undoubtedly received the bulk of British captures. Table 8.6 lists the 711 captures adjudicated in Halifax by year of capture and vessel type, while table 8.7 separates the prizes by adjudication.

The 629 valid prizes adjudicated at Halifax seem to indicate that the blockade experienced great success in its interdiction efforts. Relatively few of the vessels, however, were the valuable high-tonnage ships—the key elements in the international carrying trade. Instead low-tonnage vessels, indicative of the coasting and fishing fleets, form the bulk of the prizes. The increase in captures of these smaller vessels in 1813 reflects the campaign in the Chesapeake Bay, while the increase in 1814 corresponds to stepped-up British activity within that bay and along the coast of New England.

The Royal Navy did not operate alone off the coast of the United States. Privateers from England and Canada cruised American waters throughout the war, and accounted for a substantial portion of the prizes taken into Halifax (table 8.8). In war one usually takes any help offered, but the most common welcome extended to those private cruisers by the Royal Navy came via impressment. In fact, British officers viewed them as competition for the prizes available, and harassed

TABLE 8.6. *Halifax: Prizes by Vessel Type*

	Ship	Sloop	Brig	Schooner	Total
1812	42	7	43	52	144
1813	45	71	79	144	339
1814	23	45	47	99	214
1815	0	2	6	6	14
TOTAL	110	125	175	301	711

Source: Essex Institute, *American Vessels Captured by the British.*

TABLE 8.7. *Halifax: Court Rulings*

	Condemned	Restored	Recaptured	Total
1812	95	18	31	144
1813	252	45	42	339
1814	163	19	32	214
1815	11	0	3	14
TOTAL	521	82	108	711

Source: Essex Institute, *American Vessels Captured by the British.*

TABLE 8.8. *Halifax: Vessels by Party Capturing*

	Royal Navy	Privateer	Other	Total
1812	119	24	1	144
1813	225	112	2	339
1814	153	59	2	214
1815	6	8	0	14
TOTAL	503	203	5	711

Source: Essex Institute, *American Vessels Captured by the British.*

those flying the "Red Jack" at every opportunity.[18] Napier's record of the relationship between Royal Navy and private navy speaks volumes: "*Shannon*, privateer, again out. Must drive her off, as she spoils our cruising ground. . . . Boarded and impressed five seamen from the *Rolla*, English privateer. . . . Impressed two men from the *Lively*, English privateer."[19]

Having discovered over six hundred vessels taken as valid prizes by British blockaders and privateers, and with the knowledge that Halifax provided only a portion of the total captures during the war, it would appear that the British actually went some way toward the "annihilation" of American commerce. An examination of imports and exports during the war (table 8.9) seems even more conclusive.

TABLE 8.9. *United States Exports and Imports,*
1812–1815 (in Millions of Dollars)

	Imports	Exports
1811	53	61
1812	77	39
1813	22	28
1814	13	7
1815	113	53
1816	147	82

Source: *American State Papers, Commerce and Navigation*
1:889, 963, 993, 1022, and 2:20, 52.
Note: Annual records run from 1 October to 30 September
of the following year.

Between 1812 and 1814, imports and exports suffered reductions of
84.4 percent and 84.2 percent, respectively. Though the reduction in
exports hindered the local economies of the United States, the loss of
trade to a government almost totally reliant on duties for income
proved nearly devastating. This outcome seems to indicate that the
blockade enjoyed great success against American commerce, and that
Mahan was correct: "It seems fairly safe, however, to say that after the
winter of 1812–13 American commerce dwindled very rapidly, till in
1814 it was practically annihilated."[20]

As an alternative to Mahan's rhetoric, consider the nature of American maritime strategy on the eve of war. That strategy was simplistic
in the extreme. Knowing that it was impossible to avoid the destruction of the American merchant marine by the superior British Navy if
it remained at sea, President Madison issued the prewar embargo and
called on all merchant vessels to hurry home or to shelter in a neutral
port until hostilities ended. American naval forces then sailed as a
squadron to distract the Royal Navy and cover the homeward bound
merchant vessels. In other words, *international commerce was voluntarily*
surrendered for the duration of the war. In that case, to paraphrase Mahan,
it seems fairly safe to say that before the winter of 1812–13 American
commerce dwindled rapidly as merchant ships found safe havens, till
in 1813 and 1814 the only commerce that continued was that allowed
by British licenses or chanced by letter of marque traders. This alternative interpretation does not deny the effectiveness of the British
blockade, or at least American fear of the hazards of a British controlled Atlantic basin, in reducing the transoceanic trade of the United

States. It does, however, clearly distinguish between "halted" and "annihilated" commerce.

Great Britain intended the commercial blockade to weaken the American economy by denying neutral carriage. The loss of imports, however, seemed less damaging to that economy than the military blockade's constriction of its coasting trade. Many Americans experienced inconvenience and frustration due to the slow inland transportation that replaced interrupted coastal traffic and certainly inflation driven by the inability of farmers to move goods to market plagued many areas; but the nation was self-sufficient, and a self-sufficient economy tends to resist disruption.[21] If not disrupted, the economy was certainly discomfited, and the literate wealthy who speculated in shipping and export provided the records that witnessed to their discomfort (not only in the pages of newspapers and in the halls of Congress, but in the minutes of the Hartford Convention of 1814).[22] Even the government suffered from shortages of funds, amassing a large public debt over the course of the war. The debt had increased from its prewar level of $39,905,183 to $88,485,995 by 31 December 1814.[23]

Such problems, however, cannot be blamed entirely on the blockade. They arose because the government of the United States failed to achieve its short, victorious war as originally planned. By December 1812, it was clear to Madison that the initial assault on Canada, the only leverage against Britain available to the United States, had failed. With that failure, Congress quickly appointed peace commissioners to seek an end to the conflict. The situation, however, was not urgent; Madison had enough faith in a renewed offensive into Canada to order that any negotiations in 1813 retain the original American demands. Meanwhile, the United States' maritime strategy changed from coastal defense to *guerre de course* for most of the Navy while making no official efforts (other than rhetoric) to reestablish international commerce.

"Annihilation" implies utter destruction. Did the British blockade destroy American carrying capacity? Table 8.10 displays the status of American commercial tonnage during the war years. "Registered" tonnage represents tonnage available for international trade, "Entered" tonnage applies to tonnage available for the coasting trade, while "Fishing" is self-explanatory. The "Duties" columns indicate the amount of available tonnage actually engaged in activity (if a registered ship sailed from an American port twice in one year, it paid duties twice, which explains the apparent aberrations in 1811 and 1816).

TABLE 8.10. *United States Merchant Tonnage (in Thousands of Tons)*

	Registered	Duties	Entered	Duties	Fishing	Duties
1811	768.8	948.4	420.4	321.9	43.3	37.6
1812	760.6	668.0	478.0	338.2	31.4	27.8
1813	674.8	237.7	471.1	252.4	20.7	18.5
1814	674.6	59.8	466.2	189.7	18.4	16.5
1815	854.3	707.0	475.7	374.8	38.2	33.2
1816	800.8	877.5	522.2	414.6	49.3	48.1

Source: American State Papers, Commerce and Navigation 1:959, 962, 998, 1001, 1018, 1021, AND 2:13, 14, 38, 39, 62, 63.
Note: Data tabulated as of 31 December of each year.

Registered tonnage suffered a loss of some 85,800 tons in the first months of the war, the equivalent of 150 to 200 large vessels. Despite the sailing of over 295,000 tons during 1813 and 1814, additional losses proved negligible, indicative of involvement in the licensed trade. Losses to the coasting trade remained small throughout the war— 11,800 tons, or perhaps 200 vessels of 50 to 100 tons each. These small losses occurred despite the fact that 70.7 percent in 1812, 53.6 percent in 1813, and 40.7 percent of available tonnage operated in 1814.[24] The fishing fleet was a different matter entirely. Between 1812 and 1814, it lost 13,000 tons, or 41.4 percent of its strength. This figure represented literally hundreds of small to medium tonnage vessels taken or destroyed by the British, and apparently constituted the bulk of British prizes.[25]

As the numbers illustrate, the commerce carriers of the United States did not suffer annihilation at British hands. Though temporarily, and to some degree voluntarily, isolated from their normal markets, they rebounded in 1815 to volumes of trade approaching those of 1811. Even the fishing fleet had recovered, with interest, by 1816. Not only does table 8.10 reveal that the American merchant marine avoided being "wiped out," as Ian R. Christie insisted, it also reveals that a substantial volume of seaborne commerce continued unfettered, if not unhindered, throughout the war.

Again, this does not indicate that the British blockade was completely ineffective. American commerce was tremendously reduced, but far from Marcus's "practically annihilated." Losses to the merchant marine proved minimal, allowing a vigorous return in 1815 to the commercial lanes from which it had been voluntarily withdrawn in 1812. The fact that 40.7 percent of American coasting tonnage operated in 1814, and did so with minimal losses, seems somewhat at odds with the traditional view of the tight blockade of the American coast. Such an overpowering blockade as that reflected in the interpretations of past historians should have virtually "annihilated" the American coasting fleet, or at least kept the greatest portion of its tonnage locked in port (without relying on Madison's help). That the British block-aders did not do so tends to indicate an effectiveness somewhat less than that currently accepted.

Examining American merchant marine activity at the microlevel is extremely difficult. Of the seven major ports of the era—Boston, New York, Baltimore, Wilmington (North Carolina), Charleston (South Carolina), Savannah, and New Orleans—only tonnage and clearance records for Baltimore and New Orleans appear to have escaped the twin ravages of fire and the purging of government records.[26]

Table 8.11 depicts vessels clearing the port of Baltimore from July 1812 to April 1815. The almost complete cessation of registered and foreign shipping from March 1813 through the end of the war attests to the effective closing of the entrance to the Chesapeake Bay. From July 1812 to February 1813, eighty-three registered vessels sailed from Baltimore: thirty-seven (44.6 percent) under British license to the Iberian Peninsula, sixteen (19.3 percent) presumably under British license to the Caribbean, twelve (14.5 percent) to France, and the remaining vessels to ports ranging from China to Africa. Note that the British licensing system subsidized almost two-thirds of these sailings. Surviving port records did not list merchantmen sailing under a letter of marque and privateers. Apparently, the bulk of the vessels recorded by Barrie as exiting the bay during the winter of 1813–14 fell into those categories, the remainder constituting a portion of the coasting trade.

The coasting trade operating from Baltimore suffered little disrup-tion to its pattern of shipping—the peak months of March, July, Sep-tember, and November differing only in volume from those present since 1809 (barring, of course, the disruption caused by the attempt to capture the port in late August of 1814). The number of the port's enrolled vessels active in the bay during the war actually decreased by less than a third compared to trade between 1809 and 1812.[27]

On the whole, Baltimore's shipping activity seems to confirm the effectiveness of the British blockade as established between the capes of the Chesapeake. It also illustrates the lack of disruption stemming

TABLE 8.11. *Baltimore Ship Clearances, July 1812–April 1815*

	July 1812	Aug.	Sept.	Oct.	Nov.	Dec.
Registered	17	14	10	17	15	5
Foreign	2	4	4	10	12	4
Coasting	36	12	23	20	16	6
TOTALS	55	30	37	47	43	15

	Jan. 1813	Feb.	Mar.	Apr.	May	June
Registered	2	3	0	0	0	0
Foreign	4	4	1	0	0	0
Coasting	6	10	44	12	13	21
TOTALS	12	17	45	12	13	21

	July 1813	Aug.	Sept.	Oct.	Nov.	Dec.
Registered	0	0	0	0	0	0
Foreign	0	0	0	0	0	0
Coasting	24	8	28	15	26	18
TOTALS	24	8	28	15	26	18

	Jan. 1814	Feb.	Mar.	Apr.	May	June
Registered	0	1	0	0	0	0
Foreign	0	0	0	0	1	0
Coasting	11	14	39	16	17	13
TOTALS	11	15	39	16	18	13

	July 1814	Aug.	Sept.	Oct.	Nov.	Dec.
Registered	0	0	0	0	0	0
Foreign	0	0	0	0	0	0
Coasting	23	10	5	14	24	14
TOTALS	23	10	5	14	24	14

	Jan. 1815	Feb.	Mar.	Apr.	Totals
Registered	0	0	3	19	106
Foreign	0	0	2	4	52
Coasting	15	2	61	30	646
TOTALS	15	2	66	53	804

Source: Baltimore Tonnage Book, 1808–1815, National Archives, Washington, D.C., RG36.

from the Royal Navy's summer campaigns in 1813 and 1814. If the most basic pattern of the region's maritime culture so graphically continued, then British operations designed to curtail the use of the Chesapeake as an American transportation system evidently failed, at least in the upper regions of the bay.

Activity at the port of New Orleans appears to have increased dra-

TABLE 8.12. *New Orleans Ship Clearances, July 1812–April 1815*

	July 1812	Aug.	Sept.	Oct.	Nov.	Dec.
Registered	11	8	5	4	5	2
Foreign	6	7	3	11	8	9
Coasting	8	2	2	4	1	4
TOTALS	25	17	10	19	14	15

	Jan. 1813	Feb.	Mar.	Apr.	May	June
Registered	3	7	5	3	7	18
Foreign	10	19	12	8	14	26
Coasting	2	6	2	3	10	16
TOTALS	15	32	19	14	31	60

	July 1813	Aug.	Sept.	Oct.	Nov.	Dec.
Registered	16	15	7	18	15	13
Foreign	14	14	11	17	10	9
Coasting	16	3	3	7	8	11
TOTALS	46	32	21	42	33	33

	Jan. 1814	Feb.	Mar.	Apr.	May	June
Registered	8	9	7	15	16	15
Foreign	5	9	8	9	13	21
Coasting	5	6	2	2	11	12
TOTALS	18	24	17	26	40	48

	July 1814	Aug.	Sept.	Oct.	Nov.	Dec.
Registered	23	17	11	10	15	6
Foreign	21	15	7	12	10	0
Coasting	18	11	7	6	11	5
TOTALS	62	43	25	28	36	11

	Jan. 1815	Feb.	Mar.	Apr.	Totals
Registered	0	0	3	32	349
Foreign	0	2	11	20	371
Coasting	0	0	2	9	215
TOTALS	0	2	16	61	935

Source: New Orleans, Record of Entrances and Clearances, 1812–1909, National Archives, Washington, D.C., RG36.

matically during the conflict (table 8.12). Surviving records begin only in July 1812, making it impossible to establish a basis for comparison of war and prewar traffic. June and July were, however, the peak shipment months for the port (a trend that continued at least through 1820), and a comparison of the activity for July 1812, 1813, and 1814 shows that port activity nearly doubled and then tripled in the last two years of the war.[28] Of particular interest is the number of foreign vessels, primarily Spanish, taking advantage of the open harbor to deliver European goods and to move American goods to distant markets.

Both foreign and registered vessels clearing the port outnumbered active coasting craft—not the sign of a successful British blockade. Even the presence of British patrollers in August 1812, June and October 1813, and September 1814 appears to have failed to discomfit the area's shipping. It was not until late December 1814 and the first two months of 1815 that the Royal Navy even attempted to interdict New Orleans, but when it did so, the interdiction was complete—at least for a few weeks. Normal maritime traffic showed signs of resuming even before official notification of the end of the war could have reached the area in mid-March 1815, a sign that the blockaders had already withdrawn from the Gulf of Mexico.

Tables 8.13 and 8.14 vividly illustrate the differences between ports suffering from the presence of a blockade and those benefiting from its absence. Every American port along the Atlantic coast should have developed shipping cycles featuring two very obvious types of peaks: one based upon the availability of agricultural goods for registered carriage (annual, occurring June to August) and a series of peak months reflecting the infrastructure supported by the coasting trade (variable, depending upon regional needs). New Orleans, a recent addition to the United States, had not yet developed a strongly delineated coasting infrastructure, partly because of the low population density along the American portion of the Gulf coast.

As table 8.13 reveals, the expected registered shipping pattern disappeared from Baltimore; the remaining peak months represent the surviving coasting infrastructure of the Chesapeake. Had this not been the case, at least one of the peak months of each year would have overlapped the heaviest shipping months of unblockaded New Orleans. If the British blockade had been fully successful, the Chesapeake Bay would have been penetrated and the pattern of coasting activity disrupted rather than the number of vessels engaged in local trade simply suffering a small reduction in quantity. Finally, as the shipping within the blockaded Chesapeake decreased in the opening months of the war, the traffic in the Gulf increased—an interesting comment on the futility of a "partial" national blockade (table 8.14 provides a comparison of total clearances during the war). Were records available for all major ports of the United States during the conflict, this shifting of traffic between the blockaded northern ports and more open southern ports would have been readily visible.

TABLE 8.13. *Activity Comparison for Baltimore and New Orleans Ship Clearances, July 1812–April 1815*

	July 1812	Aug.	Sept.	Oct.	Nov.	Dec.
Baltimore	55	30	37	47	43	15
New Orleans	25	17	10	19	14	15

	Jan. 1813	Feb.	Mar.	Apr.	May	June
Baltimore	12	17	45	12	13	21
New Orleans	15	32	19	14	31	60

	July 1813	Aug.	Sept.	Oct.	Nov.	Dec.
Baltimore	24	8	28	15	26	18
New Orleans	46	32	21	42	33	33

	Jan. 1814	Feb.	Mar.	Apr.	May	June
Baltimore	11	15	39	16	18	13
New Orleans	18	24	17	26	40	48

	July 1814	Aug.	Sept.	Oct.	Nov.	Dec.
Baltimore	23	10	5	14	24	14
New Orleans	62	43	25	28	36	11

	Jan. 1815	Feb.	Mar.	Apr.		Totals
Baltimore	15	2	66	53		804
New Orleans	0	2	16	61		935

Source: Baltimore Tonnage Book, 1808–1815, National Archives, Washington, D.C., RG36; New Orleans, Record of Entrances and Clearances, 1812–1909, National Archives, Washington, D.C., RG36.

TABLE 8.14. *Baltimore and New Orleans Total Ship Clearances, July 1812–April 1815*

	Registered	Foreign	Coasting	Total
Baltimore	106	52	646	804
New Orleans	349	371	215	935

Source: Baltimore Tonnage Book, 1808–1815, National Archives, Washington, D.C., RG36; New Orleans, Record of Entrances and Clearances, 1812–1909, National Archives, Washington, D.C., RG36.

Historians have introduced two other aspects of the war relative to the effectiveness of the blockade. The first was the question of New England and its special treatment by the British. The second concerned the drain of specie out of sections of the United States and out of the United States in general. Both arguments appear to have been somewhat overstated, where not purely fallacious.

The British government decided in 1812 that the coasts of New England should not be placed under commercial blockade. This

dispensation facilitated provision and grain shipments to the Peninsula, the Maritime provinces of Canada, and the Caribbean. Also, the
British hoped that the apparent sentiments behind the split in Congress over the declaration of war, especially long-smoldering resentment at the Restrictive System, would result in the withdrawal of New
England from the Union. The government even ordered Warren to
make a separate peace with the region if possible. That many New
Englanders resented the war was obvious. Amos A. Evans, surgeon of
the *Constitution*, recorded the antiwar attitude of Bostonians in his
journal, while anti-Madison rhetoric abounded in many of the section's newspapers. Yet other New England hands took 142 privateers
and letter of marque traders to sea, and though they sailed for personal
profit, neither the first nor the last to profit from war, they performed a
valuable service for their country. It is difficult to imagine the crews, or
their families, or their investors willingly abandoning the Union. It is
also difficult to imagine that sentiment in the citizens of Eastport, who
in early 1813 sheltered an American prize from an irate British frigate,
not only refusing to surrender it, but exchanging cannon fire with the
frigate to prevent its recapture.[29] Similarly, when given the option to
swear allegiance to King George or leave, fully 25 percent of the population in occupied Maine chose to leave. Consider their dilemma
closely: rather than abandon their country, they gave up all they possessed to the British and walked south.

Graham wrote: "In the case of New England it can be safely
affirmed that the neutrality of this wealthy ship-building area saved
British North America."[30] There is, however, tremendous difficulty in
understanding his perception of a region that supported numerous privateers, safely harbored American naval assets, claimed over a third of
the nation's standing army as native sons, and provided monetary support to the federal government as "neutral."[31] Perhaps the efforts of the
Hartford Convention, dying unheralded with war's end, prompted the
statement. Even then, the convention did not produce a document of
secession, only proposals for constitutional change to strengthen
defense and increase the power of individual states.[32]

Possibly the best contemporary assessment of New Englanders
came from the hand of Napier: "Federalists pretend to be friendly to
the English. They hate the war on their own account, hate the war
because it prevents their making money, and like the English as a
spendthrift loves an old rich wife; the sooner we are gone the better."[33]
New England not only lacked neutrality, except that envisioned by
the British government, it remained the heart of American maritime

activity throughout the war. By failing to blockade New England from the start of the conflict, Great Britain created a haven for privateers and American warships, as well as a source of revenue for the United States, that lasted into 1814.

Specie, or silver and gold coinage, constituted an important measure of wealth in the early nineteenth century. A measure of the success of the blockade frequently observed by historians has been the drain of specie from the southern and middle regions of the United States to New England, and thence to Canada, or directly from the south via Amelia Island.[34] Unfortunately, all claims lack provenance or even logical support, quite probably because no such drain of specie existed.[35]

Where did this perception originate? The *American State Papers* trace a decrease in specie held by the U.S. Treasury from an 1808 high of $13,846,717 to a 1814 low of $577,207. Apparently the state of the national government's finance has been confused with the state of its people's fiscal resources—a perception not unlike viewing the current national debt and then claiming that all Americans suffer severe credit problems. Secretary of the Treasury A. J. Dallas, in his report to Congress of 17 October 1814, illuminated the government's true dilemma: "The recent exportations of Specie have considerably diminished the fund of gold and silver Coin; *and another considerable portion of that fund has been drawn, by the timid and the wary, from the use of the Community, into the private coffers of Individuals.*"[36]

The possibility of discovering the exact transactions that precipitated a projected drain of specie almost two hundred years ago remains remote, but some readily available data and the application of knowledge of period logistics offer a refutation to existing perceptions. Specie entered the United States during the War of 1812 by two routes, the bulk of it through trade and the remainder via prizes, both of which an effective blockade should have stopped. Table 8.9 noted the export value of trade leaving the United States during the war, an apparent national income of $71 million plus or minus foreign market value. Of this, $42.2 million represented trade with the peninsula, a portion of the licensed trade. Wellington wrote in 1813, "The exporters of specie, to the great distress of the army and the ruin of the country, are the American merchants . . . these merchants cannot venture to take in payment bills upon England . . . they must continue therefore to export specie from Portugal."[37] Such would have been the case in virtually all licensed transactions, as Britain forbade licensees to return to the United States with non-British goods, while the American nonimportation law forbade their returning with British goods. This certainly produced a specie drain—only *from* Great Britain *into* the United States, primarily through the open door of New England.

Trade through Amelia Island operated as any normal market, other than during the embargo. Americans sold cotton, then purchased foreign goods quite legally, as Spain controlled the island and the British dared not interdict it nor interfere with their Spanish allies. This market, the only real one open to the United States, not only accounted for the tremendous coasting trade often escorted by vessels at St. Marys but also brought specie into the South due to the high value of cotton (driven by British textile manufactories).

As for the Canadian border, there is little doubt that American provisions fed British forces in Canada. It is illogical, however, to conclude that Americans traded most of their agricultural products for British goods—how could they have transported them through the extensive northern forests to viable markets? The ports stood closed to coasting and the northern woods lacked even rudimentary roads. Donald Hickey related the story of a Maine husbandman driving his cattle to the Canadian border. Prevented by law from crossing with them, he waited while a Canadian compatriot used a basket of corn to lure them across the border. The only thing that Hickey omitted was the bag of silver that magically fell onto American soil as the cattle ambled north.[38] Though the trade balance may have run against the United States in certain locales, on the whole tremendous quantities of specie entered the country through trade and—as no documentation exists to prove differently—the bulk of it apparently remained there until normal trade resumed. Certainly a negative trade imbalance did not exist in 1813 and 1814 to absorb American specie.

Prizes, as part of their cargo, brought quantities of specie into the country. Naval vessels and privateers recorded $1.1 million officially seized as well as, at a minimum, $500,000 extorted in ransoms.[39] Additionally, the large number of prizes captured stimulated local economies. Investors earned millions of dollars in profits from prize sales. In Baltimore, twenty-six of the major investors realized profits of over $200,000 each, while numerous minor investors among less wealthy citizens also benefited.[40] It was the same up and down the seaboard. Rather than draining specie, licensing and the failure of the blockade to contain the nation's navies and stop their prizes from reaching port actually seem to have brought specie into the United States.[41]

From 1812 through early 1815, Britain attempted to enclose the coasts of the United States in a wooden wall. The military blockade failed to contain the American public and private navies, resulting in an estimated loss of fifty-two British merchantmen per month of the war. Even during the second half of the long Anglo-French conflict, 1803–14, French naval resources (public and private) had averaged only thirty-nine captures per month.[42] And when the first two months of 1815 alone are considered, average British losses of over one hundred vessels per month seem to indicate that American efforts had not yet peaked. Nor had the economic blockade been totally successful, with Great Britain actually subsidizing a portion of the American merchant marine through most of the war via the licensed trade, while leaving New England uninterdicted until the last ten months of the struggle.

That the same men who refused the mediation of the Russian tsar in early 1813 in their desire to punish America signed a treaty in which they gained little except an end to the war in December 1814 speaks volumes.[43] Many factors played a part in that decision: war-weariness, political chaos in Europe, popular unrest at taxation, rising unemployment, a tremendous national debt, discontent of merchants, and the failure of the 1814 offensive from Canada, among others.[44] Regardless of the reasons Great Britain sought peace, the inefficiency of the blockade played its part, and any inefficiency of the Royal Navy inevitably returned to Whitehall, where the first lord staved off two serious attempts at censure in Parliament during the last months of the war.[45] Room for challenge existed because the Admiralty had failed to implement its blockade effectively, that failure falling into five categories— force allocation, extent of blockade, command conflict, confusion of objectives, and command selection.

Despite warnings of imminent war, the Admiralty failed to take steps reallocating forces to the North American command.[46] Though a question of naval resources, the decision not to allocate additional vessels to Halifax also represented a choice of priorities, and the threat potential of Napoleon carried more weight than that of Madison. With the declaration of war, the Admiralty's solution to the problem of ship availability— combining the Jamaica, Leeward Islands, and Halifax Stations—offered no succor to its hard-pressed commander in Halifax, despite the appearance on ship lists of an adequate blockading force in the theater of war. This disparity between the vision of the Admiralty, the needs of the station admiral, and the reality of vessels actually on blockade remained a problem throughout the war, as illustrated in table 8.15.

TABLE 8.15. *British Ship Availability, Halifax, 1812–1815*

	Admiralty	On Station	On Blockade
July 1812	23	7	0
February 1813	97	28	6
July 1813	112	52	11
March 1814	75	61	25
August 1814	75	61	25
January 1815	85	73	21

Source: Ships in Sea Pay, Admiralty Office, 1 July 1812, UkLPR, D, Adm. 8, Public Records Office, London; Croker to Warren, 10 February 1813, Dudley, *Naval War of 1812* 2:16–19; Ships in Sea Pay, 1 July 1813, Dudley, *Naval War of 1812* 2:168–78; Cochrane to Croker, 8 March 1814, UkLPR, Adm. 1/505; Disposition of Ships on North American Station, 26 July 1814, Hotham Papers; Public Orders Issued by Commodore Hotham, August 1814–March 1815, Hotham Papers.
Note: The January 1815 Admiralty estimate is based on compilations from primary and secondary sources. "On Station" and "On Blockade" are also calculated from a comparative search of the primary and secondary sources cited in this study.

The dates in table 8.15 were selected from primary source documents listing the ship strength used by the Admiralty and/or the strength actually available to the admiral on station. Blockade strength was a matter of tallying the average number of documented vessels physically blockading American ports. As can be seen, the numbers vary tremendously and forces that appeared more than adequate to the Admiralty sitting at table in London dwindled to a minimal coverage of the American coast.

Except for 1813, when most of the "missing" vessels resided in the Caribbean, the difference in "Admiralty" and "On Station" numbers included vessels in transit to or from the command, serving as convoy escorts, undergoing long-term refits, or lost and not yet reported. "On Station" ships unavailable for blockade included those on antiprivateer patrols, a varying amount on short term refit before relieving blockaders, vessels carrying dispatches, and warships designated for offensive actions.

This meant a shortage of ships interdicting American ports. As a comparison of the consolidated numbers from Cochrane's recommendation to the Admiralty (table 8.16) and the actual number of ships available (table 8.15) illustrate, that shortage was severe. Total ships on station, much less those on blockade, never approached the ninety vessels deemed necessary for a successful blockade. Even in the last month of the war, actual blockaders totaled only 23.3 percent of Cochrane's required blockaders. As these tables reveal, regardless of

TABLE 8.16. *Number of Vessels Required to Blockade the Coast of the United States*

Location	Vessels
New England	10
Boston	10
New York area	24
Delaware Bay	8
Chesapeake Bay	14
North Carolina	4
South Carolina	7
Georgia	6
Gulf	7
TOTAL	90

Source: Vice Admiral Sir Alexander Cochrane to Secretary of the Admiralty John W. Croker, 8 March 1814, UkLPR, Adm. 1/505, 633.

the numbers quoted by the Admiralty, the amount of force allocated to the North American command never approached the necessary minimum requested by its station admirals.

The beginning of the military blockade, meant to deny (within limits) the world's oceans to American maritime forces and sea power, can be traced to documents preceding the declaration of war and remained a continuing subject in Admiralty missives throughout the war's duration. Its failure tied directly to ship availability, as well as to timing. If early military blockades of major American ports had been established, then the swarms of privateers would have been reduced, allowing the additional British ships committed to protect convoys and patrol sea-lanes to have been used instead to blockade minor ports or to patrol American coastlines. The failure to anticipate the force allocations needed to establish and to maintain the blockade proved pivotal to its ultimate level of effectiveness.

The economic blockade, declared in four separate stages, remained less than fully efficient throughout the war, though if the war had continued, 1815 could have been a different story. By February of that year, the New England coast had been closed to neutrals for several months, and Cockburn had demonstrated that Amelia Island could be isolated by the seizure of St. Marys. As implemented through 1814, however, the economic blockade—working around licensing, Spain's Amelia Island, and a shortage of blockading vessels—had been unable to force the United States to sue for peace under any terms.

The tendency to give conflicting orders and to misdirect and criticize subordinates was one of the Admiralty's most devastating faults, especially in the first eighteen months of the war. From the initial orders that urged Warren to destroy the enemy while not endangering peace negotiations through the final decision in early 1814 to split the North American command as Warren had requested months earlier, the Admiralty weakened the blockading effort by sowing confusion (and possibly despair) in its chosen commander's mind. That confusion of objectives led to the Chesapeake Bay campaign of 1813, an operation that removed valuable vessels from the blockade yet achieved little.

The last full year of the war brought a change in strategic objectives along the Atlantic seaboard. The Admiralty intended the massive raids along the Atlantic shores and in the Chesapeake as a diversion, distracting American troops from reinforcing against the British invasions from Canada (intended both to capture and to hold ground) and simultaneously weakening the American will to resist. It expected the New Orleans expedition to capture and hold the mouth of the Mississippi, either permanently or as a bargaining chip at the peace conference. Nonetheless, warships assigned to these campaigns lessened the already insufficient number of vessels available for the blockade, and the concentration of force for the latter operation certainly played a part in the large number of prizes taken by the Americans in early 1815.

The diversion of warships from blockading stations during the last months of the war is very evident in the journal of former Captain of the Fleet Henry Hotham, then serving as commodore of the squadron off New York from August 1814 through the dissolution of the blockade in March 1815. In early August, Hotham's squadron of twenty to twenty-two vessels interdicted the coast from north of Boston through the Delaware Bay; his area of responsibility expanded as offensive fleets concentrated along the coast of Maine and in the Chesapeake Bay. During the second half of August, Hotham's squadron shrank to ten ships, the others supporting the invasion of Maine. They returned in early September, and the squadron retained a strength of twenty to twenty-one vessels through October. By mid-November, available vessels averaged thirteen to fifteen as several ships departed to join the New Orleans expedition or to replace blockaders accompanying Cochrane to the Gulf. By the end of January, all offensive action at an end, Hotham's area of responsibility had shrank to the blockade of New York and New London. His squadron's strength averaged only five warships for the remainder of the war—a little short of the twenty-four ships Cochrane thought necessary for the blockade of the New York area.[47] In truth, Hotham had seldom commanded half of the necessary ships required for a successful blockade, as estimated by Cochrane (table 8.16). But then, that had been the norm along the American coast for every officer from commodore to commander in chief since the war began.

Aside from Sawyer, whom fate unkindly placed at the cruel point of decision in the first three months of the struggle, the Admiralty selected only two men to control the North American command during the war. Adm. Sir John Borlase Warren, a solid officer, earned an undeserved reputation during his time in command. Thrown into the fire of conflict with mixed orders, privateers running freely, too few ships locally to patrol the coast adequately (much less blockade it), and numerous ships in the Caribbean which the Admiralty refused to let him control, he nonetheless brought order out of chaos, installed a weak blockade, and even continued to work toward peace negotiations. The Admiralty ridiculed his pleas for additional ships and demanded the destruction of the U.S. Navy with the forces at his disposal. Warren then attempted to do just that in the Chesapeake. On 13 March 1814, a young British officer, distraught because his powerful frigate had been anchored in port for four months awaiting repairs while numerous brigs and schooners refitted ahead of it, mused on Warren's reasons for such commands: "The conduct of Sir John Warren, since he has commanded on this station, has been so very inexplicable that *his* reasons must be *very secret* indeed, as there is not a person able to form a conjecture on the subject; so secret are these reasons, that some people even begin to fancy that he never had any."[48]

As many authors have done since, Napier criticized the apparent indecision of Warren; and like them, he was wrong. In this case, the smaller vessels refitted faster and served an immediate need on the convoy lanes, while the frigate, unable to stand alone against the larger Americans, could wait. This was typical of Warren's decision-making skills, skills which with proper support from the Admiralty could have built a wooden wall around the United States.

On the surface, Vice Adm. Sir Alexander F. I. Cochrane appeared a poor choice on the Admiralty's part to command the blockade. His hatred for Americans distracted him from the mundane duty of interdicting their coasts. That seems, however, to have been exactly the type of commander Lord Melville felt he needed in North America, one who could and would take the war home to the American people, forcing them to the treaty table on bended knees. Certainly the Admiralty supported the harsh measures authorized by their admiral, and Cochrane personally selected the targets for the Chesapeake and Mississippi campaigns of 1814. As fate dictated, his taking the war to the American people accomplished little except the weakening of the blockade, despite major reinforcement of his forces.

Though primary accountability for the splintered wall rests with the Admiralty, other sources certainly contributed. The attitude of officers in the Royal Navy, especially their scramble for prize money and their early denigration of the U.S. Navy's abilities, played a part in the permeability of the blockade. The aura of invincibility surrounding the Royal Navy, shattered in three brief frigate actions and mocked by the seemingly unstoppable cuts of American privateers and public cruisers alike, also contributed. More important than either, however, was the war with France. The continuation of that conflict necessitated the licensing policy, thereby contributing to keeping the ports of New England open. The fear of a French breakout from one of the blockaded Channel ports loomed large in the mind of the Admiralty and Warren and had an impact on command structure and force allocation. The need for a Spanish ally negated any thought of taking action against Amelia Island, and the overall alliance situation made dealing with any neutral shipping tricky indeed. The ports of France and its allies greatly extended the range of American raiders operating in European waters, highlighting the critical need for a successful military blockade. Finally, it was the ending of the war with France, or rather the chaos and war-weariness following that ending, that cleared a path to the Treaty of Ghent.

The British blockade of the United States during the War of 1812 was never the overwhelmingly successful operation painted by Mahan and numerous other historians. Nonetheless, to present convincing performance measures for any isolated historical event is difficult. Fortunately, 1793–1815 saw Britain conduct three blockades, so the opportunity for comparison of these very similar events exists. Chapter 9 briefly discusses each of the blockades of France, then compares and rates all three blockades in an effort to determine their comparative efficiency.

9
❦

Comparison to
Contemporary Blockades

The British blockades of France, 1793–1802 and 1803–14, interdicted a far stronger enemy (often an alliance of strong enemies) than did the blockade of 1812–15. Nonetheless, blockade theory remained the same and the techniques Capt. Thomas Hardy employed off New York differed little from those he had practiced off Calais, allowing a valid comparison of the three British blockades of the late age of sail.

BRITAIN AND FRANCE, 1793–1802

The French fleet numbered some eighty-two ships-of-the-line, seventy-eight frigates, and a few dozen unrated vessels in 1793. Its main bases of Brest on the Atlantic and Toulon on the Mediterranean lacked adequate stockpiles of both marine stores and provisions, thanks to the bankrupt state of the French treasury and the maritime apathy of France's revolutionary politicians. Revolutionary fervor had also gripped the fleet as a whole, so much so that a state of collective undiscipline bordering upon anarchy reigned on most vessels. The majority of France's experienced naval officers, especially at the critical rank of *capitaine des vaisseaux*, had taken the path of the émigré, retaining their heads at the expense of their careers. Their *sans culottes* replacements faced a difficult challenge once Paris declared war on Great Britain on 1 February 1793.[1]

The Royal Navy, including ships rapidly removed from ordinary, consisted of eighty-eight ships-of-the-line, seventy-one frigates, and almost three dozen smaller vessels concentrated in home ports. Additionally, five small ships-of-the-line, fourteen frigates, and fifteen unrated craft patrolled foreign stations. Britain's small quantitative superiority, bolstered by Dutch and Spanish allies during the critical initial stage of the war, was enhanced by its well-stocked dockyards and its excellent cadre of officers and warrant officers.[2] The latter, often staying with a single vessel for their entire career (including maintaining it while in ordinary), proved amazingly adept at turning volunteers and pressed men alike into efficient sailors.

Admirals, however, are more important than sailors in determining strategy, and two schools of naval thought—both centered on the blockade—developed during the first war against France. Adm. Richard Lord Howe, commanding the Channel Fleet in 1793, instituted a policy of distant blockade continued by his successor Admiral Lord Bridport, Alexander Arthur Hood, and implemented by Adm. William Hotham in the Mediterranean. Howe refused to risk his vessels to the inevitable damage of close blockade, claiming that a severe gale would force a crippled British fleet to harbor for repairs while the French escaped anyway. He felt that it was better to respond to the inevitable French sortie in well-founded ships once the light units observing French ports reported the escape.[3] Adm. Sir John Jervis, later Lord St. Vincent, disagreed. Where he commanded, Jervis instituted a rigorous close blockade in echelon. If gales forced the fleet off station, it reunited at a specified rendezvous and renewed the blockade. Should significant enemy forces effect an escape, pursuit began from that point. Smaller forces could be ignored by the blockaders, as roving patrols or convoy escorts could destroy them.[4]

Both Jervis and Howe believed in roving patrols to handle escaped enemy light units or privateers and in the convoy system as a final line of defense for Britain's merchant marine. Throughout the Anglo-French contests the Channel, western approaches, and often the Mediterranean swarmed with British frigates and smaller vessels, making it increasingly hazardous for privateers and French naval forces to operate as single units. Those evading the patrols still faced convoy escorts. The Convoy Act of 1793 (followed by even more stringent requirements in 1798 and 1803) formed the final segment of Britain's system of interlocking maritime defenses. The act required any merchantman lacking special permission (granted to fast or well-armed ships, especially those belonging to the West and East India Companies) to sail in an escorted convoy or forgo insurance. Of the approximately 5,500 vessels registered for the trade at the beginning of the war, almost 1,500 cleared for distant ports, while nearly 900 sailed for southern Europe, and 3,100 sailed for northern Europe (most to the Baltic). These vessels required escorts during their return voyages, while coasting vessels also received escorts if a sufficient number of vessels collected in a port and requested convoy. Straggling convoys of 200 to 500 ships were typical, while the great convoys to and from the Baltic often massed 1,000 or more vessels. The rates and numbers of escorts varied, from 2 ships-of-the-line to a battle squadron plus frigates to 2 or 3 hired auxiliaries, depending upon ship availability and the importance of the convoy.[5]

Between 1793 and 1797, when Bridport officially supplanted Howe as commander in chief of the Channel Fleet, the policy of distant blockade consistently failed to stop the sailing of French squadrons, often with disastrous results. The Glorious First of June (1 June 1794) was an exception, to some degree. A French convoy of merchantmen had sailed from Brest (unintercepted) and returned to Brest (unintercepted) with grain desperately needed by the Committee of Public Safety to feed Paris, its escort capturing a British frigate and ten merchantmen while crossing the Atlantic. Lord Howe met the French covering force, recently sailed from Brest (unintercepted), at sea. The Channel Fleet captured seven ships-of-the-line, a superb tactical victory, but the convoy reached Brest safely, while its covering force had captured almost the entire Dutch Lisbon convoy in mid-May, before being brought to battle.[6]

In November 1794, a French squadron intercepted a convoy escort of two ships-of-the-line, capturing one. Two months later, the Brest fleet sortied, one squadron to reinforce Toulon while the remainder of the fleet disrupted British shipping. Bad weather forced both groups back to port by early February, losing five ships-of-the-line (exclusively to poor seamanship) but capturing a British sloop and over seventy merchantmen. The Brest force repeated the effort later, the fleet safely escorting the Toulon reinforcement squadron out of the Bay of Biscay as well as disrupting British shipping.[7] These examples (and there are others through 1800) illustrate the ineffectiveness of the convoy system against enemy battle squadrons. Escorts adequate to preserve the convoy from the depredations of single raiders and privateers went in the bag along with their nicely collected charges when the blockade did not contain the French squadrons.

The distant blockade's failure to contain or to intercept major French fleet elements in a timely fashion also harmed British efforts against French colonial possessions and threatened the safety of Britain's own colonies. Britain initiated operations against French commerce in the West Indies in 1794, capturing several islands, the most important being Guadeloupe. While British forces attempted to conquer Saint Domingue, a small French squadron out of Brest recaptured Guadeloupe. The island remained a threat to British shipping until its reconquest in 1810. French successes against British trade in North America and the West Indies mounted through 1796: French frigate squadrons gutted two Jamaican convoys in 1795, capturing fifty-eight prizes, and in the next year Admiral de Richery (out of Toulon with a stop at Cadiz) destroyed the Newfoundland fishing fleet, taking or burning over one hundred vessels and destroying the fleet's supporting shore establishments. Nor were British possessions in Africa safe. A French squadron temporarily captured Sierra Leone in September 1794, basing there for a month until fever decimated its crews. Returning unmolested to Brest, it claimed 210 British and British-allied merchantmen taken. Finally, a fleet, carrying an army commanded by General Hoche for the invasion of Ireland, sailed from Brest in late 1796. It neither saw nor suffered interference from the British fleet. Fortunately for the Royal Navy, bad weather prevented a landing.[8]

French successes on land in 1795 increased the operational demand upon the Royal Navy. Military defeat forced Prussia, Holland, and Spain to make peace with France, the last two coerced into a military alliance against Great Britain by late 1796. Still, the Royal Navy had accomplished quite a bit—between the Royal Navy and the weather, the French fleet had suffered large losses; its bases had been isolated from their primary supply sources (the Baltic for Brest and Corfu for Toulon—the latter captured by the British in 1794); and several of France's colonial possessions now flew British colors. In response, the Committee of Public Safety, after reviewing the state of its Navy near the end of 1795, officially declared that *guerre de course* should be employed from that point forward. Only small squadrons or single vessels would sail against the British, and then only against British trade.[9]

Between Spain's alliance with France and the Italian successes of a young French general, Napoleon Bonaparte, the British were compelled to withdraw their fleet under Jervis from the Mediterranean in late 1796. This redeployment led directly to Jervis's victory over a Spanish fleet off Cape St. Vincent in February 1797, his institution of a close blockade of Spanish ports, and the Battle of the Nile in August 1798, upon the return of a British squadron under Nelson to the Mediterranean. The last not only isolated a French Army in Egypt, but allowed the close blockade of Toulon, virtually guaranteeing that the Army would not be rescued. Thus, by 1798, Jervis had implemented close blockades throughout his command. Unfortunately, he often had to lift his blockades as the naval situation in the Mediterranean remained fluid because of frequent incursions by major French squadrons from the Channel ports, most notably the squadrons of Bruix and Ganteaume.[10]

The question must be asked: Why did Howe and Bridport cling to an obviously inefficient distant blockade when close blockade offered superior containment of the enemies' forces? First, they did not cling all that tightly. A close blockade of Texel, established shortly after Holland's shift of alliance, continued throughout the war, setting the stage for minor skirmishes as the Dutch attempted to escort Baltic convoys of marine stores to Brest, and for the fleet battle of Camperdown, handily won by a superior British force.[11] Second, both were victims of a past conflict—the American War of Independence. As flag officers in that struggle, they had shouldered their share of the blame for the temporary loss of command of the Channel and thence of the sea, resulting in the loss of Britain's colonies. Overextension caused that loss, so is it any wonder that they refused to scatter the Channel Fleet in close blockades? Jervis, Lord St. Vincent after his victory off those capes of the same name, was a mere post captain during the American struggle. His perspective of that war was far different from that of Howe and Bridport. Jervis's patrol and blockade duty off the port of Brest had brought fame and prize money—it had also convinced him that the place to hurt France's maritime power was at its points of origin. Thus he developed and implemented a blockade strategy to do exactly that.[12]

By 1800, the Admiralty's displeasure with the conduct of the Channel Fleet had reached such a point that Bridport was forced to resign, St. Vincent being installed in his place in April. The latter immediately instituted a close blockade from the Baltic to the northern coast of Spain, including an echeloned blockade of Brest. Moreover, he worked diligently to increase the efficiency of the fleet and to correct the attitudes of captains who regarded and used their ships as private yachts—an insufferable misuse of his majesty's valuable warships. A grateful government rewarded his efforts with an appointment as the first lord of the Admiralty in February 1801.[13]

The capture or destruction of most of the Danish fleet in its harbor at Copenhagen (2 April 1801) marked the last major action in Britain's war against the French revolutionary governments and their successor, the Consulate.[14] France and Britain signed the Peace of Amiens on 24 March 1802. Significantly, Great Britain did not negotiate from a position of strength as the Continent stood neutral or arrayed behind France (barring tiny and ever-faithful Portugal). Though La Marine de la France had been reduced to only thirty-nine ships-of-the-line and thirty-five frigates by the Royal Navy (as well as a bit of lackluster seamanship), and though French commerce had been driven from its coasts and the high seas with estimated heavy losses, the close blockade had simply not been in effect long enough to affect the peace negotiations. Nor had the Royal Navy been overly successful in protecting its own merchantmen, 3,466 of which fell prize to Britain's enemies (an average of approximately 34 ships per month). What the Royal Navy did very well indeed was to assist in the capture of the colonial possessions of France, Spain, and Holland. Unfortunately, the price of an immediate peace was the return of all but Trinidad and Ceylon to their previous owners.[15] The final price of peace was almost twelve more years of war.

THE NAPOLEONIC WAR, 1803–1814

It is easy to divide the second naval struggle between Great Britain and France (and their varying allies) into two segments, split on or slightly after 21 October 1805. The battle of Trafalgar, fought on that date, manages to eclipse everything that came before, while afterward, with no further fleet actions in the war, Napoleon's struggles throughout Europe and Wellington's tramp across the Iberian Peninsula loom large in the spyglass of history. Alan Schom challenged the first half of this perspective in his narrative of the Trafalgar campaign, tying the battle into the strategic planning meant to thwart Napoleon's invasion of England rather than treating it as a singular event. He did not, however, present the campaign as a segment of existing blockade theory directly traceable to the close blockade of St. Vincent, nor did he take the story of the blockade beyond 1805.[16] Both continuity and story certainly exist.

Failed negotiations over the fate of the Low Countries and Malta catalyzed Great Britain's return to a state of war against France on 16 May 1803, though numerous other reasons—ranging from colonial possessions to the status of Napoleon as a ruler—contributed to Anglo-French tension during the short-lived Peace of Amiens. Though Great Britain had reduced its fleet during the peace, its battle line still outnumbered that of France and probable French allies, Spain and Holland, by 115 to 112. Considering the poor state of the French fleet and the abysmal condition of the Spanish fleet, the qualitative advantage was far greater than revealed by the actual numbers. In addition, the British enjoyed a quantitative superiority of roughly 50 percent in non–battle line vessels, and the failure of Spain to enter the war until December 1804—and then only after being monumentally provoked by the British capture of its annual treasure fleet—shifted the Royal Navy's initial quantitative superiority well beyond 2 to 1.[17] Napoleon returned a two-part response to Britain's declaration of war: he increased naval building (a policy continued throughout his reign) and took immediate steps to invade England. Meanwhile, the Royal Navy reestablished its system of close military blockade.

Napoleon ordered an invasion camp prepared at Boulougne and expanded its harbor to accommodate the mass of shipping needed to transfer a force of 114,000 men and 7,000 horses to England. He ordered the shipping gathered from the coasts of France and Holland to be supplemented by quick-to-build flat-bottomed boats. Realizing that concentrating vessels for the amphibious effort would be difficult against the British close blockade, Napoleon ordered the coasts of France fortified—at least a gun per league—and backed the batteries with fast-response forces of cavalry and mobile artillery to discourage raiding forces. His efforts were largely successful; by late 1804 only one final step remained: achieving temporary control of the Channel. To accomplish that, Napoleon prepared no fewer than nine invasion plans, all failures, attempting to force his admirals and those of his allies to concentrate their squadrons at Boulougne. All the squadron sailings before Trafalgar formed parts of the invasion scheme.[18] In the end, the blockade frustrated Napoleon's plan.

Between May 1803 and January 1805, not a single French battle squadron escaped harbor, despite Napoleon's numerous orders to do so. The severe winter of 1804–5, however, achieved what the French could not, battering the blockaders until chinks eventually appeared in their wooden cordon. On 10 January, a squadron of ten vessels commanded by Admiral de Burgues Missiessy, including five ships-of-the-line, braved the strong gale which had driven the British from Rochefort. Though undermanned and suffering severe damage to its spars from the same weather which had facilitated its escape, the squadron made for the West Indies. The British squadron assigned to chase the escapees never made contact—not surprising considering the several days' head start by the French. Missiessy delivered some thirty-five hundred troops and tons of supplies to Martinique, then raided British commerce, taking thirty-three prizes before being ordered to return to France. Despite damaged vessels and crews averaging less than half strength, the squadron successfully returned to Rochefort, the British having removed their blockading ships-of-the-line in the absence of the French.[19]

For ten months Admiral Nelson conducted a close blockade of Toulon. By December 1804, accumulated wear and tear forced him to move his few ships-of-the-line to a sheltered anchorage, leaving light units to monitor the harbor. On 17 January 1805, French admiral Villeneuve used a division of his forces to drive off those pickets and sallied with his entire fleet. Once word reached Nelson, he began an aggressive pursuit of the French force; unfortunately, he pursued in the wrong direction. His light forces having lost contact with Villeneuve, Nelson assumed that Napoleon planned a repeat of the invasion of Egypt. Meanwhile, Villeneuve had been driven back to a now-unwatched Toulon by a damaging gale. He sailed again, for Cadiz, on 29 March. The now severely outnumbered commander of the British forces blockading Cadiz, unaware that Nelson was at last pursuing in the correct direction, fled to the Channel Fleet rather than remain and observe the enemy. Reinforced by the French and Spanish forces in the port, Villeneuve sailed for Martinique on 9 April. While there he unloaded reinforcements, captured a convoy of fifteen sail, and forced the surrender of HMS *Diamond Rock* (one of the more interesting sloops of war in the Royal Navy—the *Diamond Rock* was actually a rock). Learning that Nelson had pursued the Combined Fleet all the way to the West Indies, Villeneuve abandoned his planned attacks on several British islands, burned his prizes, and fled to Ferrol. He engaged a large British squadron on 22 July, losing two old ships-of-the-line before breaking off the action. The British force, despite getting its prizes away and spending time looking for Nelson off Cape Finisterre, actually returned to reinforce the blockade of Ferrol before the arrival of the Combined Fleet. Forced from their position by strong winds on 1 August, the blockaders returned to find the Combined Fleet in Ferrol. Rather than risk piecemeal destruction by a now numerically superior foe, the British joined the Channel Fleet on 14 August, a day before Nelson appeared after his long and fruitless pursuit of Villeneuve. Observing a greatly reinforced Channel Fleet between his forces and Brest, Villeneuve sailed for Toulon via Cadiz on 20 August. The French fleet at Brest, finally responding to Napoleon's proddings, sortied in a half-hearted attempt to join Villeneuve on 21 August. The blockading squadron easily repulsed the effort. Villeneuve successfully reached Cadiz, then sailed for Toulon—and into the waiting arms of Nelson—on 19 October. With the defeat of the Combined Fleet on the twenty-first, Napoleon's dream of invasion came to an abrupt end.[20]

The story of Trafalgar is a testament to the effectiveness and implementation of the close blockade. First, French and allied squadrons could not sail independently and rendezvous at sea. Missiessy escaped in bad weather, while Villeneuve's escape(s) from Toulon, logistically the most precarious of blockading stations during the war, may well have been bad judgment on the part of Nelson (considering the eastward chase when all roads led to the invasion of England and the fact that ships too battered to maintain the close blockade of Toulon managed to sail across the eastern Mediterranean, to the West Indies, and back to the Channel, where most stayed with the fleet).[21] But Nelson, in keeping with the operational plans of the close blockade, did pursue the French force, maintaining a pressure that upset Villeneuve's (to say nothing of Napoleon's) plans.

Because of the local strength of the blockade, Villeneuve could be reinforced only if he lifted it with his own superior (in numbers) fleet, as at Cadiz. Even there, the blockaders escaped to join the main fleet in the Channel, so the overall balance of forces suffered little change. Had weather not intervened, Trafalgar could well have been fought off Ferrol as the blockading force had already beaten Villeneuve once. Had Villeneuve tried to reach Brest, he would have met a Channel Fleet reinforced by the former blockaders of Toulon, Cadiz, and Ferrol and would have been no closer to joining French naval forces in Brest. So he sailed for Toulon, not realizing that a force built around the new blockade of Cadiz and led by Nelson waited ahead. Behind him, the blockading forces returned. The strength and flexibility of the close military blockade should share an equal measure of glory for the defeat of Villeneuve.

Few successful escapes by French squadrons occurred after Trafalgar. Two squadrons sailed from Brest on 13 December 1805 by roundabout routes to the West Indies. A pursuing British squadron destroyed one at St. Thomas on 6 February, while the second had little luck as commerce raiders and fell victim to a hurricane in mid-August. On 23 February 1806, a frigate squadron sortied from Cadiz, partially evading a trap set by the blockaders. Its survivors eventually arrived safely at Toulon. A squadron sailed from Rochefort in severe weather (losing one ship-of-the-line in the process) on 17 January 1808, arriving at Toulon on 6 February as reinforcements for the most successful cruise by a French fleet during the war. The reinforced Toulon fleet sailed the next day, delivering supplies to Spain and engaging in commerce raiding that cost the British one-quarter million pounds sterling in prizes. It returned untouched to Toulon on 10 April. This failure of the blockade caused the Admiralty to place an increased emphasis on the Mediterranean for the remainder of the war.[22]

A squadron successfully sailed during bad weather (one ship-of-the-line lost aground) from Brest for Rochefort on 21 February 1809. Three frigates sailed from Lorient for Rochefort at the same time but were isolated and destroyed by British blockaders. The Brest squadron, reinforced by ships-of-the-line from Rochefort, anchored in the Aix Roads. The British attacked them on 11 April with fire ships and lighter vessels, resulting in a French loss of five ships-of-the-line, an incomplete victory considering that all French vessels were aground at one point.[23]

Beginning in April 1809, the French squadron in Toulon twice made efforts to supply its Army in Barcelona by sea. The first such expedition was successful, though it almost fell prey to a superior British force while returning to Toulon. A second convoy in October was intercepted and defeated at sea by the blockading fleet. Its survivors fled to Rosas Bay, and were all destroyed or taken prize by a massive cutting-out expedition on 1 November. The effort had cost the French three ships-of-the-line, two frigates, five unrated vessels, and a dozen merchantmen. The Toulon fleet sortied only once more during the war, and then did no damage during its week at sea. The honor of the last squadron sortie of the war went to a force in Lorient which escaped under the cover of bad weather on 8 March 1812, avoided an aggressive pursuit, and captured a few small prizes before returning to Brest in late March.[24]

TABLE 9.1. *French Captures of British Merchantmen, 1803–1814*

	1803	1804	1805	1806	1807	1808
Captures	222	387	507	519	559	469
	1809	1810	1811	1812	1813	1814
Captures	571	619	470	400	371	145

Source: G. J. Marcus, *The Age of Nelson, the Royal Navy 1793–1815* (New York, 1971), pages 382 and 404. The losses for 1812 are estimated.

Though the close blockade managed to keep the French fleet in check throughout the war, the Royal Navy experienced its greatest challenge in the aggressive *guerre de course* adopted by France from the outset of the conflict. Privateers—of several national backgrounds—operated from ports along the Adriatic through the Baltic as well as from the numerous colonial possessions of France and its allies. As table 9.1 illustrates, the French assault on British merchantmen accelerated through 1810, then dropped dramatically. In examining these numbers, three questions beg answers: Why were the French so successful in *guerre de course?* What brought that success to an end? And what role did the close blockade play in the scenario?

Four distinct groups of raiders operated against Great Britain. As has been shown, naval raiders operating in squadron strength achieved limited successes against British shipping (certainly when compared to their successes against the distant blockade of 1793–1800). Individual French naval vessels, especially frigates, seem to have achieved slightly better results on a per ship basis, especially when they cruised on distant stations (the West and East Indies, Indian Ocean, and Atlantic seaboard of North America).[25] The remaining raiders were privateers: those operating from French home ports, those sailing from colonial ports, and those basing in the Baltic—primarily the Danes. The first group gained a level of notoriety beyond their actual achievements because their captures were highly visible to British citizens, often occurring along England's bays and headlands. These privateers dashed from harbor on dark nights and waited along coastal shipping routes, often disguised as fishing vessels, until a convoy or coasting vessels appeared. They would then snatch a prize or two and flee to a friendly port. Becalmed convoys formed their special prey—the privateers carried sweeps as well as sails—and escorts often watched helplessly as raiders cut the richest prizes from their charges. Still, these privateers operated in the most thickly patrolled of maritime environments and faced the close blockade at the beginning and end of their voyage. When Lloyd's of London, primary insurer for Great Britain's merchant marine, voiced concern at losses in March 1809, part of the Admiralty's response included the fact that only 48 vessels had been lost from convoys in the Channel over the previous six months—out of a potential 3,762 sail operating within the convoy system. Clearly, the layered defensive system of blockade, patrol, and convoy worked well in the Channel. In addition, the blockaders conducted numerous cutting-out expeditions against known privateers, capturing or destroying those vessels before they became a threat.[26]

The final two groups of raiders achieved the most captures—and the most damaging captures—of the war. French privateers operating from friendly ports in the East and West Indies (as well as the occasional neutral port) ravaged British trade. Several of these privateers were frigate-built or ex-French naval frigates able to overpower smaller convoy escorts, causing the then unprotected merchantmen to scatter—easy prey for smaller raiders.[27] These privateers sometimes worked in groups, almost always conducted short duration missions, and seldom sailed far from the defenses of a sheltering harbor. The British countered these raiders by increased convoy protection, aggressive patrols, and the seizure of French, Dutch, and Spanish (until it became a British ally) colonial possessions. Unable to succor these bases after 1805, France watched the capture of its colonies completed by 1810. The last Dutch colony, Java, fell in 1811.[28]

The final group of raiders operated in the Baltic. Most prevalent of them were the Danes; and the Danes, their capital at Copenhagen, had little love for Britain (having one's fleet ignominiously captured or destroyed in its own harbor—twice—tends to arouse feelings of ire). They used small, fast, and heavily crewed gunboats to dash to the most vulnerable section of a convoy, snatch a prize or two, and get them away before the escorts could respond. Becalmed convoys sometimes suffered heavy losses as the sweeps of the gunboats made them almost as handy as galleys. When operating in numbers, as they frequently did, Danish privateers also had little fear of engaging the Royal Navy directly, capturing several of its vessels during the war. Other than increase convoy escorts, Britain could do little against this final group of raiders. Prizes taken by Baltic raiders formed the bulk of Britain's European losses after 1811.[29]

The close military blockade confined the French regular Navy, assisted in controlling French privateers along blockaded coasts, and certainly prevented interference with the capture of French colonial bases. It could not, however, accomplish one thing: ending neutral trade with France. The difficulties inherent in defining contraband, searching neutral vessels for it, and smoothing the ruffled political feathers of nations suffering from seizures of their supposedly neutral vessels had reached a crisis level by 1806. In an effort to simplify the problem, Minister of Foreign Affairs Charles James Fox requested support for a new form of blockade—a *commercial blockade*. The order in council of 16 May established what became known as the Fox Blockade, once and for all eliminating, or so it was hoped, the need to define contraband. The order stated that neutral ships could not trade at any ports between the mouth of the Seine River and Ostend (eventually extended to the mouth of the Elbe River). Beyond those limits, ships could trade with the continent if they had not been loaded at ports hostile to Great Britain and did not plan to return to such ports. On 21 November, Napoleon responded with the Berlin Decree. He argued that blockades on the sea should follow the rules for sieges on land—only fortresses (naval bases) should be so invested—and that sufficient force should be available along the entirety of a blockade line to guarantee its success. Napoleon found the Fox Blockade to be illegal on both counts. The Berlin Decree met illegality with illegality, declaring a shipless blockade of the British Isles and possessions which forbade all trade between them and France, including French dependents. The document declared all British commerce legal prize and all British citizens eligible for imprisonment. This decree formed the cornerstone of Napoleon's Continental System, an attempt to force Britain to terms by denying its merchants access to continental markets, thus achieving an economic victory in place of his aborted military conquest.[30]

Britain responded in 1807 with no fewer than fourteen orders in council aimed at commercial interests. Three of those, one dated 7 January and two dated 2 November, had tremendous impact. The first declared that Great Britain certainly had the vessels to exert a physical blockade outside the Seine-Ostend limit (in fact, much of that area was already blockaded) but chose to allow trade to continue for the sake of true neutrals (more accurately would have been "for the sake of British merchants"). Additionally, it reaffirmed the Fox Blockade. The second document ordered neutrals to desist from trading with all ports at which Britain could not trade, regardless of the presence of blockaders, or be subject to seizure. In addition, any merchant vessel bearing certificates of origin guaranteeing their cargoes to be non-British would be seized as attempting to circumvent the British orders in council. Lastly, Britain declared the sale of belligerent vessels to neutral nations to be illegal. Enemy-built hulls would be confiscated regardless of flag.[31]

Napoleon responded with the Milan Decree of 17 December. It declared any neutral vessel touching at a British port or allowing itself to be searched by a British vessel to be legal prize, either at sea or upon entering a French controlled port. Two additional decrees, that of Bayonne on 17 April 1808 and of Rambouillet on 23 March 1810, directly targeted the largest neutral carrier, the United States. These ordered French harbor masters to seize American vessels as violators of their own embargo and nonimportation acts.[32]

Between Britain's military and commercial blockades and Napoleon's Continental System, the economy of France suffered dramatically. First hurt were the maritime towns and industries. Crippled by the loss of overseas markets and by raw material shortages, industrial output in Marseilles alone fell from a prewar value of 50 million francs to 12 million francs by 1813. Shipbuilding and related industries declined; as an example, the rope makers of Tonneins fell from seven hundred in 1783 to two hundred in 1801 to none in 1811. The population in maritime towns actually decreased during the war, at least partly in response to the deterioration of economic conditions hinging upon the blockade. Economic historian François Crouzet determined: "Moreover the 'Atlantic' sector of the European [French and French-allied] economy was not to recover when peace had been restored in 1815. There was of course a revival of traffic in the ports, but even where a fairly high level was attained, most of them had lost their position as international entrepôts and had become mere regional ports. As for their industries, they were relatively far less active."[33]

The impact of the blockade reached beyond the maritime regions, however. Cotton printing was virtually eliminated while the linen industry throughout the continent decreased (in many locations without a postwar recovery) by as much as 90 percent. Industrial dislocation and the runaway inflation evident by 1810–11 brought long-term change to France's economy. As Crouzet explains, "Because of the permanent injury on many Continental industries by interruption of overseas trade, the war brought about a lasting deindustrialization or pastorialization of large areas (with, in some areas of France and Holland, a definite shift of capital from trade and industry towards agriculture)."[34]

By extending the concept of blockade into a new area, interdiction of all neutral commerce, Great Britain unwittingly (or uncaringly) expanded the war. By June 1812, France had lost its colonies and any hope of challenging the might of Great Britain at sea even though Napoleon's armies stood at the pinnacle of their success, preparing to invade Russia. Both British close and commercial blockades strangled France, and the largest navy in the world had achieved a strong measure of control over the world's sea-lanes. Perhaps too strong a measure, for in the same month that Napoleon invaded Russia, James Madison asked Congress for a declaration of war upon Great Britain— for free trade, sailors' rights, and perhaps a little Canadian soil.

THREE BLOCKADES: A COMPARATIVE ANALYSIS

Any attempt to compare the blockades of 1793–1802, 1803–14, and 1812–15 must be strongly subjective because of the tremendous differences in the duration of the conflicts, the varying forces of the belligerents, the geographical placement of the blockades, the complexity of period economics, and, perhaps most important, the difficulty in gathering accurate numerical data on the structure and impact of the blockades. Still, blockading theory, as applied by the Admiralty, offers several potential measures of the degree of success attained by British efforts. Careful consideration suggests seven principles—those first introduced in chapter 2—against which blockades can be rated:

1. The military blockade, as part of a three-tiered defensive system, holds friendly merchant marine losses to enemy squadrons and *guerre de course* to an acceptable level. Methods of measure include comparative losses, varying insurance rates, economic dislocation, and public outrage. (Protect)[35]

2. The greater the duration of the military blockade, the less effective the enemy navy becomes as losses experienced by raiders, inability to gain the sea, and the debilitating effects of prolonged, forced stays in port weaken it. This is best measured by the number of enemy vessels at sea across the duration of the blockade, and by the performance of those vessels when in action. (Enemy Navy)

3. The ability of the enemy navy to interfere with the tactical options of the military blockade is impaired or eliminated. The ability of the blockading forces to conduct successful raids, and the impact of those raids on the enemy, measures degree of success. (Control)

4. The enemy's coasting trade is virtually eliminated or severely retarded by the military blockade. Measures include percent of normal trade occurring, reduction of enemy tonnage, diversion of potential cargoes to land transport, and public outrage. (Coasting)

5. The enemy merchant marine is held in port or destroyed by the military blockade. Measures are percent of normal exports, tonnage lost, varying insurance rates, and public outrage. (Merchant)

6. A successful commercial blockade stops unfavorable neutral trade with the enemy. Measures of success include the elimination of imports and exports carried in neutral hulls, as well as the establishment of trade favorable to the blockader. (Neutral)

7. Successful military and economic blockades assist in causing visible dislocation to an enemy's economic, political, and even social infrastructures. This will be readily apparent at the end of the conflict, and the degree of blockade efficiency can be roughly measured by the terms of the peace treaty and the length of time the enemy nation takes to recover from its maritime losses. (Victory)

Table 9.2 rates the three blockades on each principle according to the following schedule: 1 = overall failure; 2 = adequate performance; 3 = near ideal performance; NA = does not apply. To allow a final comparison, an average of all scores is included in the table. What follows is a principle-by-principle discussion of the ratings. For the sake of readability, each principle and related scores will be restated immediately before discussion of the reasoning behind the ratings.

DISCUSSION

1. The military blockade, as part of a three-tiered defensive system, holds friendly merchant marine losses to enemy squadrons and *guerre de course* to an acceptable level. Methods of measure include comparative losses, varying insurance rates, economic dislocation, and public outrage. 1793–1802: 1; 1803–14: 2; 1812–15: 1.

The desire to protect the homeland and commerce of Great Britain formed the cornerstone of blockade theory. Both conflicts with France found the Royal Navy providing adequate protection for commerce against raiders, once it is considered that most losses to raiders in the second of the wars occurred away from blockaded ports, but the dis-

TABLE 9.2. *Comparative Ratings of British Blockades, 1793–1815*

	Protect	Enemy Navy	Control	Coasting	Merchant	Neutral	Victory	Average
1793–1802	1	2	2	2	3	NA	2	2
1803–14	2	3	3	3	3	2	3	2.7
1812–15	1	1	3	2	2	2	1	1.7

Note: 1 = overall failure; 2 = adequate performance; 3 = near ideal performance; NA = does not apply.

tant blockade of 1793–1800 simply failed to contain French naval squadrons. The close blockade of 1803–14 could have received even higher marks if not for the lapses in 1804–5, allowing interference with the capture of French possessions in the West Indies (shelters for raiders), and the post-1805 rampage of the Toulon fleet. As for the War of 1812, every British vessel lost constituted a failure of the close blockade as every American raider sailed from a (nominally, at least) blockaded port. Average monthly losses across the three wars were: 1793–1802, 36 ships; 1803–1814, 41 ships; and 1812–1815, 53 ships. Clearly, the failure of the American close blockade proved even more damaging to the British merchant marine than the distant blockade's inability to control French squadrons. The protests of merchants and shipowners as well as the highest marine insurance rates of the era underscore that failure.[36]

2. The greater the duration of the military blockade, the less effective the enemy navy becomes as losses experienced by raiders, inability to gain the sea, and the debilitating effects of prolonged, forced stays in port weaken it. This is best measured by the number of enemy vessels at sea across the duration of the blockade and by the performance of those vessels when in action. 1793–1802: 2; 1803–14: 3; 1812–15: 1.

By the end of each war against France, the blockades (coupled with Napoleon's need for infantry in the second struggle) had reduced the French Navy to a shell. Admittedly, a large number of hulls existed in 1814—the legacy of Napoleon's post-Trafalgar extensive naval building program—but they were mere hulls. Not only were naval stores in short supply due to the British blockade, but Napoleon had began turning crews into infantry as early as 1808, when he sent twenty-five hundred seamen to the peninsula. In 1813 (after the Russian debacle), he diverted all naval conscripts to the Army, and roughly twenty thousand sailors served as infantry in the campaign in Germany alone. The conscripts of 1814 were again diverted by Napoleon, and an additional five thousand sailors transferred to the artillery in January—records are unclear as to how many joined the infantry in the last-ditch defense of France. Needless to say, the relatively few men remaining with the fleet by spring of 1814 were not prime seamen—the best had marched to the eagles.[37]

French losses among state and private ships speak for themselves. Even more noteworthy was the paucity of French naval vessels at sea after 1810, and the declining quality of French crews throughout the second conflict—a result of staggering losses of seamen coupled with idleness enforced by the close blockade. The U.S. Navy, on the other hand, increased its strength and experience throughout the War of 1812, possessing 33 percent more vessels by early 1814 and having its first battle squadron of three ships-of-the-line almost ready for sea at the cessation of hostilities.[38] On the date of the Senate approval of the Treaty of Ghent, five naval vessels were at sea (50 percent of ready raiders, five others were under orders to sail or completing fitting out for extended voyages). Two of those met and defeated more or less equal vessels of the Royal Navy. Based upon the hundred British ships per month loss in January and February 1815, an estimated two dozen or more privateers also cruised at war's end—and did so successfully. At no point during the War of 1812 did the close blockade approach containment of the American state and private navies, both of which continued to improve in performance throughout the war.

3. The ability of the enemy navy to interfere with the tactical options of the military blockade is impaired or eliminated. The ability of the blockading forces to conduct successful raids, and the impact of those raids on the enemy, measures degree of success. 1793–1802: 2; 1803–14: 3; 1812–15: 3.

The close blockade was a springboard for raids—usually cutting-out expeditions into protected enemy anchorages, but also against other military targets. Neither the French nor American navies proved capable of stopping these raids, while local defense forces fared little better. Frequently, raids targeted enemy naval vessels, privateers, and vessels taken from the Royal Navy. In the American war, the British concentrated on military stores and foundries along the Chesapeake and local shipping or fishing craft hidden in harbors and along rivers. The blockade of 1793–1802 received a lower rating because the distant blockade failed to provide the offshore platform needed for constant raiding.[39]

4. The enemy's coasting trade is virtually eliminated or severely retarded by the military blockade. Measures include percent of normal trade occurring, reduction of enemy tonnage, diversion of potential cargoes to land transport, and public outrage. 1793–1802: 2; 1803–14: 3; 1812–15: 2.

In a time of limited roads, the bulk of internal shipments moved via a maritime nation's coasting trade. Small coasters plied inshore waters, traveling port to port. Stoppage of this trade isolated coastal communities and, more important, reduced the supply of marine stores to naval bases to a trickle. From 1793 to 1802, the distant blockade hindered the coasting trade of France, certainly to a great degree isolating its naval facilities from their Baltic- and Corfu-based suppliers. Yet the coasting trade still progressed under convoy away from those ports until the introduction of the close blockade. The close blockade of 1803–14 not only stopped virtually all coasting trade within the blockaded area, the Royal Navy actually went into French ports to burn or cut out known coasting vessels. The close blockade of the United States halted most north-south coasting at the mouths of the Chesapeake and Delaware Bays; however, escorted convoys regularly continued to run the Maine–to–New York route through the fall of 1813 and more sporadically after April 1814.[40] Coasting vessels, often convoyed, streamed back and forth between the southern ports of Charleston, South Carolina, and St. Marys, Georgia (gateway to the Spanish trade at Amelia Island, Spanish Florida), with lesser trade to Wilmington, North Carolina. The only major British assault on this chain was the temporary capture of St. Marys in early 1815, and trade there resumed as soon as the British withdrew.[41] Though the coasting trade of the United States suffered interruption and some small loss (table 8.10 in chapter 8), the close blockade failed to seal the American inshore highway.

5. The enemy merchant marine is held in port or destroyed by the military blockade. Measures are percent of normal exports, tonnage lost, varying insurance rates, and public outrage. 1793–1802: 3; 1803–14: 3; 1812–15: 2.

During all three blockades, the interdicted merchant marines largely disappeared from the seas with the onset of war. For all practical purposes, the French merchant marine had been lost—reflagged, destroyed, or rotted at anchor—by 1802 and again by 1814. Its recovery was slow until spurred in the last quarter of the nineteenth century by neocolonialism.

As tables 8.9 and 8.10 (in chapter 8) illustrated, the blockade's performance during the War of 1812 was somewhat different. The American merchant marine, unlike that of France, not only received warning of the coming war, but found its long-term well-being a matter of deliberate government policy and foresight. Still, a goodly portion of the public voiced complaint; the term "Madison's nightcaps" in reference to the baskets up-ended over mast heads of harbored merchant vessels was hardly complimentary. Regardless of any public outrage (and Madison, nightcapped or not, was reelected during the war), the merchant marine continued to function at minimal levels and surpassed its prewar performance by the end of the first full year of peace. This accounts for the assignment of a lower British performance rating in this category.

6. A successful commercial blockade stops unfavorable neutral trade with the enemy. Measures of success include the elimination of imports and exports carried in neutral hulls, as well as the establishment of trade favorable to the blockader. 1793–1802: NA; 1803–14: 2; 1812–15: 2.

The commercial blockades of the Napoleonic era sought less to deny succor to the enemy than to guarantee that trade favored Great Britain. Ideally, pressure forced direct trade with Britain or the carriage of British goods in neutral hulls. Thus, French and American grains, the former via neutral shipping, supplied Britain at different stages of the respective conflicts, while French soldiers often wore British woolens as they struggled against Continental opponents. The system of licensing which allowed this trade was nonetheless a weakness, draining more British specie into French and American coffers than it collected. Additionally, American trade with neutrals through unblockaded New England continued into early 1814. The port of New Orleans remained uninterdicted for all but a few weeks of the conflict, and trade through Spanish Amelia Island spanned the war, barring one brief interruption of a few days. In the last case, local officials appear to have neglected to record all business transactions (an early concept of duty-free goods); thus the full extent of the trade may never be known. Still, when all is considered, both commercial blockades seem to have accomplished at least the bare minimums for success.

7. Successful military and economic blockades assist in causing visible dislocation to an enemy's economic, political, and even social infrastructures. This will be readily apparent at the end of the conflict, and the degree of blockade efficiency can be roughly measured by the terms of the peace treaty and the length of time the enemy nation takes to recover from its maritime losses. 1793–1802: 2; 1803–14: 3; 1812–15: 1.

The struggle of 1793–1802 certainly contributed to the concentration of power in the hands of Napoleon. The failure of the revolutionary governments to counter British interference on the continent, to protect its holdings abroad, and to shift goods and food by sea—all because of the blockade—assisted in their downfall. Unfortunately, Britain's politicians surrendered too many colonial gains at the conference table, and in the next round of war, their nation paid the price for their decisions.

That round, 1803–14, found a close blockade virtually eliminating France's maritime economy. The French Navy, isolated in its bases and more often than not destroyed when it sailed, could not prevent the British from capturing the entirety of its colonial possessions, nor could it interfere with the struggle in the Iberian Peninsula. Victory saw Napoleon replaced by a monarchy and the French fleet so crippled that it barely participated in the Hundred Days of 1815.

The American conflict, 1812–15, constituted as near an opposite to the second stage of the French wars as one can imagine. Peace returned the belligerents to the *status quo antebellum*. The U.S. Navy increased in size throughout the war and remained strong for another decade. The Republican government, far from falling, dispatched its Federalist opponents on the strength of somewhat dubious wartime successes and entered into that period labeled the Era of Good Feelings. The American merchant marine quickly and effectively returned to business, while prices dropped to near normal levels with the news of a potential peace—not after supply had responded to demand.[42] The rise of industry, already underway in textiles during the conflict, would be partially financed by private income from successful privateering and the licensed trade during the war.[43] Clearly, the results speak rather poorly for the overall efficiency of the second close blockade.

The average ratings—1793–1802: 2.0; 1803–14: 2.7; 1812–15: 1.7— find only the blockade of the United States to rate less than successful (2.0). Four overarching reasons, none of which concern any real or imagined superiority of American ships and crews, seem to lie behind the comparative ineffectiveness of the 1812–15 blockade. First, despite knowledge of a possible declaration of war by the United States, Britain did not have sufficient ships on station to guarantee the initial quantitative superiority required for immediate institution of a close blockade of American ports. Second, the Admiralty never allocated sufficient vessels to the blockade. Third, the Admiralty demanded a campaign to hurt the U.S. Navy in 1813 and campaigns in support of the invasion from Canada in 1814 which strained the small pool of ships technically available for the blockade. Finally, and partly because of the shortage of vessels, the Admiralty implemented the commercial blockade in a piecemeal fashion, thereby reducing its negative impact upon the American economy. Without some risk in Europe, risk that the Admiralty proved, perhaps understandably, unwilling to take, the blockade of the United States never had the opportunity to match the efficiency of those that crippled France.

Conclusion

One should be leery of David and Goliath stories—the little guy always wins, and that is not the way of the world. Storytellers forget the more frequent times when the stone misses and the sword connects, or the occasional instance when the sling breaks and the sword shatters, giving Goliath a technical victory because tiny David is unable to physically shift the giant from his chosen ground—or sea. And sometimes we discover that the storyteller's perception of Goliath's six cubits and a span may have been overstated by a cubit or so.

The blockade of the United States never approached the six cubits and a span portrayed by Mahan. In truth, by the measures of that day it proved less than fully effective when compared to the blockades of France, and it certainly placed Britain in a more precarious seat at Ghent's bargaining table than the chair that country enjoyed in Paris and, later, at Vienna. The United States' inability to quickly secure Canada (a broken sling) and Great Britain's less-than-effective blockade and its failed offensives from Canada (a shattered sword) cloud the question of victory which should have been decided at Ghent.

It is debatable whether anyone won the War of 1812; that popular perception in the United States viewed the British as not winning the war is a fitting final comment on the effectiveness of the blockade. Yet the Treaty of Ghent addressed none of the issues originally set forth by James Madison; instead, it returned the belligerents to the *status quo antebellum*. That those issues disappeared of their own accord as time ran its course has projected a sense of triviality and unimportance on the war, until what remains in common knowledge is Washington burning, the defense of Fort McHenry, Andrew Jackson winning at New Orleans, and the *Constitution*. That splintered British wall, misinterpreted by historians until it became the overwhelming force it never was, lies forgotten.

The blockade, however, has been and remains the most damaging naval stratagem against a maritime opponent. It is both a defensive and an offensive strategy—defensive because it locks the enemy fleet into its ports and, when combined with aggressive patrols and convoys, it effectively counters enemy raiders; offensive because it is a ready platform for littoral raiding and allows naval operations away from the blockade to occur without interference by the enemy fleet. Economically, the blockade is potentially devastating, more so now than in the age of sail, especially if the enemy can be isolated from key raw materials (foodstuffs, nitrates, oil). Both Germany during World War I and the British Isles during World War II bear testimony to the potential inherent in an interdictive strategy.

Though the concepts of distant and close blockade must be redefined for modern naval operations—the Mark I Eyeball has been enhanced by numerous electronic sensor suites and "infernal devices" abound—four things remain the same: the blockade must be established quickly, it must be as tight as possible and in as much depth as needed, a sufficiency of force must be available to maintain it through the duration of the conflict, and the risks necessary to support those three dictates must be accepted. If blockaders fail to envision, analyze, and weigh their risks, see the War of 1812 for their projected results.

Notes

INTRODUCTION

1. President James Madison's War Message to Congress of 1 June 1812, *National Intelligencer,* 18 June 1812.

2. Brackenridge, *History of the Late War;* Ingersoll, *History of the Second War;* Lossing, *Pictorial Fieldbook;* Roosevelt, *Naval War of 1812;* Adams, *History of the United States of America.*

3. Mahan, *Sea Power.* Mahan also stressed the Francophilia and Anglophobia stemming from the Revolutionary War as a cause of the conflict.

4. Hacker, "Western Land Hunger and the War of 1812," 365–95; Pratt, *Expansionists of 1812.*

5. Taylor, "Agrarian Discontent in the Mississippi Valley," 471–505; Latimer, "South Carolina," 914–29.

6. Risjord, "1812," 196–210; Perkins, *Prologue.*

7. Hickey, *Forgotten War.*

8. Clowes, *Royal Navy* 6:25; Ships in Sea Pay, Admiralty Office, 1 July 1812, UkLPR, D, Adm. 8, Public Record Office, London. All unarmed hulls and vessels in ordinary were removed.

9. James, *Full and Correct Account;* Clowes, *Royal Navy* 6:1–180; Graham, *Empire;* Graham, *Sea Power.*

10. Marcus, *Age of Nelson,* 467.

11. Kennedy, *Naval Mastery,* 163.

12. Christie, *Wars and Revolutions,* 320.

13. Mahan, *Sea Power* 2:21.

14. *Times* (London), 30 December 1814.

15. Napier, *Journal,* 24.

16. As this treatise focuses to seaward, the land campaigns of the War of 1812 are not discussed in detail. For an excellent study of military activities, see Quimby, *U.S. Army in the War of 1812.*

CHAPTER 1. *The Royal Navy and the Practice of Blockade, 1642–1783*

1. The major wars, by their European titles, were the Anglo-Dutch Wars (three separate struggles, 1652–74), War of the League of Augsburg (1688–97), War of Spanish Succession (1701–14), Great Northern War (1700–1721), War

of Austrian Succession (1740–48), Seven Years' War (1756–63), War of the American Revolution (1775–83), and War of the First Coalition (the first war resulting from the French Revolution, 1792–1800). There were, of course, other conflicts.

2. Clowes, *Royal Navy* 2:118–36.

3. Ibid. 2:310–22; Jones, *Anglo-Dutch Wars*, 180, 201–7. Jones described De Ruyter's command during the final war as "perhaps the most effective defensive strategy ever undertaken by a fleet of inferior strength." This sound assessment highlights the importance of an enemy's response to the threat of blockade.

4. Harding, *Naval Warfare*, 104–5.

5. Ibid., 65–107.

6. Morriss, *Royal Dockyards*, 1–20. Morriss briefly discusses the evolution of the dockyards.

7. Jones, *Anglo-Dutch Wars*, 174–78.

8. Black and Woodfine, *British Navy*, 71.

9. Ibid., 73.

10. Lloyd, *Health of Seamen*, 6–25, 132–289; Watt, Freeman, and Bynum, *Starving Sailors*, 9–12; Admiral Sir Edward Hawke to Secretary of the Admiralty John Clevland, 27 May 1759, Mackay, *Hawke Papers*, 218. For a history of medicine in the U.S. Navy, see Langley, *History of Medicine*.

11. Black and Woodfine, *British Navy*, 163.

12. Lavery, *Nelson's Navy*, 20; Babits and Tilburg, *Maritime Archaeology*, 28–30.

13. Secret Instructions from the Lords of the Admiralty to Hawke, 18 May 1759, Mackay, *Hawke Papers*, 212–13; Mackay, *Admiral Hawke*, 200–263.

14. Hawke to First Lord of the Admiralty Sir George Anson, 19 May 1759; Hawke to Clevland, 20 May 1759, Mackay, *Hawke Papers*, 214–17.

15. Hawke to Clevland, 27 May 1759; Secret Instructions from the Lords of the Admiralty to Hawke, 1 June 1759, ibid., 218–22.

16. Hawke to Clevland, 4 June 1759, 6 June 1759; Hawke to Commissioner Rogers at Plymouth, 6 June 1759; Hawke to Clevland, 8 June 1759, ibid., 223–28.

17. Hawke to Clevland, 12 June 1759 and 20 June 1759, ibid., 230, 237.

18. Hawke to Clevland, 3 July 1759, ibid., 238.

19. Hawke to Clevland, 3 July 1759, ibid., 250–51.

20. Hawke to Clevland, 28 August 1759, ibid., 271–74.

21. Report by Captain Michael Clements to Hawke, 29 August 1759; Hawke to Clevland, 12 August 1759; Report by Clements, 31 August 1759; Captain Sir Augustus Hervey to Hawke, 17 September 1759; Hawke to Clevland, 1 October 1759, ibid., 265–305.

22. Various reports from his captains to Hawke and from Hawke to the Admiralty, 1 November to 17 November 1759, ibid., 317–39.

23. Hawke to Clevland, 10, 12, and 17 November 1759; ibid., 336–41.

24. Hawke to Clevland, 24 November 1759, ibid., 344–50; Mackay, "Edward Hawke," 158–69.

25. Admiralty Minute, 7 February 1760; Hawke to Anson, February 1760; Hawke to Clevland, 16 December 1759, Mackay, *Hawke Papers*, 360–63.

26. Burrows, *Life of Edward Lord Hawke*, 491–92.

27. Black and Woodfine, *British Navy*, 110–27.

28. For detailed discussions of British strategy and performance, see Harding, *Naval Warfare*, 234–55, and especially Mackesy, *War for America*.

29. Memorandum, July 1775, Barnes and Owens, *Private Papers of John, Earl of Sandwich* 1:64–66 (hereafter cited as *Sandwich Papers*).

30. Memorandum from Admiral Sir Hugh Palliser, December 1775, ibid. 1:76–80.

31. Barnes and Owens, *Sandwich Papers* 1:42–46.

32. Mackesy, *War for America*, 156; Barnes and Owens, *Sandwich Papers* 1:47.

33. Sandwich to Admiral Samuel Graves, 25 August 1775, Barnes and Owens, *Sandwich Papers* 1:70–72. Also see Mackesy, *War for America*, 101–2.

34. Buel, *In Irons*, 77–216. Buel contends that Britain's efforts at blockade, from an economic standpoint, were ineffective through 1777 and less than fully effective through 1781.

35. Mackesy, *War for America*, 99.

36. Vice Admiral Molyneux Shuldham to Sandwich, 13 January 1776, Barnes and Owens, *Sandwich Papers* 1:104–7. Note that the four volumes of the *Sandwich Papers* detail numerous problems with American privateers and naval vessels through the end of the war.

37. Shuldham to Sandwich, 23 March 1776, ibid. 1:123–25.

38. Sandwich to Vice Admiral Richard Howe, 17 October 1776, ibid. 1:159–62.

39. William Northcote, Surgeon, to Sandwich, 19 August 1781, ibid. 4:178–79.

40. A Paper sent to Lord North on 8th December 1777 relative to the American war and urging more efforts to be made at home, ibid. 1:327–35.

41. Ibid. 1:324.

42. Buel, *In Irons*, 217–39.

43. The terms *shallow draft*, *medium draft*, and *deep draft* will appear frequently in the following pages. Numerically, these terms convert to twelve or less feet draft, twelve to twenty-four feet draft, and over twenty-four feet draft, respectively.

CHAPTER 2. *The Blockade in Theory and Practice*

1. Tracy, *Naval Chronicle* 1:317–19. Two letters, from 1804 and 1808, discuss perceptions of the close blockade. The first correctly defines several of the objectives of the blockade but criticizes the close blockade as wasteful of resources. The second rambles through the logistical constraints of year-around interdiction, suggesting that the blockade be abandoned during winter's inclement weather.

2. Petrie, *Prize Game;* Grotius, *Commentary;* Grotius, *Law of War;* Vattel, *Law of Nations.* Grotius and Vattel are also the most frequently quoted authorities in prize cases before the United States Supreme Court from its founding through the War of 1812: see Scott, *Prize Cases.*

3. A certain irony surrounds the writing of *Commentary on the Law of Prize and Booty*. According to translator Gwladys L. Williams, Grotius meant his words for the ears of a powerful Dutch religious sect rather than for the international community. The wealthy sect viewed the seizure of prizes and goods as theft, and verged upon refusing to support the Dutch Navy. Thus the concepts which entered into international law had as their origin little less self-interest than that of the English Navigation Acts.

4. Mahan, *Sea Power* 1:9–41; Harper, *Navigation Laws*.

5. Tracy, *Naval Chronicle* 2:92–93; Hill, *Prizes of War,* 20–33, 130–37. For example, the *Chronicle* reported the British seizure of neutral Danish and Swedish convoys, including their naval escorts, on 24 July and 29 August 1800, respectively; while Hill acknowledges the difficulty of dealing with neutrals and the occasional overstepping of legal bounds by individual captains and crewmen in his study of the British prize system.

6. Great Britain employed limited blockades frequently throughout the nineteenth century. The blockade of Dahomey, July 1876 to May 1877, is an excellent example. Neither declaration of war nor naval opposition existed, the blockade's entire purpose being to force a bloodless acceptance of British policy; Clowes, *Royal Navy* 7:282–83. Tactical blockades possess a specific short-term objective; for example, the blockade of Bahia by the *Constitution* and the *Hornet* in December 1812 hoped to bag the packet *Bonne Citoyenne* and its cargo of British specie; Consul Frederick Lindeman to Captain Charles Stewart, 1 January 1813, UkLPR, Adm. 1/503, 431, Public Record Office, London. The terms *limited blockade, tactical blockade, linear blockade, echeloned blockade, military blockade*, and combined forms thereof have been introduced in an effort to provide some consistency to the examination of blockade theory and practice. The terms *distant blockade, close blockade*, and *commercial* or *economic blockade* are already in common usage and require only careful definition.

7. Tracy, *Naval Chronicle* 1:210–24; Murray, "Admiralty, Part VI," 341. Though low pay and poor service conditions certainly stimulated these mutinies of British sailors, the constant anchoring in sight of home shores which their feet could not touch catalyzed the crews to attempt their misguided action.

8. More terminology: the typical military blockade consisted of one or two vessels watching smaller ports (those without major enemy naval assets) while other craft patrolled the coast between those harbors. Since it lacked depth at the point of contact, this disposition is best termed a *linear military blockade* or a *simple military blockade* to distinguish it from the complex *echeloned military blockade*, which evolved off Brest, Toulon, and Cadiz.

9. The weather frequently deteriorated, the charts were often incorrect, but the French sortied far less than one would imagine; see Leyland, *Blockade of Brest*. Losses to weather and navigational hazards far outnumbered the losses to hostile action; see Gossett, *Lost Ships*.

10. Richmond, *Statesmen*, 338–43. Most historians have captured the layered structure of the blockade, but Richmond defines its defensive purposes most clearly, supporting his assertions with references to period documentation.

11. Mahan, *Sea Power* 2:306–13; Rathbone, *Wellington's War,* 181 ff; Graham, *Empire,* 247–48; Albion and Pope, *Sea Lanes,* 108–9.

12. Tracy, *Naval Chronicle* 2:235–36. In 1804, a year before the implementation of the commercial blockade against France, the *Chronicle* printed a protest from the United States' House of Representatives directed against illegal seizure of American vessels by the Royal Navy. That the declaration of the economic blockade did not deter American captains from attempting trade with France is obvious in the increased ship seizures, in Jefferson's embargoes, and, ultimately, in the War of 1812.

13. Robert Saunders Dundas Melville to Admiral Sir John B. Warren, 23 March 1813, InU, War of 1812 Manuscripts, Lilly Library, Indiana University, Bloomington. In this letter addressing the capabilities of the North American command, Melville reflected the Admiralty's understanding of this logistical reality. He calculated that 120 ships should allow Warren the vessels required for "blockading, convoy, & cruising services, & also for a full third in port refitting & repairing."

14. Lavery, *Nelson's Navy,* 300–305. This is a simplification. Several larger classes of frigates carried supplies for as much as a six-month cruise without touching land. Ships-of-the-line, however, increased firepower and crew size while maintaining little more room for stowage of food and water than the large frigate—obviously reducing the available time on station. Smaller frigates, and particularly sloops of war, lost storage space while maintaining large crews, again sacrificing cruising time. In the end, duration of voyages depended upon the balance between hold space and crew size of individual ships.

15. Captain Edward Codrington to William Codrington, 1805, in Marcus, *Age of Nelson,* 427.

16. Gardiner, *Nelson Against Napoleon,* 164–65.

17. Clowes, *Royal Navy* 5:2–3, 18–20. See also Adm. Sir John B. Warren, Standing Orders on the North American Station, 6 March 1813, Dudley, *Naval War of 1812* 2:59–60—an order to increase gunnery exercise—and the appended note of 23 March 1813 calling for a specific reduction in a useless bit of "spit and polish."

18. Neither contemporaries nor historians have attempted to establish a methodology for the evaluation of blockade effectiveness, much less any form of comparative evaluation. The isolation of these key principles from the sources listed in the bibliography is a tentative step in that direction.

19. Perkins, *Prologue,* 64.

CHAPTER 3. *Assessing Maritime Potential*

1. Lavery, *Nelson's Navy,* 245–51; McKee, *Naval Officer Corps,* 29. The honorific "commodore," in both the United States and Royal navies, constituted a temporary rank usually assigned to the senior non-flag-rank officer of a squadron and symbolized by a swallow-tailed pennant flown from the mast of his flagship. In the Royal Navy, the designation was mission specific, the

commodore reverting to his normal rank at its completion or when superseded by an admiral. In the United States, which did not create the rank of admiral until the Civil War, the title of commodore assumed semipermanence. It marked the ranking officers within the service and provided them with increased prestige if not with greater pay.

2. For examples of these reports and public commentary see *Gentlemen's Magazine* and the *Times* (London) for 1793–1815, and Tracy, *Naval Chronicle.*

3. Chapelle, *American Sailing Navy,* 118–34; Fowler, "America's Super-Frigates," *Mariner's Mirror* 59:49–56.

4. Gossett, *Lost Ships;* Emmons, *Navy,* 11–13.

5. Lavery, *Nelson's Navy,* 25, 273–74, overviews naval use of merchant vessels. Lyon, *Navy List,* lists a number of these auxiliaries. Clowes, *Royal Navy,* refers to hired ships throughout volumes 4–6. Hill, *Prizes of War,* 133–34, discusses hired merchantmen in relation to prize money.

6. Captain John H. Dent to Secretary of the Navy Paul Hamilton, 4 June 1812, Dudley, *Naval War of 1812* 1:128–30, provided a listing of numerous stores needed at Charleston and Wilmington. Commodore Thomas Tingey to Hamilton, 22 June 1812, ibid. 1:145, requested quick delivery of spars to the Washington Navy Yard for *Congress.*

7. Guttridge and Smith, *Commodores,* 172.

8. Symonds, *Naval Policy Debate,* 107–8. This is the definitive study of the debates.

9. Hamilton to Commodore John Rodgers, 21 May 1812, Dudley, *Naval War of 1812* 1:118–19; Rodgers to Hamilton, 3 June 1812, ibid. 1:119–22; Commodore Stephen Decatur to Hamilton, 8 June 1812, ibid. 1:122–24; Hamilton to Rodgers, 22 June 1812, ibid. 1:148–49. The last constituted a set of undelivered orders that would have initially steered Rodgers to the penny-packet approach instead of sailing as a combined squadron in June 1812.

10. Smith, *Purposes of Defense,* 73–93.

11. Symonds, *Naval Policy Debate,* 420–21; Lossing, *Pictorial Fieldbook,* 235–38; Lewis, *Seacoast Fortifications* (Annapolis, Md., 1993), 5–13, 21–36.

12. *New York Evening Post,* 21 April 1812; *Columbian Centinel,* 20 May 1812; *Niles',* 30 May 1812.

13. Hacker, "Western Land Hunger and the War of 1812: A Conjecture," *MVHR,* 365–95; Pratt, *Expansionists of 1812;* Stagg, *Mr. Madison's War.*

14. King and Hattendorf, *Every Man;* Baugh, "Eighteenth Century Navy as a National Institution," 150–56.

15. King and Hattendorf, *Every Man,* 6–8.

16. Rodger, *Wooden World;* King and Hattendorf, *Every Man.*

17. Clowes, *Royal Navy* 5:18–31; Baugh, "Eighteenth Century Navy as a National Institution," 143–50.

18. Henderson, *Sloops and Brigs,* 41. According to Henderson, the daily ration of grog may well have been deadlier than combat. Of the estimated 100,000 men lost by the Navy during the Napoleonic era, 50 percent died from disease, 30 percent from alcohol-induced accidents, 13 percent from the perils of the sea, while only 7 percent fell to enemy action.

19. As quoted in Forester, *Age of Sail*, 129–30.

20. Henderson, *Frigates*, 31–37.

21. Baugh, "Eighteenth Century Navy as a National Institution," 144–48.

22. Lewis, *Navy in Transition*, 232; Loffin, *Jack Tar*, 72–73; Hill, *Prizes of War*.

23. Robert Saunders Dundas, 2d Viscount Melville, served as first lord of the Admiralty, 1812–27. The first lord of the Admiralty was a member of the Cabinet, the advisory committee to the king. The Cabinet was a decision-making group in its own right, issuing laws termed "orders in council," several of which were central to the causation and prosecution of the war. John W. Croker, whose name appeared most frequently on communications to officers off North America, occupied the office of first secretary of the Admiralty during the War of 1812. J. N. Barrow served as private secretary of the Admiralty.

24. Corbett, *Principles*, 95–96. Though speaking and writing in the opening decade of the twentieth century, Corbett accurately echoed the opinions of the long dead British officers of the Napoleonic era: "[Privateering] greatly increased the difficulty of manning the navy, and the occasional large profits had a demoralizing influence on detached cruiser commanders." His happiness at the international banning of this "barbarous" practice at the Treaty of Paris of 1856 certainly reflected his humanitarian interests, but it should be remembered that the world's largest merchant marine, that of Great Britain, had historically suffered the greatest losses to such legalized piracy.

25. Mitchell, *European Statistics*, 488, 613; Marcus, *Age of Nelson*, 423; Great Britain, House of Commons, *Sessional Papers*, 1811–16 (New York, 1965), 1812, 10:27. Tonnage and number of vessels under British registry are as of 31 December 1812. The estimated size of the fishing fleet is based upon Marcus's quotation of 2.5 million tons total for the British merchant marine. The estimated size of the international trade is based upon data reported to Parliament in 1812 and Mitchell's tables of British exports, reexports, and imports.

26. Lavery, *Nelson's Navy*, 273. The term *support* includes the import of naval stores, the redistribution of naval materiel via the coasting trade, the maintenance of Royal Naval bases abroad, and the direct support of naval activities as hired ships.

27. A summary of Royal Navy captures and their disposition between 1793 and 1812 (or 1815) has not been compiled, but over nine hundred American vessels were seized between 1803 and 1812. As the merchant marines of France and the Batavian Republic almost ceased to exist during the conflict, while other French allies (Denmark, Spain, Naples) and neutrals (notably Sweden) also suffered losses, a rough guess of perhaps five thousand to sixty-five hundred captures seems appropriate. A large proportion of these vessels would have been purchased at auction by shippers and added to the British merchant marine.

28. *American State Papers, Commerce and Navigation* 1:959, 962; Martin, *American Merchant Marine*, 19–28; Essex Institute, *Vice-Admiralty Court at Halifax*. Registered tonnage in 1811 recorded clearances totaling 948,446 tons, and enrolled tonnage listed 420,362 tons in the coastal trade. "Tonnage" refers to

carrying capacity instead of displacement, as appropriate for the period. Also, tonnages were not equivalent across national boundaries, though the difference between British and American measurements was small. Based upon the given sources and numerous but scattered references to individual merchant vessels, 370 and 50 seemed appropriate for the respective average tonnages of American transatlantic carriers and coasting vessels. Division into the tonnages listed for 1811 (and appropriate rounding) provided the estimate of merchant hulls.

29. Hickey, *Forgotten War,* 19–24; Perkins, *Prologue.*

30. Martin, *American Merchant Marine,* 122–23; *New York Evening Post,* 26 January 1812, 21 April 1812; *Washington National Intelligencer,* 14 April 1812; *Columbian Centinel,* 20 May 1812; *Niles',* 30 May 1812.

31. Albion and Pope, *Sea Lanes,* 70. Except for the Boston Marine Insurance Company, American records of the era seem to have vanished. Apparently most insurance companies suspended premiums to destinations within the Atlantic basin for the duration of the war—a solid comment upon contemporary perception of the effectiveness of the Royal Navy.

32. As quoted in Marcus, *Age of Nelson,* 460–61.

CHAPTER 4. *The Geography of the Blockade*

1. Tucker, *Gunboat Navy,* 115; *New Chart of the Coast of North America* (1780).

2. Napier, *Journal,* 11.

3. Henderson, *Sloops and Brigs,* 44.

4. Tannehill, *Hurricanes,* 11–34; Lavery, *Nelson's Navy,* 267–68; Lieutenant R. Basset to Captain J. S. Dent, 2 July 1814, Brannan, *Official Letters,* 373–74. Basset reported USS *Alligator* sunk by a waterspout at Port Royal, South Carolina (later raised).

5. Brown, *Dismal Swamp Canal,* 48–49.

6. *American State Papers, Commerce and Navigation* 1:959, 962, 998, 1001, 1018, 1021, and 2:13, 14, 38, 39, 62, 63. It is impossible to measure the percentage of total tonnage carried by coasting and export trades during the years under study, or, for that matter, even the total volume of goods moved domestically. International shippers paid duties on each ton transported; thus a 500-ton vessel sailing for Portugal twice in one year would have been recorded as 1,000 tons in duties. A 20-ton coaster, however, paid duties only once per year despite the fact that it potentially moved 20 tons of cargo each week of that year (1,040 tons). Though later discussion will focus upon American commerce by duties paid, it should be kept in mind that, for example, the 189,700 tons of duties recorded for domestic trade in 1814 potentially translated to an upper limit of 9,864,400 tons of freight moved.

7. Bureau of the Census, *Statistical History,* 905, lists American exports for 1811 as $61 million, with $14 million sold directly to the British Isles. An additional $24 million fell in the "Other" European countries category. Over 66 percent of this trade went to Portugal, supplying the British war effort. Finally,

$21 million in trade occurred outside Europe, and by 1811, British colonies formed the only significant markets remaining for American produce and products outside Europe.

8. Steele, "Time, Communications and Society: The English Atlantic, 1702," *Journal of American Studies* 1:1–21. Set more than one hundred years before the War of 1812, Steele's study remains highly relevant: the speed of maritime transport did not appreciably change before the introduction of the steamship, and the pace of *normal* communication along the Atlantic basin remained tied to the speed of sail-driven vessels. Though that pace seems agonizingly slow in this day of the World Wide Web, it was an accepted and defining parameter of communications in the late age of sail. The turnaround time for communications is verified by examination of Royal Navy communications and comparison of the dates on which they were dispatched and received. Some, of course, had a faster transit, while communications from the Admiralty to the North American Station suffered several days' delay if the admiral had personally taken command of a campaign or was shifting between Halifax and Bermuda.

9. Morriss, *Royal Dockyards*, 1–20. Morriss discusses locations, accessibility, and capability of home dockyards.

10. Symonds, *Historical Atlas*, 43. Transit time is calculated assuming eight knots of speed (probably high) and favorable wind (certainly optimistic). Though ships sometimes recorded transits in four to five days, a week may well be a better estimate. Couple that with the time needed to restock provisions and materials and to conduct essential repairs, and the ship is away from the blockade for two to three weeks under the best of conditions.

11. Lohnes, "British Naval Problems at Halifax," 317–19.

12. Ibid. The Royal Navy maintained a small squadron off Newfoundland, primarily protecting the region's fisheries and local shipping. As the squadron remained small and operated independently for much of the war, it is not directly addressed in this manuscript.

13. *Times* (London), 19 July 1814.

14. Clowes, *Royal Navy*. Volumes 4–6 details the intensity of both British interest and naval action in the Caribbean, as well as (in volume 6) the tremendous efforts required to suppress American *guerre de course* from 1812 to 1815.

15. Babits and Tilburg, *Maritime Archaeology*, 45–290; Shomette, "Londontown: The Reconnaissance of a 17th–18th Century Tidewater Riverport Complex," *Beneath the Waters of Time*, 167–74. These works examine change along the land-sea interface and the rapidity with which such change occurs.

CHAPTER 5. *1812: Birth of a Blockade*

1. Coggeshall, *American Privateers*, 5; Martin, *American Merchant Marine*, 122–23.

2. Admiralty to Commanders of Newfoundland, Halifax, Jamaica, and Leeward Islands Stations, 9 May 1812, UkLPR, Adm. 2/163, Public Record Office, London; Graham, *Empire*, 247.

3. *Niles'*, 12 September 1812. Some thirty to forty ships reached neutral ports. Tonnages reported in *American State Papers, Commerce and Navigation* (Washington, D.C., 1832), support the idea that these vessels actually continued a coasting trade in the Baltic during the war.

4. Knox, *USN*, 83; Mahan, *Sea Power* 1:322; Secretary of the Navy Hamilton to Commodore John Rodgers, 22 June 1812, Dudley, *Naval War of 1812* 1:148–49.

5. The *Essex* sailed 3 July, the *Nautilus* attempted to sortie 16 July, and the *John Adams*, though eventually converted to a corvette to improve its handling, remained at New York for the duration of the war. For the aggressiveness potential of Rodgers, see Paullin, *Commodore John Rodgers*, 13–277.

6. Captain Richard Byron, to Vice Admiral Herbert Sawyer, 27 June 1812, Dudley, *Naval War of 1812* 1:157–60.

7. Lohnes, "British Naval Problems at Halifax, During the War of 1812," *Mariner's Mirror* 59:318.

8. *Gentlemen's Magazine* 64:658; Tucker and Reuter, *Injured Honor;* Rodgers to Hamilton, 23 May 1811, Dudley, *Naval War of 1812* 1:44–49.

9. Fowler, *Jack Tars*, 168.

10. Ships in Sea Pay, Admiralty Office, 1 July 1812, UkLPR, D, Adm. 8. The Caribbean stations as well as Newfoundland possessed responsibilities of their own, and the Admiralty had not yet established a joint local command structure.

11. Marcus, *Age of Nelson*, 413; Colley, *Britons*. Both London and Manchester had the strongest ties to importation of any British cities—they are the worst case scenario instead of the tip of the iceberg.

12. *Parliamentary Debates* 22:1, 212, 329, 424, 1057, 1058, 1118, 1152, and 23:202, 219–20, 232.

13. Knox, *USN*, 84; Lieutenant William M. Crane to Hamilton, 29 July 1812, Dudley, *Naval War of 1812* 1:209–11.

14. Hamilton to Captain Isaac Hull, 18 June 1812, Dudley, *Naval War of 1812* 1:209–11.

15. Martin, *Fortunate Ship*, 145–51; Hull to Hamilton, 21 July 1812, Dudley, *Naval War of 1812* 1:161–65.

16. Knox, *USN*, 84.

17. Mahan, *Sea Power* 1:388; *Gentlemen's Magazine* 82:77. The latter used the words "calmly accepted" in describing government reaction to the unofficial announcement.

18. Stephen and Lee, *Dictionary of National Biography* 20:869–72; Woodman, *Sea Warriors*, 37–59, 97–111, 147, 215.

19. As quoted in Gardiner, *Admiralty*, 222.

20. Mahan, *Sea Power* 1:381; *British and Foreign State Papers* 1:1345. The order in council is dated 31 July 1812.

21. Wellington to Stuart, 17 December 1811, Rathbone, *Wellington's War,* 181.

22. As quoted in Forester, *Age of Sail*, 182.

23. Graham, *Empire*, 247–48, 252; Albion and Pope, *Sea Lanes*, 108–9; Mahan, *Sea Power* 1:265, 409–12; Ingersoll, *History of the Second War,* 39–43.

Ingersoll states that the British ambassador, Andrew Allen, ended his stay in the United States by fleeing American authorities attempting to stop the dispensing of licenses. He was less than eager, however, to answer to his superiors, who had discovered the kickbacks Allen had accepted to fatten his own purse. Britain did not place a new ambassador in Washington until after the war and relied primarily upon neutral diplomats in American ports to dispense licenses through early 1814.

24. *Niles'*, 4 September 1813.

25. As quoted in Albion and Pope, *Sea Lanes*, 116.

26. Ingersoll, *History of the Second War*, 40; Crawford, "Navy's Campaign against the Licensed Trade," 165–72. Crawford mentions court cases being decided as early as summer of 1813, though the only specific case mentioned was that of the *Julia*, whose condemnation was upheld by the Supreme Court on 7 March 1814.

27. Ingersoll, *History of the Second War*, 39; Madison to Congress, 24 February 1813, Brannan, *Official Letters*, 136–37.

28. As quoted in Forester, *Age of Sail*, 79–80; my italics.

29. Note that several historians misconstrued this action. For example, Albion and Pope, *Sea Lanes*, 116, states that Warren arrived at Halifax with 101 ships. Historians also differ on the number of reinforcements to Halifax in 1812. Marcus, *Age of Nelson*, 455, states that they consisted of 3 ships-of-the-line, 21 frigates, and 37 unrated vessels. That is almost double the number of vessels that actually arrived at Halifax in 1812. Apparently Marcus included ships dispatched to the Caribbean and ships ordered to but not arriving at Halifax in 1812.

30. Graham, *Empire*, 247; Mahan, *Sea Power* 1:381–88.

31. Coker, *Heritage*, 156.

32. Martin, *Fortunate Ship*, 155–65; Hull to Hamilton, 30 August 1812, Brannan, *Official Letters*, 49–51.

33. Rodgers to Hamilton, 1 September 1812, Dudley, *Naval War of 1812* 1:209–11. Scurvy, despite the knowledge of its cause, remained a problem for navies during the late age of sail—a question of not having the cure to hand. *Parliamentary Debates* 24:576–77: Earl Bathurst, secretary of state for the Department of War and the Colonies, in a speech to the House of Lords on 18 February 1813, confused the convoy pursued by Rodgers with the one escorted by Broke. He claimed that the timing of the declaration of war was meant to facilitate "intercepting our homeward-bound fleet from the West Indies" by Rodgers, but "by the judicious management of our force in that quarter, our fleet was protected, and commodore Rodgers returned disappointed to port." He was, at least, correct about the commodore's disappointment.

34. Coker, *Heritage*, 156.

35. Lieutenant Daniel S. Dexter to Captain John Shaw, 23 August 1812, Dudley, *Naval War of 1812* 1:403–5; Tucker, *Gunboat Navy*, 155.

36. Captain David Porter to Hamilton, 3 September 1812, Dudley, *Naval War of 1812* 1:443–47; Porter to Hamilton, 17 August 1812, Brannan, *Official Letters*, 44.

37. Hamilton to Rodgers, 9 September 1812, Dudley, *Naval War of 1812* 1:470–72.

38. Rodgers to Hamilton, 17 September 1812, ibid. 1:494–96.

39. Pack, *Cockburn*, 143; Lohnes, "British Naval Problems at Halifax, During the War of 1812," *Mariner's Mirror* 59:330–21. Exact returns for the crew strength of vessels operating out of Halifax are unavailable, though, according to Barry Lohnes, Sawyer had wrestled with the problem throughout his tenure. Reinforcements arriving in 1813 brought drafts of men, but the demands for sailors on the Great Lakes consumed many of the replacements. Only the abdication of Napoleon in 1814 and the transfer of sailors to North America from ships going into ordinary finally stabilized the manpower situation.

40. Maclay, *American Privateers*, 241.

41. Warren to Secretary of State Monroe, 30 September 1812, Palmer, *Historical Register* 1:23–25.

42. Clowes, *Royal Navy* 6:38–41; Lieutenant Commander Jacob Jones to Hamilton, 24 November 1812, Brannan, *Official Letters*, 92–93.

43. Mahan, *Sea Power* 2:9.

44. Ibid. 2:15; Captain John H. Dent to Hamilton, 17 October 1812, Dudley, *Naval War of 1812* 1:534–35; Lieutenant Charles F. Grandison to Hamilton, 20 December 1812, ibid. 1:610–11.

45. Kay, *Frigate Macedonian*, 45–99; Decatur to Hamilton, 30 October 1812, Brannan, *Official Letters*, 87–88.

46. Monroe to Warren, 27 October 1812, Palmer, *Historical Register* 1:25–27.

47. Pack, *Cockburn*, 145.

48. Coker, *Heritage*, 157–60; Dent to Hamilton, 5 November 1812, Dudley, *Naval War of 1812* 1:584.

49. Captain James L. Yeo, to Vice Admiral Charles Stirling, 22 November 1812 and 11 December 1812, ibid. 1:594–95.

50. Mahan, *Sea Power* 2:9.

51. Rodgers to Hamilton, 2 January 1813, Dudley, *Naval War of 1812* 2:5; Master Commandant Arthur Sinclair to Hamilton, 2 January 1813, ibid. 2:7–9.

52. Martin, *Fortunate Ship*, 171–79; Bainbridge to Secretary of the Navy, 3 January 1813, Brannan, *Official Letters*, 118–19.

53. Mahan, *Sea Power* 2:11.

54. Admiralty to Admiral Sir John B. Warren, 26 December 1812, Dudley, *Naval War of 1812* 1:633–34.

55. Proceedings of 12th Congress—2d Session, Palmer, *Historical Register* 1:70–73; Symonds, *Naval Policy Debate*, 184.

56. Marcus, *Age of Nelson*, 467; Coggeshall, *American Privateers*, 81. Coggeshall listed 266 vessels for New York.

57. Gossett, *Lost Ships*, 84–87. Emmons, *Navy*, 56–74.

58. Graham, *Empire*, 236. Graham gives 318 as the number of privateers. That was the number of letters of marque issued in 1812, though how many actually made it to sea and how many times they actually sortied is debatable. Contemporary sources, much less the historians cited in this study, do not agree on captures. These estimates were taken from the *Niles'*, 1812 editions.

59. Matloff, *American Military History* 1:122–47.

60. Master Commandant Charles Ludlow to Hamilton, 29 September 1812, Dudley, *Naval War of 1812* 1:502–3.

61. Gossett, *Lost Ships*, 84–87; Ships in Sea Pay, 1 July 1813, Dudley, *Naval War of 1812* 2:168–78. Sailing dates and transit times were used to calculate reinforcements, with 18 June and 1 December as end points.

62. Graham, *Empire*, 235; Essex Institute, *Vice-Admiralty Court at Halifax*. Warren's primary interest in hastening the admiralty court may well have been a desire for the prize money from each sale that automatically went to the admiral commanding, or he may have been pressured by his officers with their desire for the money. Also, delays in handling the cases were not necessarily a matter of incompetent court officers, as the directions from the Admiralty as to what constituted a legal prize did not arrive until the very last days of 1812.

63. As quoted in Forester, *Age of Sail*, 133.

64. Warren to Secretary of the Admiralty John W. Croker, 29 December 1812, Dudley, *Naval War of 1812* 1:649–51.

CHAPTER 6. *1813: The Grip Tightens*

1. Pack, *Cockburn*, 145–46.

2. Captain John R. Lumley to Warren, 17 January 1813, Dudley, *Naval War of 1812* 2:631.

3. Croker to Warren, 9 January 1813, ibid. 2:14–15.

4. Ibid. Secretary of the Admiralty J. N. Barrow to Captain Henry Hotham, July 1813, 8 November 1813, March 1814, 16 April 1814, Papers of Admiral Sir Henry Hotham, County Records Office, Beverly, Yorkshire, England (hereafter cited as Hotham Papers); Hotham to Melville, 6 November 1813, Hotham Papers. Barrow's letters to Hotham record the receipt of numerous private communications to the Admiralty, letters delivered by Barrow "directly into their hands."

5. Croker to Warren, 9 January 1813, Dudley, *Naval War of 1812* 2:14–15.

6. Croker to Warren, 10 February 1813, ibid. 2:16–19.

7. Marcus, *Age of Nelson*, 361–405.

8. Coggeshall, *American Privateers*, 156, 225.

9. Chartrand, *Sea Soldiers*, 8–40; Delmas, *Histoire Militaire* 2:371–407.

10. *Times* (London), 30 July 1814. The *Times* listed the number of French ships-of-the-line (including those building) as of 1 April as 104, its information derived from the French newspaper, *Moniteur*. The *Times* quantified neither the condition of completed vessels, the launch dates of the unfinished hulls, nor the lack of availability of crews, thus contributing to alarm in the minds of British leaders and naval officers at the potential menace of French activity.

11. By late 1814, as the first American ships-of-the-line approached readiness, the Admiralty would begin to question the capability of the Royal Navy's three-deckers. Croker issued a secret circular in November of that year advising British captains of the superiority of the American third rates and ordering them not to engage those (untested!) vessels in single combat. Secret

Circular from Croker to Post Captains, UkLPR, Adm. 8, 1/1381, 46, Public Record Office, London.

12. Warren to Croker, 28 March 1813, Dudley, *Naval War of 1812* 2:80–81.

13. Croker to Warren, 20 March 1813, UkLPR, Adm. 2/1376, 341–67, Public Record Office, London.

14. Ibid.; Melville to Warren, 26 March 1813, Dudley, *Naval War of 1812* 2:78–79.

15. Stewart to Jones, 5 February 1813, Dudley, *Naval War of 1812* 2:311–13; Mahan, *Sea Power* 2:9–16.

16. Proclamation of Blockade by Admiral Sir John B. Warren, 6 February 1813, UkLPR, Adm. 1/503, 221.

17. Circular from Secretary of the Navy Jones to Commanders of Ships Now in Port Refitting, 22 February 1813, Dudley, *Naval War of 1812* 2:48–49.

18. Lieutenant Henry D. Chads to Croker, 31 December 1812, ibid. 1:646–49; Lieutenant Frederick A. Wright, to the Admiralty, 26 March 1813, ibid. 2:70–75.

19. *Times* (London), 26 February 1813.

20. Pack, *Cockburn*, 146–47; Lossing, *Pictorial Fieldbook*, 669–71. The force includes only ships verifiable by name. Both authors imply that other unrateds may have been in the bay. Vessels were: ships-of-the-line—*Santo Domingo, Marlborough, Dragon, Victorious;* frigates—*Acasta, Junon, Statira, Maidstone, Narcissus;* sloops—*Laurestinus, Tartarus;* brigs—*Fantome, Mohawk;* tenders—*Dolphin, Racer, Highflyer.*

21. Proceedings of 13th Congress—1st Session, Palmer, *Historical Register* 1:100–102; Symonds, *Naval Policy Debate*, 187.

22. Proceedings of 13th Congress—1st Session, Palmer, *Historical Register* 1:104; Lossing, *Pictorial Fieldbook*, 471–72.

23. Croker to Warren, 17 May 1813, Dudley, *Naval War of 1812* 2:356–57.

24. *Gentlemen's Magazine* 84:65–71. Italics added.

25. Warren, Standing Orders on the North American Station, 6 March 1813, Dudley, *Naval War of 1812* 2:59–60.

26. Lord Commissioners of the Admiralty to Warren, 26 March 1813, UkENG, Cochrane Papers, Library of Congress (hereafter cited as Cochrane Papers); Melville to Warren, 26 March 1813, Dudley, *Naval War of 1812* 2:78–79.

27. Croker to Warren, 28 April 1813, UkLPR, Adm. 2/1376, 320–22.

28. Pack, *Cockburn*, 153–57; Warren to Admiralty, 28 May 1813, reprinted in *Gentlemen's Magazine* 84:375–76.

29. Captain James Lawrence to Jones, 19 March 1813, Dudley, *Naval War of 1812* 2:70–72.

30. Mahan, *Sea Power* 2:129–34; Tucker, *Gunboat Navy*, 158; Lossing, *Pictorial Fieldbook*, 591.

31. Captain the Honorable Thomas Bladen Capel to Warren, 11 May 1813, Dudley, *Naval War of 1812* 2:105–6. British vessels were *La Hogue, Shannon, Tenedos, Nymphe,* and *Curlew.*

32. Pack, *Cockburn*, 155.

33. Henderson, *Sloops and Brigs*, 41; *Niles'*, 4 September, 4 December, 11 December 1813.

34. Stewart to Jones, 21 May 1813, Captains' Letters (hereafter cited as CL), 1813, Vol. 3, No. 58, RG 45, National Archives, Washington, D.C. (hereafter cited as NA).

35. Article 25, Port Standing Orders, Nova Scotia, 1 October 1813, Hotham Papers; Griffith to Hotham, Circular, 28 November 1814, Hotham Papers.

36. Decatur to Jones, June 1813, Dudley, *Naval War of 1812* 2:135–36; Decatur to Jones, 6 June 1813, ibid. 2:136–37; Captain Robert Dudley Oliver, to Warren, 13 June 1813, ibid. 2:137–38; Mahan, *Sea Power* 2:147–48. Mahan states that three ships-of-the-line, four frigates, and three sloops challenged Decatur's breakout. The actual force, as recorded by those involved, consisted of one ship-of-the-line and one frigate; by the time that the full squadron of two ships-of-the-line, two frigates, one sloop, and three tiny tenders united, Decatur had found safety. Errors such as that of Mahan lend a strength to the blockade that simply did not exist.

37. Captain Philip B. V. Broke to Lawrence, 1813, Dudley, *Naval War of 1812* 2:126–29; An Account of the *Chesapeake-Shannon* Action, 6 June 1813, ibid. 2:129–33; Lieutenant George Budd to Jones, 15 June 1813, ibid. 2:133–34.

38. Croker to Edward Griffith, 9 July 1813, UkLPR, Adm. 2/1377, 140–42, Public Record Office, London.

39. Jones to Lieutenant William Henry Allen, 5 June 1813, Dudley, *Naval War of 1812* 2:141–42; Dye, *Cruise of the Argus*, 117–290.

40. Jones to Master Commandant George Parker, 8 December 1813, Dudley, *Naval War of 1812* 2:294–96. Several letters with similar paragraphs exist, all after the loss of the *Chesapeake* and the *Argus*.

41. Dye, *Cruise of the Argus*, 280–90.

42. Pack, *Cockburn*, 157; Mahan, *Sea Power* 2:162–68; Ships in Sea Pay [Extract], 1 July 1813, Dudley, *Naval War of 1812* 2:168–78.

43. Captain John Cassin to Jones, 23 June 1813, Dudley, *Naval War of 1812* 2:359–60; Warren to Croker, 24 June 1813, ibid. 2:360–61; Mahan, *Sea Power* 2:163–66; Pack, *Cockburn*, 157–58.

44. Napier, *Journal*, 39–40; Cassin to Jones, 26 June 1813, Dudley, *Naval War of 1812* 2:361–62; Colonel Sir Thomas Sidney Beckworth, British Army, to Warren, 28 June 1813, ibid. 2:362–64; Beckworth to Warren, 5 July 1813, ibid. 2:364–65; *Gentlemen's Magazine* 84:375–76.

45. Pack, *Cockburn*, 158–59; Warren to Croker, 29 July 1813, Dudley, *Naval War of 1812* 2:368–69.

46. Cockburn to Warren, 12 July 1813, Dudley, *Naval War of 1812* 2:184–86; Cockburn to Warren, 19 July 1813, ibid. 2:365–66; *Gentlemen's Magazine* 84:601.

47. Pack, *Cockburn*, 159–61; Warren to Croker, 23 August 1813, Dudley, *Naval War of 1812* 2:382–83.

48. Pack, *Cockburn*, 162; Captain Robert Barrie to Mrs. George Clayton, 4 September 1813, Dudley, *Naval War of 1812* 2:384–85.

49. Hull to Jones, 14 June 1813, as quoted in Mahan, *Sea Power* 2:186.

50. Hull to Jones, 24 June 1813, Dudley, *Naval War of 1812* 2:160.

51. Tucker, *Gunboat Navy*, 114.

52. Lieutenant David McCrery, R.N., to Commander Alexander Gordon, 6 September 1813, Dudley, *Naval War of 1812* 2:234–35; Lieutenant Edward R.

McCall to Hull, 7 September 1813, ibid. 2:235–38; Albion and Pope, *Sea Lanes,* 117–18. Albion and Pope's narrative is the most recent retelling of this incident, borrowed from interviews of local residents recorded by Lossing. Its authenticity is somewhat dubious, as it is not verified by the official reports. The story, however, does fit the grasping actions of some British naval captains during the blockade.

53. Rodgers to Jones, 27 September 1813, Dudley, *Naval War of 1812* 2:251–54; Warren to Croker, 16 October 1813, ibid. 2:261.

54. Tucker, *Gunboat Navy,* 114; Mahan, *Sea Power* 2:192.

55. Circular from Warren to British Captains, 16 November 1813, UkLPR, Adm. 1/504, Public Record Office, London; Warren to Croker, 20 November 1813, Dudley, *Naval War of 1812* 2:262–63.

56. Captain Jonathan Hayes to Warren, 25 October 1813, UkLPR, Adm. 1/504.

57. Captain Robert Dudley Oliver to Swedish Council at New York Henry Gahn, 2 December 1813, Huntington, Misc. War of 1812.

58. Captain John Smith to Jones, 14 December 1813, Dudley, *Naval War of 1812* 2:300–301; Martin, *Fortunate Ship,* 184.

59. Tucker, *Gunboat Navy,* 158–60.

60. Coker, *Heritage,* 165–68; *Niles',* 14 September 1813; Dent to Jones, 26 August 1813, Area File of the Navy Records Collection, M625, NA. *Niles'* reports the sloop and brig as two brigs, while Dent names *Colibri*'s consort as the *Charybdis* instead of the *Moselle.*

61. Tucker, *Gunboat Navy,* 148.

62. *Niles',* 6 November 1813; Captain John Dent to Mayor Thomas R. Smith, 29 October 1813, NcU-W, Elliot-Gonzales Papers, Wilson Library, University of North Carolina, Chapel Hill; Coker, *Heritage,* 168.

63. *Niles',* 11 December 1813.

64. Warren to Croker, 20 November 1813, UkLPR, Adm. 1/504; Warren to Croker, 20 December 1813, Dudley, *Naval War of 1812* 2:307–8; Napier, *Journal,* 3; *Niles',* 4 September 1813 and 11 December 1813; *Gentlemen's Magazine* 84:390–91, *Times* (London), 25 December 1813. Interestingly, the letter to Croker of 20 November, unlike that of 30 December, does not mention the damage incurred in Halifax from the storm. Rather, Warren assigned sixteen vessels under Griffith to blockade Boston, cover convoys, and patrol New England and Canadian coastal waters "during my absence." On the twentieth, however, two-thirds of those vessels required repairs—at least one did not sail until April 1814. Though Warren's letter specifies its origin as Halifax, a good guess places him at or nearing Bermuda on 12 November, oblivious to his new nightmare.

65. Warren to Croker, 28 March 1813 (Enclosure), Dudley, *Naval War of 1812* 2:80–81.

66. As of that moment, only the northern entrance to Long Island Sound and the coast of New England remained free of economic interdiction, at least on paper.

67. Melville to Warren, 26 March 1813, Dudley, *Naval War of 1812* 2:78–79.

68. Croker to Warren, 10 July 1813, ibid. 2:183–84. Not, of course, that any

prompting should have been needed after the frigate losses of the previous year.

69. Hotham to Melville, 6 November 1813, Hotham Papers.

70. Proceedings of 13th Congress—1st Session, Palmer, *Historical Register* 1:147–48. Of the $22 million in exports for 1813, virtually all constituted licensed trade with Great Britain. This, however, formed only a portion of Madison's concern. An indeterminate amount of illicit trade across the Canadian border as well as voluntary supply of the Royal Navy's blockaders also existed. See Hull to Lieutenant William Burrows, 28 August 1813, Dudley, *Naval War of 1812* 2:233; U.S. District Attorney Asher Robbins to Jones, 14 September 1813, ibid. 2:244; Napier, *Journal;* Hickey, "American Trade Restrictions during the War of 1812," *Journal of American History* 68:517–38.

71. Navy Department Circular, 30 July 1813, Dudley, *Naval War of 1812* 2:205–6.

72. Proceedings of 13th Congress—2d Session, Palmer, *Historical Register* 2:79–81.

73. Schom, *Trafalgar,* 84–88, 261, 383; Robert Fulton to Hamilton, 22 June 1812, Dudley, *Naval War of 1812* 1:146–47.

74. Pack, *Cockburn,* 156; Lossing, *Pictorial Fieldbook,* 693.

75. Master Commandant Jacob Lewis to Jones, 28 June 1813, Dudley, *Naval War of 1812* 2:161; Warren to Croker, 22 July 1813, ibid. 2:162–63; General Order of Admiral Warren, 19 July 1813, ibid. 2:164.

76. Lossing, *Pictorial Fieldbook,* 693; *Gentleman's Magazine* 84:390.

77. Skaggs and Altoff, *Signal Victory;* Decatur to Jones, 18 February 1813, Dudley, *Naval War of 1812* 2:428–29; Bainbridge to Jones, 27 April 1813, ibid. 2:429–30; Jones to Commodore Isaac Chaucey, 3 July 1813, ibid. 2:509–12; *Gentlemen's Magazine* 85:75.

78. Lord Castlereagh to Monroe, 4 November 1813, SP, Palmer, *Historical Register* 3:19–20; Monroe to Castlereagh, 5 January 1814, SP, ibid. 3:22–24.

79. Stagg, *Mr. Madison's War,* 300–302.

80. Coggeshall, *American Privateers,* 128–69.

81. As quoted in Forester, *Age of Sail,* 90.

82. Rathbone, *Wellington's War,* 324.

83. *Niles',* 1 January 1814; Barrie to Warren, 14 November 1813, UkLPR, 1/505, 131.

84. Warren to Croker, 30 December 1813, Dudley, *Naval War of 1812* 2:307–8.

CHAPTER 7. *1814–1815: The Wooden Wall Complete?*

1. Whitehorne, *Baltimore,* 87–90.

2. Pack, *Cockburn,* 164–66; *Niles',* 6 February 1814. The *Sceptre* returned to Bermuda, out of the war for good.

3. Dent to Jones, 31 January 1814, Brannan, *Official Letters,* 305–6; Captain Charles Morris to Jones, 29 April 1814, ibid., 329; *Niles',* October 1813 to March 1814.

4. Mahan, *Sea Power* 2:178, 255; Marcus, *Age of Nelson*, 474; L. Warrington to Jones, 29 April 1814, Brannan, *Official Letters*, 329–30.

5. Knox, *USN*, 100–108; Porter to Secretary of Navy, 2 July 1813 and 3 July 1813, Brannan, *Official Letters*, 175–79, 347–58.

6. Hickey, "American Trade Restrictions during the War of 1812," *Journal of American History* 68:517–38; New Orleans, Record of Entrances and Clearances, 1812–1909, RG 36, NA.

7. General Bond Required of Vessels Confined to the Bay, RG 36, NA; Embargo Bonds, Savannah, Georgia, 1812–1815, RG 36, NA; Embargo Bonds for New York, 1814, RG 36, NA; Embargo Bonds, Charleston, South Carolina, 1812–1815, RG 36, NA.

8. *Niles'*, 22 January 1814.

9. Napier, *Journal*, 18.

10. Hickey, "American Trade Restrictions during the War of 1812," *Journal of American History* 68:517–38.

11. Captain C. Upton to Rear Admiral Edward Griffith, 6 April 1814, UkENL, Cochrane Papers.

12. Napier, *Journal*, 10. The date given by the American fisherman was inaccurate.

13. Ibid., 24.

14. Ibid., 22, 27, 31, 33.

15. Apparently, a "Ships in Sea Pay, July 1, 1814" was not completed due to the rush to demobilize (per communication with Public Record Office, London, August 1996). Approximate strength for 1814 was determined from analysis of vessel names and numbers mentioned in available primary and secondary sources.

16. Stephen and Lee, *Dictionary of National Biography* 4:615–16; Whitehorne, *Baltimore*, 88.

17. Cochrane to Croker, 8 March 1814, UkLPR, Adm. 1/505, 633, Public Record Office, London. A portion of the letter, as well as the ship list, is missing. Possibly, the slight difference between the quantity of vessels listed by location and those enumerated in his commentary is explained in the missing section.

18. Barrow to Hotham, 16 April 1814, Hotham Papers. Hotham had requested the new assignment sometime in February or March of that year. Considering the failure of the 1813 campaign, the Admiralty's approval of the transfer reflected either considerable faith in the captain's abilities or the repayment of a debt to a chosen man.

19. Croker to Cochrane, 25 January 1814, UkLPR, Adm. 2/1376, 916–18.

20. *Niles'*, 30 April 1814: 20 vessels burned. Napier, *Journal*, 24, describes a similar raid on Scituate Harbor, netting two prizes and burning eight hundred tons of shipping.

21. *Niles'*, 9 July 1814.

22. As quoted in Pack, *Cockburn*, 166–67.

23. By the Honorable Sir Alexander Cohrane [Cochrane], A Proclamation, 25 April 1814, UkENL, Cochrane Papers; Mahan, *Sea Power* 2:11. An order in council of 31 May 1814 gave official blessing to the extension.

24. Proclamation of James Madison, 29 June 1814, MiU-C, Goulburn Collection.

25. Martin, *Fortunate Ship*, 184–88.

26. Lieutenant John B. Nicholson to Jones, 1 May 1814, Brannan, *Official Letters*, 330–31; Knox, *USN*, 129; Captain J. Blakeley to Jones, 8 July 1814, Brannan, *Official Letters*, 376–77; Blakeley to Jones, 11 September 1814, ibid., 410–12; Mahan, *Sea Power* 2:261–62.

27. Lieutenant J. Lewis to Jones, 29 May 1814, Brannan, *Official Letters*, 336–37; Hull to Jones, 15 July 1814, ibid., 378; Hull to Jones, 24 June 1814, CL, 1814, Vol. 4, No. 100, RG 45.

28. Tucker, *Gunboat Navy*, 143, 150.

29. Lohnes, "British Naval Problems at Halifax, During the War of 1812," *Mariner's Mirror* 59:317–19. The absence of a dry dock certainly slowed repairs after so many ships were driven aground in the same storm. The lack of proper facilities compounded the continuing problem of a shortage of skilled artificers and general laborers at Halifax.

30. Napier, *Journal*. A careful reading of Napier's words drives both points—weather and focus—home.

31. Cochrane to Secretary for War and Colonies Earl Bathurst, 14 July 1814, UkENL, Cochrane Papers; Cochrane to Croker, 18 July 1814, UkLPR, Adm. 1/506, 915, Public Record Office, London. The communiqué of 18 July carried the same information to the Admiralty, minus much of the invective present in the earlier letter.

32. Captain Hugh Pigot to Cochrane, 20 June 1814, UkLPR, Adm. 1/504, 320; Rear Admiral George Cockburn, to Cochrane, 5 October 1814, UkLPR, Adm. 1/504, 703–5. Escaped American slaves under British officers formed Cockburn's Colonial Corps.

33. Pack, *Cockburn*, 179.

34. As quoted in Mahan, *Sea Power* 2:266.

35. Ingersoll, *History of the Second War*, 122.

36. John Armstrong to Brig. General McClure, 4 October 1813, Brannan, *Official Letters*, 329; Shepard, *Plunder, Profit, and Paroles*. Prevost referred to the burning of Newark by retreating Americans on 10 December 1813, an act approved in advance by the American War Department. It sparked a new wave of retaliation and counter-retaliation along the Canadian frontier. Shepard conveys the escalating hatred along the border in great detail.

37. Cochrane to Croker, 18 July 1814, UkLPR, Adm. 1/506; General Orders from Vice Admiral Cochrane, 18 July 1814, UkENL, Cochrane Papers; Secret Memorandum from Vice Admiral Cochrane, 18 July 1814, UkENL, Cochrane Papers.

38. *Niles'*, 10 September 1814; 1 October 1814.

39. Shomette, *Flotilla;* Norton, *Barney*, 168–84.

40. Cockburn to Barrie, 11 July 1814, MiU-C, Barrie, Robinson, Chew Papers.

41. Pitch, *Burning of Washington;* Pack, *Cockburn*, 180–90; Tingey to Jones, 27 August 1814, *American State Papers, Military Affairs* 1:578–79, *Gentlemen's Magazine* 86:372–85.

42. *Gentlemen's Magazine* 86:385, 585.

43. Major General S. Smith to Monroe, 19 September 1814, Brannan, *Official Letters*, 422–30; Lieutenant Colonel G. Armistead to Monroe, 24 September 1814, ibid., 439–41; Lord, *Dawn's Early Light;* Whitehorne, *Battle for Baltimore,* 159–94.

44. Mahan, *Sea Power* 2:350–51.

45. *Gentlemen's Magazine* 86:583–85.

46. Message of the President of the United States, on the Opening of Congress, 20 September 1814, *British and Foreign State Papers* 1:1547–51.

47. Matloff, *Military History* 1:130–32. American soldiers had looted and burned the public buildings of York, capital of Upper Canada, in late April 1813.

48. *Parliamentary Debates* 24:16–18. The speaker, Lord Grenville, directly compares the excesses in the United States to those of Napoleon.

49. Perkins, *Castlereagh,* 96–97.

50. *Niles'*, 6 October 1814; Ingersoll, *History of the Second War,* 116.

51. Morris to Jones, 22 August 1814, Brannan, *Official Letters,* 392–94; *Gentlemen's Magazine* 86:475–81. The last source reprints British dispatches recording the capture of Eastport, Castine, and Machias, as well as the burning of the *Adams.*

52. Graham, *Empire,* 260; *Niles'*, 6 October 1814; Ingersoll, *History of the Second War,* 116.

53. Matloff, *Military History* 1:143–44; Marcus, *Age of Nelson,* 480–81; Perkins, *Castlereagh,* 97–99. The news was particularly devastating because it followed on the heels of the failure at Baltimore.

54. *Republican and Savannah Evening Ledger,* 30 July 1814; 16 August 1814; 27 August 1814; 8 October 1814; 13 October 1814.

55. Campbell to Jones, 3 September 1814, CL, 1814, Vol. 7, No. 2, RG 45, NA; Tucker, *Gunboat Navy,* 150–52; Campbell to Jones, 26 October 1814, CL, 1814, Vol. 7, No. 2, RG 45, NA; Campbell to Jones, 12 September 1814, Area File of the Navy Records Collection, M625, NA.

56. Campbell to Jones, 11 November 1814, CL, 1814, Vol. 7, No. 2, RG 45, NA.

57. Cochrane to Griffith and Hotham, 5 January 1815, UkLPR, 1/508, 4:543.

58. Captain A. A. Massias to Brigadier General Floyd, 11 January 1815, Brannan, *Official Letters,* 471; Massias to Floyd, 13 January 1815, ibid., 472–74; Pack, *Cockburn,* 270; Tucker, *Gunboat Navy,* 171.

59. Mahan, *Sea Power* 2:236–37.

60. Colonel William Lawrence to Major General Andrew Jackson, 15–16 September 1814, Brannan, *Official Letters,* 424–26; *Niles'*, 22 October 1814.

61. Lieutenant Commander Thomas AP Catesby Jones to B. W. Crowninshield, 12 March 1815, ibid., 487–90. Benjamin W. Crowninshield succeeded William Jones as Secretary of the Navy in early 1815.

62. Jackson to Monroe, 27 December 1814, ibid., 453–55; Jackson to Monroe, 29 December 1814, ibid., 455; Jackson to Monroe, 9 January 1815, ibid., 455–57; Jackson to Monroe, 19 January 1815, ibid., 459–61; *Niles'*, 13 February

1815; Lawrence to Jackson, 12 February 1815, Brannan, *Official Letters*, 484–85; Brigadier General J. Winchester to Monroe, 17 February 1815, ibid., 483–84.

63. Martin, *Fortunate Ship*, 191.

64. Captain John Hayes to Hotham, 17 January 1815, UkLPR, Adm. 1/508, 387–90; Decatur to Crowninshield, 18 January 1815, Brannan, *Official Letters*, 481–83. The *United States* had taken damage to its bottom while attempting to cross the bar off Sandy Hook the previous evening, though obviously not enough damage, in its captain's judgment, to force a return to New York. The brig later joined the *Hornet* and the *Tom Bowline* (though sharing a name with the captured frigate, this *Macedonian* was only a humble brig).

65. Coggeshall, *American Privateers*, 301–3; *Niles'*, 22 October 1814; Forester, *Age of Sail*, 219.

66. Perkins, *Castlereagh*, 99; *Parliamentary Debates* 29:1–18, 41–75; *Times* (London), 18 November 1814; Mitchell, *European Statistics*, 697, 708. Beginning in November 1814, Parliament intensely debated the much despised income and property taxes. Perkins provides a brief examination of the tax burden, drawn from Castlereagh's correspondence during the negotiations at Ghent. Mitchell records the annual deficits accompanying Britain's wars with France and the United States: 25 million pounds in 1812, 36 million pounds in 1813, and pounds in 1814. Reduction in taxation did not occur until 1815, after the end of the War of 1812. Mitchell reflects the sharp drop in revenue between 1815 and 1816 as the government reduced income and property taxes.

67. Schroeder, *European Politics*, 535; Perkins, *Castlereagh*, 100. The issue was the Polish-Saxon question, and on 3 January 1815, Great Britain, France, and Austria actually signed a secret treaty promising 150,000 men each to use against expected Russian aggression. The threat of a French revolt against the Bourbons also raised British anxiety levels.

68. Captain Charles Stewart to Secretary of the Navy, May 1815, Brannan, *Official Letters*, 492–94; Martin, *Fortunate Ship*, 195–207.

69. Lieutenant Commander J. Biddle to Secretary of the Navy, 25 March 1815, Brannan, *Official Letters*, 490–92; Biddle to Decatur, 10 June 1815, ibid., 494–96.

70. Fowler, *Jack Tars*, 248; Knox, *USN*, 129.

CHAPTER 8. *Challenging the Efficiency of the Blockade*

1. A "good risk" offers a high percentage chance of success, a "bad risk" affords a low percentage chance, and an "unrecognized risk" is not perceived as a risk at all. For example, a woman lives in a house just across a river, driving over the bridge each evening to reach home. One day she finds a warning sign, Central Span Out, investigates, and discovers two wooden planks extending across the missing span. Problem solving ensues, with a good risk being to abandon the car and walk across the planks and a bad risk being, rather obviously, an attempt to drive across the two planks. Suppose, however, that the warning sign had been removed to adorn the wall of her son's bedroom—the

risk factor would have been unknown and unrecognized until too late to do anything but suffer the consequences.

2. *Gentlemen's Magazine* 84:229–31.

3. Porter to Hamilton, 17 August 1812, Brannan, *Official Letters*, 44. Porter wrote from the frigate *Essex* that the outgunned *Alert* "ran down on our weather quarter, gave three cheers and commenced an action (if so trifling a skirmish deserves the name), and after eight minutes firing struck her colours with seven feet water in her hold."

4. Average U.S. Naval vessels available for cruising were compiled from primary and secondary sources listed in the bibliography (notably the *Captain's Letters to the Secretary of the Navy*, the *American State Papers*, and Emmons, *Navy*) usually on a ship by ship basis. Guardships, ships fitting out for most of a quarter or otherwise not ready for sea, ships stripped of guns and crew for the Great Lakes, and vessels assigned to convoy or coastal patrol duties were not included. Ships under close blockade but also under sailing orders (*Constellation*, *United States*) were considered available for *guerre de course*.

5. Roosevelt, *Naval War of 1812*, 69–70, 105–36, 282–301, 386.

6. Gossett, *Lost Ships*, 1–95.

7. Garitee, *Private Navy*, xvi, gives "over 500" as the number, while Knox, *USN*, 95, offers 526, and Maclay, *American Privateers*, 506–7, uses 515. Coggeshall, *American Privateers*, 460, states that only 253 were actually privateers. The remainder were letter of marque traders.

8. *Niles'*, 6 January 1816; *Parliamentary Debates* 29:649–50.

9. Emmons, *Navy*, 56–200. Prizes taken on the Great Lakes as well as barges, launches, and fishing smacks are not included. Also remember, the total number of prizes taken exceeded Emmons's final figure—possibly by several hundred vessels. Those captures simply could not be verified.

10. *Niles'*, 3 June 1815, reported sixteen hundred prizes safely arrived in the United States during the war, with perhaps one hundred still at sea in June. Contemporary reports of Lloyd's of London as well as myriad scattered records support the general accuracy of this figure.

11. Baltimore Tonnage Book, 1808–1815, RG 36, NA; New Orleans, Record of Entrances and Clearances, 1812–1909, RG 36, NA. The volume for Baltimore appears to be the only surviving major port record from the War of 1812 which lists the arrival of prizes. Except for New Orleans, the remaining tonnage records apparently have been lost, either destroyed by fire or possibly purged by the government. In the case of New Orleans, the clerk recorded only minimal information, and failed to list any arriving prizes. Fifteen prizes arrived in Baltimore in 1812 while two made port in 1813.

12. Perkins, *Castlereagh*, 99–100.

13. Jones to Parker, 8 December 1813, Dudley, *Naval War of 1812* 2:294–96; Jones to Master Commandant John O. Creighton, 22 December 1813, ibid. 2:296–97.

14. Emmons, *Navy*, 60–65.

15. Mitchell, *European Statistics*, 488, 613. The tonnage registry for Great Britain reflected a continual increase in merchant shipping between 1793 and 1815, barring dips in 1796 and 1807. Between 31 December 1812 and

31 December 1814, 151,000 tons are recorded as having joined the merchant shipping fleet. This statistical evidence (as with tonnage figures introduced later in this chapter for registered vessels in the United States) should be considered with care. Ships are removed from the national register only when papers of registration are surrendered by the owners, when the loss of vessels are otherwise made known to the government, or when the responsible agency goes to the expensive and time-consuming effort to physically compare records and existing ships—such as the United States did in 1817 (for the first time in its brief history). A dip similar to those of 1796 and 1807 also appears in British records for 1817, possibly indicating periodic adjustments to the registry. This conjecture is supported by the absence of a proportional decrease in imports and exports for those years.

16. Garitee, *Private Navy*, 244; Fairburn, *Merchant Sail* 2:821; Marcus, *Age of Nelson*, 462; Forester, *Fighting Sail*, 218; Coggeshall, *American Privateers*, 300.

17. Essex Institute, *Vice-Admiralty Court at Halifax*. All Halifax related tables are drawn exclusively from this work. In order to compile a complete British prize list, up to a dozen Vice-Admiralty Court sites as well as numerous Admiralty letters would need to be found and analyzed, though just having Bermuda's records would add tremendously to the evaluation. Unfortunately, almost all Vice-Admiralty Court records have been lost. J. R. Hill recently confirmed this in *Prizes of War*, xviii.

18. Snider, *Red Jack;* Kert, *Prize and Prejudice*.

19. Napier, *Journal*, 23, 35, 37.

20. Mahan, *Sea Power* 2:21.

21. The term "self-sufficiency" refers to a nondependence upon maritime trade for vital raw materials, including food. Contrast the position of the United States with that of the British empire, forced to depend upon its new enemy to feed its populations in the Canadian maritime provinces and the Caribbean, as well as its army in Spain. Portions of the empire lacked self-sufficiency, whereas Madison felt confident enough of the United States' ability to maintain its people to declare another embargo in 1813–14.

22. For near continuous criticism of the war effort, see the *Columbian Centinel*, the *New York Evening Post*, and the *Philadelphia Aurora;* for a contemporary discussion of the Hartford Convention, see Dwight, *History of the Hartford Convention*.

23. A. J. Dallas, Treasurer, to the House of Representatives, 25 February 1815, *American State Papers, Finance* (Washington, D.C., 1832), 2:912. This debt was internal to the United States. The government did not borrow internationally during the War of 1812.

24. The impact of the 1813–14 embargo on coasting should be kept in mind; without it, well over 50 percent of tonnage would have operated in 1814. The same reasoning applies to transoceanic trade.

25. Actual tonnage losses most likely exceeded the numbers arrived at due to purchase and conversion of prizes to trade as well as newly built vessels entering the lanes, though the bulk of building activities during the war centered on naval and privateer vessels. It would be nice to compare the tonnage losses from tables 11 and 16; it would also be inappropriate. To avoid serious

skewing in favor of the United States, a table similar to 11 would need to be created from total British captures and average tonnage. Unfortunately, both statistics remain unavailable.

26. Baltimore Tonnage Book, 1808–1815, RG 36, NA; New Orleans, Record of Entrances and Clearances, 1812–1909, RG 36, NA.

27. Baltimore Tonnage Book, 1808–1815, RG 36, NA.

28. New Orleans, Record of Entrances and Clearances, 1812–1909, RG 36, NA. Less information is provided in this volume than in the records for Baltimore, thus reducing the amount of potential comparative analysis available to the historian.

29. Sawtell, *Amos A. Evans, Surgeon,* 160–62, 381, 385; *Columbian Centinel; Boston Globe;* Maclay, *American Privateers,* 506–7; Coggeshall, *American Privateers,* 154.

30. Graham, *Empire,* 248.

31. Morison, Merk, and Freidel, *Dissent in Three American Wars,* 1–31; *American State Papers, Finance* 1:661. Morison addresses the difference between the reality of New England dissent and popular perceptions of the section as "neutral" and even "rebellious." The list of banks participating in the war loan of 2 May 1814 included Portsmouth, Salem, Boston, Providence, Bristol, Newport, Norwich, Hartford, and New Haven.

32. Dwight, *History of the Hartford Convention;* Banner, *To the Hartford Convention;* Morison, Merk, and Freidel, *Dissent in Three American Wars,* 1–31.

33. Napier, *Journal,* 23.

34. Historians addressing the drain of specie include Henry Adams, Francis Beirne, A. L. Burt, Gerald S. Graham, Donald R. Hickey, Dudley Knox, Alfred T. Mahan, Albert Marrin, J. C. A. Stagg, and Patrick C. T. White.

35. *American State Papers, Finance* 2:365, 909.

36. Ibid. 2:236. Emphasis added.

37. As quoted in Forester, *Age of Sail,* 84. An article in the *Times* (London), 22 March 1813, expressed similar sentiments, noting that the specie drain extended to those colonies requiring American provisions.

38. Hickey, "American Trade Restrictions during the War of 1812," *Journal of American History* 68:535.

39. Emmons, *Navy,* 56–200; Coggeshall, *American Privateers.* Unreported specie captured and ransoms taken would increase the stated totals.

40. Garitee, *Private Navy,* 240.

41. Table 15 also supports, at least tentatively, the hypothesis of a non-shortage of specie in the United States at the end of the war. Note the sharp increase in imports from the 1812 level of $77 million to $113 million in 1815 and $147 million in 1816. This represented a considerable trade imbalance, the difference quite probably requiring hard cash to subsidize.

42. Marcus, *Age of Nelson,* 382. French numbers are from Marcus; the American average is based on seventeen hundred prizes taken during the war (a low-end estimate).

43. Treaty of Peace, signed at Ghent on 24 December 1814, Coggeshall, *American Privateers,* 439–51. Great Britain realized some small territorial gains in the northeast United States. A commission to adjudicate the long-running

boundary disputes between the two nations was also established. The treaty resolved none of the major issues voiced in Madison's declaration of war.

44. Schroeder, *European Politics*, 574; *Times* (London), 25 November 1814; *Gentleman's Magazine.* Schroeder centers the change of heart on the lack of victories in America and Wellington's refusal to accept command of the forces in the United States. The *Times* refers to petitions (protesting ship losses) directed to the Prince Regent from the merchants and shipowners of Liverpool, Glasgow, Port-Glasgow, Greenock, and London. Finally, the "Proceedings in the Present Session of Parliament" from July 1812 to the end of the war in each issue of the *Gentlemen's Magazine* reflect an increasing discontent with war in general and the American conflict in particular (though never strong enough to force a change of cabinet).

45. *Parliamentary Debates* 26:173–83, 29:10–18, 905–14; *London Times*, 24 March and 9 November 1814. Relevant motions occurred in May 1813 and from November 1814 into February 1815. Without doubt, a strong political motivation backed the challenges by Whigs in the House of Lords, but there certainly existed reason enough for legitimate concern over the American war.

46. *Gentlemen's Magazine* 84:268. Whether from true belief or denial of guilt, the Admiralty never admitted that the Halifax squadron was unprepared at the onset of war. Members of Parliament certainly made that challenge, as in a March 1813 session: "Lord *Melville* said, whenever the detail was entered into, it was capable of proof that at the time of the breaking out of the war, the force on the American station was amply sufficient for all the purposes required of it." Though searched for diligently in the records of Parliament and the Admiralty, that "proof" remains well hidden. Even if discovered, its political necessity would taint its value as an indication of strategic policy formulation by the Admiralty in early 1812.

47. Public Orders Issued by Commodore Hotham, Hotham's Journal, August 1814 to March 1815, Hotham Papers.

48. Napier, *Journal*, 3.

CHAPTER 9. *Comparison to Contemporary Blockades*

1. Mahan, *French Revolution* 1:1–69; Gardiner, *Fleet Battle*, 9–10; Arthur, *Remaking of the English Navy*, 7–15.

2. Clowes, *Royal Navy* 4:197–98.

3. Mahan, *French Revolution* 1:101–2, 165–66.

4. Arthur, *Remaking of the English Navy*, 114–15, 143–51, 187–99, 205–7; Mahan, *French Revolution* 1:212, 232, 368–76.

5. Kennedy, *Naval Mastery*, 132; Gardiner, *Fleet Battle*, 61; Graham, *Empire*, 247.

6. Mahan, *French Revolution* 1:122–61; Clowes, *Royal Navy* 4:216–17.

7. Mahan, *French Revolution* 1:163–64; Clowes, *Royal Navy* 4:241–42, 253–54.

8. Gardiner, *Fleet Battle*, 59–61; Mahan, *French Revolution* 1:347–67; Clowes, *Royal Navy* 4:251–304.

9. Gardiner, *Fleet Battle,* 86–89; Mahan, *French Revolution* 1:170–72, 202–3.

10. Gardiner, *Fleet Battle,* 118–37; Clowes, *Royal Navy* 4:279–394, 447–54; Mahan, *French Revolution* 1:184–287.

11. Clowes, *Royal Navy* 4:325–31, 407–8; Gardiner, *Fleet Battle,* 174–75.

12. Mackesy, *War for America.* See especially chapters 10, 15, 17, and 22. This theory seems to make more sense than the "general incompetence of the elderly" hypothesis too often put forth by contemporaries and naval historians regarding Howe and Bridport.

13. Mahan, *French Revolution* 1:368–80; Arthur, *Remaking of the English Navy,* 143–208.

14. Mahan, *French Revolution* 2:41–77.

15. Clowes, *Royal Navy* 4:473; Mahan, *French Revolution* 2:71–73.

16. Schom, *Trafalgar.*

17. Richmond, *Statesmen,* 214–18; Mahan, *French Revolution* 2:76–100; Clowes, *Royal Navy* 5:10, 48.

18. Schom, *Trafalgar,* 63–127, 160–81, 373–77.

19. Ibid., 184–86; Mahan, *French Revolution* 2:141–48.

20. Clowes, *Royal Navy* 5:88–174; Schom, *Trafalgar,* 200–356. This brief summary does not do justice to the intricacies of the campaign. See Schom or Corbett, *Campaign of Trafalgar,* for detailed coverage.

21. The precarious logistical situation of Toulon blockaders (not to mention all British fleet elements in the Mediterranean) was a matter of distance from supply sources and the utter lack of locally available naval stores in the opening years of the war. The major bases at Gibraltar, Malta, and Port Mahon had to be stocked from Britain, itself dependent on raw materials arriving from the Baltic and North America. As serious as the lack of spars, powder, and provisions was the shortage of men—both replacement seamen and the shipwrights and artificers needed to repair major damage to vessels. The lack of a dry dock at any of the Mediterranean bases also severely hindered repairs. Note that this situation is analogous to that of Halifax and Bermuda during the War of 1812. See Lavery, *Nelson's Navy,* 221–44, for additional discussion of the British logistical infrastructure.

22. Clowes, *Royal Navy* 5:183–245.

23. Ibid. 5:252–70.

24. Ibid. 5:278–81, 296, 303–4.

25. Richmond, *Statesmen,* 243; Clowes, *Royal Navy* 5:540–48.

26. Marcus, *Age of Nelson,* 402–4; Clowes, *Royal Navy* 5:472–87.

27. Clowes, *Royal Navy* 5:341. *Egyptienne,* thirty-six, was a former naval frigate while *Blonde,* thirty, was keel-built as a frigate. The latter took HMS *Wolverine,* thirteen, escorting a Newfoundland convoy in March 1804. Two of the convoy's merchantmen were also captured, while six successfully scattered.

28. Marcus, *Age of Nelson,* 399–401; Richmond, *Statesmen,* 244; Clowes, *Royal Navy* 5:451, 457–61. France's inability to defend its overseas possessions hinged upon the successes of the British close blockade, including Trafalgar.

29. Clowes, *Royal Navy* 5:510, 514, 523, 553; Marcus, *Age of Nelson,* 370–75.

30. Mahan, *Sea Power* 1:108–10, 272–73; Richmond, *Statesmen,* 228–30.

31. Richmond, *Statesmen*, 344–45.

32. Mahan, *Sea Power* 1:290–92.

33. Crouzet, *Britain Ascendant*, 300, 302–16.

34. Ibid., 300–301. Crouzet concludes that the "maritime war and British blockade" definitely caused a "collapse of the 'Atlantic sector' in the Continental economy, which had serious and lasting consequences" while treating the Continental System as the secondary causation of the economic woes of France. For alternative views stressing the Continental system see Ellis, *Napoleon's Continental Blockade*, and Heckscher, *Continental System*.

35. The words in parentheses are used in table 19 to identify the categories being evaluated.

36. Garitee, *Private Navy*, 244; Marcus, *Age of Nelson*, 473; Coggeshall, *American Privateers*, 301–3.

37. Chartrand, *Sea Soldiers;* Clowes, *Royal Navy* 4:548–61, 5:549–67; Marcus, *Age of Nelson*, 404.

38. List of the Naval Forces of the United States, Delivered to Congress by William Jones on 4 March 1814, *British and Foreign State Papers* 1:1452–54. From its initial strength of 16 reliable vessels, the U.S. Navy had grown to 8 frigates, 10 sloops-of-war, 4 brigs, and 2 schooners (omitting 2 vessels serving as guardships and 1 as a cartel) despite its losses to combat. One-third of these warships were engaged in *guerre de course* or readying (under orders or refitting) to leave port in early March 1814. Also, 126 gunboats, 32 barges, and 11 armed vessels served in a coastal defense capacity. Additionally, several hulls neared completion in various ports: 3 ships-of-the-line, 3 frigates, and 59 barges.

39. *Gentlemen's Magazine* (London), vols. 66–86. This journal provided consistent coverage of the three wars of the era. Its editor attempted to report unbiased news, and faithfully reproduced the gazettes from the Admiralty without change. By comparing monthly reports, it appears that raids based upon the blockade almost quadrupled in rate between the first and second wars against France. For the quantity of raids against the United States, see *Niles'*.

40. Hull to Jones, 14 June 1813, as quoted in Mahan, *Sea Power* 2:186; Hull to Jones, 24 June 1813, Dudley, *Naval War of 1812* 2:160; Tucker, *Gunboat Navy*, 114.

41. Tucker, *Gunboat Navy*, 150–52, 171; Campbell to Jones, 11 November 1814, CL, 1814, Vol. 7, 2, RG 45, NA; Pack, *Cockburn*, 270.

42. *New York Evening Post*, 14 February 1815. For example, sugar in New York fell from $26.00 to $12.50 per hundredweight and a pound of tea from $2.25 to $1.00 overnight after the announcement of the signing of the Treaty of Ghent but before the blockade had been lifted. This hints that a significant percentage of inflation during the war was a question of profiteering instead of shortages caused by a successful blockade.

43. *Niles'*, 20 November 1813, celebrated the tremendous growth in the previous year in the cotton spinning industry of Baltimore. Additional mentions of industrial growth can be found in 1815 and 1816 editions.

Bibliography

PRIMARY SOURCES

Memoirs

Gleig, George. *Narrative of the Campaigns of the British Army at Washington, Baltimore, and New Orleans, under Generals Ross, Pakenham, & Lambert, in the Years 1814 and 1815; with Some Account of the Countries Visited.* Philadelphia: M. Carey & Sons, 1821.

Jones, Noah. *Journals of Two Cruises Aboard the American Privateer Yankee, by a Wanderer.* New York: Macmillan, 1967.

King, Dean, and John B. Hattendorf, eds. *Every Man Will Do His Duty: An Anthology of Firsthand Accounts from the Age of Nelson.* New York: Henry Holt, 1997.

Napier, Henry E. *New England Blockaded in 1814: The Journal of Henry Edward Napier, Lieutenant in H.M.S. Nymphe.* Edited by Walter Muir Whitehill. Salem, Mass.: Peabody Museum, 1939.

Sawtell, William D., ed. *Journal Kept Onboard the Frigate Constitution, 1812 by Amos A. Evans, Surgeon, U.S.N.* Concord, Mass.: Bankers Lithograph, 1967.

Thursfield, H. G., Rear-Adm. *Five Naval Journals, 1789–1817.* London: Naval Records Society, 1951.

Published Documents

American State Papers. Commerce and Navigation, vols. 1 and 2; *Finance,* vol. 1.; *Military Affairs,* vol. 1. Washington, D.C.: Gales and Senter, 1832.

Barnes, G. R., and J. H. Owen, eds. *The Private Papers of John, Earl of Sandwich, First Lord of the Admiralty, 1771–1782.* 4 vols. London: Navy Records Society, 1932.

Brannan, John, ed. *Official Letters of the Military and Naval Officers of the United States, During the War with Great Britain in the Years 1812, 13, 14 and 15.* 1823. Reprint, New York: Arno Press, 1971.

Dudley, William S., ed. *The Naval War of 1812: A Documentary History.* 2 vols. Washington, D.C.: Naval Historical Center, 1985.

Essex Institute. *American Vessels Captured by the British During the Revolution and the War of 1812.* Records of the Vice-Admiralty Court at Halifax, Nova Scotia. Salem, Mass.: Essex Institute, 1911.

Leyland, John, ed. *Dispatches and Letters Relating to the Blockade of Brest, 1803–1805.* 2 vols. London: Navy Records Society, 1899–1902.

Mackay, Ruddock F. *The Hawke Papers: A Selection, 1743–1771*. Brookfield, Vt.: Scholar Press (Navy Records Society), 1990.

Palmer, T. H., ed. *The Historical Register of the United States*. 4 vols. Philadelphia: G. Palmer, 1814–16.

Scott, James Brown, ed. *Prize Cases Decided in the United States Supreme Court, 1789–1918, Including Also Questions on the Instance Side in Which Questions of Prize Law Were Involved*. Vols. 1 and 2. Oxford: Oxford University Press, 1923.

United Kingdom. Foreign Office. *British and Foreign State Papers*. 2 vols. 1839. Reprint, Washington, D.C.: Microcard Editions, 1968.

United Kingdom. House of Commons. *Sessional Papers*. 1811–16. New York: Readex Microprint, 1965.

United Kingdom. Parliament. *Parliamentary Debates*. (Also known as *Hansard's Parliamentary Debates*.) Vols. 22–29. 1803.

Unpublished Documents

County Records Office, Beverly, England

Papers of Admiral Sir Henry Hotham, DDHO 7/1–7/2

Library of Congress

Alexander F. I. Cochrane Papers

Lilly Library, Indiana University, Bloomington

War of 1812 Manuscripts

National Archives and Records Administration

Area File of the Navy Records Collection, M625
Baltimore Embargo Bonds, 1814, RG 36
Baltimore Foreign and Coasting Entrances and Clearances, January 7, 1813–July 11, 1815, RG 36
Baltimore Tonnage Book, 1808–1815, RG 36
Captains' Letters to the Secretary of the Navy, 1813, Vol. 3, RG 45
Captains' Letters to the Secretary of the Navy, 1814, Vol. 4, RG 45
Captains' Letters to the Secretary of the Navy, 1814, Vol. 7, RG 45
Charleston Embargo Bonds, 1812–1815, RG 36
New Orleans, Record of Entrances and Clearances, 1812–1909, RG 36
New York Embargo Bonds, 1814, RG 36
Savannah Embargo Bonds, 1812–1815, RG 36

Public Record Office, London, England

Adm. 8, 1/503, 1/504, 1/505, 1/506, 1/508, 1/1381, 2/163, 2/1376, 2/1377.

William L. Clements Library, University of Michigan, Ann Arbor

Barrie, Robinson, Chew Papers
Goulborn Collection

Wilson Library, University of North Carolina, Chapel Hill

Elliot-Gonzales Papers

Newspapers and Periodic Journals

Charleston (S.C.) Daily Courier
Columbian Centinel (Boston)
Gentlemen's Magazine and Historical Chronicle (London), vols. 66–86
Georgetown (D.C.) Federal Republican
National Intelligencer (Washington, D.C.)
New York Evening Post
Niles' Weekly Register (Baltimore)
Philadelphia Aurora
Republican and Savannah (Ga.) Evening Ledger
Richmond (Va.) Enquirer
Times (London)
Tracy, Nicholas, ed. *The Naval Chronicle: The Contemporary Record of the Royal Navy at War.* 2 vols. Mechanicsburg, Pa.: Stackpole Books, 1998.

Maps

Atlas of United States History. Maplewood, N.J.: Hammond, 1995.
Jeffreys, Thomas. *The Caribbee or Leeward Islands, the Virgin Islands, and the Isle of Porto Rico.* 1794. Reproduction, Ithaca, N.Y.: Historic Urban Plans, 1990.
Kelly, Victor J., John W. Lothers, and Ellie Sabban. *Ghost Fleet of the Outer Banks.* Washington, D.C.: National Geographic Society, 1970.
A New and Accurate Map of New Jersey from the Best Authorities. From the *Universal Magazine of Knowledge and Pleasure* 66 (June 1780). Library of Congress, Washington, D.C.
New Chart of the Coast of North America. Salem, Mass.: Samuel Lambert, 1818.
Northern Provinces of the United States. 1817. Reproduction, Ithaca, N.Y.: Historic Urban Plans, 1990.
Royal Navy. *Roberts and Gauld Chart of the Gulf of Florida or New Bahama Channel.* 1794. Reproduction, Ithaca, N.Y.: Historic Urban Plans, 1990.
Southern Provinces of the United States. 1817. Reproduction, Ithaca, N.Y.: Historic Urban Plans, 1990.
Tanesse, Jacques. *Plan of the City and Suburbs of New Orleans from an Actual Survey Made in 1815.* 1817. Reproduction, Ithaca, N.Y.: Historic Urban Plans, 1990.

SECONDARY SOURCES

Articles

Barrett, Craig. "Living Off the Land." *Command: Military History, Strategy, & Analysis* 8 (February 1998): 80–83.
Baugh, Daniel A. "The Eighteenth Century Navy as a National Institution, 1690–1815." In *The Oxford Illustrated History of the Royal Navy,* ed. J. R. Hill, 150–56. New York: Oxford University Press, 1995.

Crawford, Michael J. "The Navy's Campaign against the Licensed Trade in the War of 1812." *American Neptune* 46 (Summer 1986): 165–72.

Fowler, William M. "America's Super-Frigates." *Mariner's Mirror* 59 (February 1973): 49–56.

Goldenberg, Joseph A. "Blue Lights and Infernal Machines: The British Blockade of New London." *Mariner's Mirror* 61 (November 1975): 385–98.

Hacker, Louis M. "Western Land Hunger and the War of 1812: A Conjecture." *Mississippi Valley Historical Review* 10 (March 1924): 365–95.

Hickey, Donald R. "American Trade Restrictions during the War of 1812." *Journal of American History* 68 (December 1981): 517–38.

Latimer, Margaret K. "South Carolina—A Protagonist of the War of 1812." *American Historical Review* 61 (November 1956): 914–29.

Lohnes, Barry J. "British Naval Problems at Halifax, During the War of 1812." *Mariner's Mirror* 59 (November 1973): 317–33.

Mackay, Ruddock F. "Edward Hawke: Risk-Taker Preeminent (1705–1781)." In *The Great Admirals, Command at Sea, 1587–1945*, ed. Jack Sweetman, 152–71. Annapolis: Naval Institute Press, 1997.

Middleton, Richard. "Naval Administration in the Age of Pitt and Anson, 1755–1763." In Black and Woodfine, *British Navy and the Use of Naval Power*.

Murray, Sir Oswyn A. R. "The Admiralty, Part VI." *Mariner's Mirror* 24 (November 1938): 329–52.

Partridge, M. S. "The Royal Navy and the End of the Close Blockade, 1895–1905: A Revolution in Naval Strategy?" *Mariner's Mirror* 75 (April 1989): 119–36.

Risjord, Norman K. "1812: Conservatives, War Hawks, and the Nation's Honor." *William & Mary Quarterly*, 3d ser., 28 (April 1961): 196–210.

Shomette, Donald G. "Londontown: The Reconnaissance of a 17th–18th Century Tidewater Riverport Complex." In *Beneath the Waters of Time: The Proceedings of the Ninth Conference on Underwater Archaeology*, by the Texas Antiquities Committee. Austin: Texas Antiquities Committee, 1978, 167–74.

Steele, Ian K. "Time, Communications and Society: The English Atlantic, 1702." *Journal of American Studies* 8, no. 1 (January 1974): 1–21.

Taylor, George R. "Agrarian Discontent in the Mississippi Valley Preceding the War of 1812." *Journal of Political Economy* 39 (September 1931): 471–505.

Books

Abbot, Willis J. *Blue Jackets of 1812: A History of the Naval Battles of the Second War with Great Britain to Which Is Prefixed an Account of the French War of 1798.* New York: Dodd, Mead, 1887.

Adams, Henry. *History of the United States of America.* 9 vols. New York: Charles Scribner's Sons, 1891–96.

Albion, Robert G., and Jennie B. Pope. *Sea Lanes in Wartime: The American Experience, 1775–1942.* New York: W. W. Norton, 1942.

Arthur, Charles B. *The Remaking of the English Navy by Admiral St. Vincent—Key to the Victory over Napoleon: The Great Unclaimed Naval Revolution (1795–1805).* Lanham, Md.: University Press of America, 1986.

Atherley-Jones, L. A. *Commerce in War.* London: Methuen, 1907.

Babits, Lawrence E., and Hans Van Tilburg, eds. *Maritime Archaeology: A Reader of Substantive and Theoretical Contributions.* New York: Plenum Press, 1998.

Bamford, Paul Walden. *Forests and French Sea Power, 1660–1789.* Toronto: University of Toronto Press, 1956.

Banner, James M., Jr. *To the Hartford Convention: The Federalists and the Origin of Party Politics in Massachusetts, 1789–1815.* New York: Alfred A. Knopf, 1970.

Beirne, Francis F. *The War of 1812.* New York: E. P. Dutton, 1949.

Bird, Eric C. F., and Mannu L. Schwartz, eds. *The World's Coastlines.* New York: Reinhold Publishing, 1985.

Black, Jeremy, and Philip Woodfine, eds. *The British Navy and the Use of Naval Power in the Eighteenth Century.* Leicester, U.K.: Leicester University Press, 1988.

Brackenridge, Henry M. *History of the Late War Between the United States and Great Britain.* Philadelphia: J. Kay, June and Brother, 1845.

Brant, Irving. *James Madison, Commander in Chief, 1812–1836.* New York: Bobbs-Merrill, 1961.

Brown, Alexander Crosby. *The Dismal Swamp Canal.* Chesapeake, Va.: Norfolk County Historical Society of Chesapeake, Virginia, 1970.

Brown, Wilbert S. *The Amphibious Campaign for West Florida and Louisiana, 1814–1815.* University: University of Alabama Press, 1969.

Buel, Richard, Jr. *In Irons: Britain's Naval Supremacy and the American Revolutionary Economy.* New Haven, Conn.: Yale University Press, 1998.

Burrows, Montague. *The Life of Edward Lord Hawke, Admiral of the Fleet, Vice-Admiral of Great Britain, and First Lord of the Admiralty from 1766 to 1771, with Some Account of the Origin of the English Wars in the Reign of George the Second, and the State of the Navy at That Period.* London: W. H. Allen, 1883.

Burt, A. L. *The United States, Great Britain, and British North America from the Beginning to the Establishment of Peace after the War of 1812.* New York: Russell and Russell, 1961.

Chandler, David G. *Atlas of Military Strategy: The Art, Theory and Practice of War, 1618–1878.* London: Arms and Armour Press, 1980.

Chapelle, Howard I. *The History of the American Sailing Navy: The Ships and Their Development.* New York: W. W. Norton, 1949.

Chartrand, René. *Napoleon's Sea Soldiers.* London: Osprey Publishing, 1990.

Christie, Ian R. *Wars and Revolutions: Britain, 1760–1815.* Cambridge: Harvard University Press, 1982.

Clary, David A. *Fortress America: The Corps of Engineers, Hampton Roads, and United States Coastal Defense.* Charlottesville: University of Virginia Press, 1990.

Clowes, William Laird. *The Royal Navy: A History from the Earliest Times to 1900.* 7 vols. 1897–1903. Reprint, London: Chatham Publishing, 1997.

Coggeshall, George. *History of the American Privateers and Letters of Marque During Our War with Great Britain in the Years 1812, 13, and 14.* New York: Edward O. Evans, 1856.

Coker, P. C., III. *Charleston's Maritime Heritage, 1670–1865.* Charleston, S.C.: Coker Craft Press, 1987.

Colley, Linda. *Britons: Forging the Nation, 1707–1837*. Avon, Eng.: Bath Press, 1992.

Cooper, James Fenimore. *The History of the Navy of the United States of America*. 1839. Reprint, Upper Saddle River, N.J.: Gregg Press, 1970.

Corbett, Julian S. *The Campaign of Trafalgar*. 2 vols. London: Longmans, Green, 1919.

———. *Some Principles of Maritime Strategy*. Introduction and notes by Eric J. Grove. 1911. Reprint, Annapolis: Naval Institute Press, 1988.

Crouzet, François. *Britain Ascendent: Comparative Studies in Franco-British Economic History*. Trans. Martin Thom. 1985. Reprint, New York: Cambridge University Press, 1990.

De Brahm, William Gerard. *The Atlantic Pilot (A Facsimile Reproduction of the 1772 Edition)*. Gainesville: University of Florida Presses, 1974.

DeHarpporte, Dean. *Northeast and Great Lakes Wind Atlas*. New York: Reinhold Publishing, 1983.

De Kay, James T. *Chronicles of the Frigate Macedonian, 1809–1922*. New York: W. W. Norton, 1995.

Delmas, Jean. *Histoire Militaire de la France*. Vol. 2, *De 1715 à 1871*. Paris: Presses Universitaires de France, 1992.

Dupuy, Trevor N., Curt Johnson, and David L. Bongard, eds. *The Harper Encyclopedia of Military Biography*. Edison, N.J.: Castle Books, 1995.

Dwight, Theodore. *History of the Hartford Convention with a Review of the Policy of the United States Government, Which Led to the War of 1812*. New York: N. & J. White, 1833.

Dye, Ira. *The Fatal Cruise of the Argus: Two Captains in the War of 1812*. Annapolis: Naval Institute Press, 1994.

Ellis, Geoffrey. *Napoleon's Continental Blockade: The Case of Alsace*. New York: Oxford University Press, 1981.

Emmons, George F. *Navy of the United States from the Commencement, in 1775, through 1853*. Washington, D.C.: Gideon, 1853.

Fairburn, William Armstrong. *Merchant Sail*. Vol. 2. Center Lovell, Maine: Fairburn Marine Educational Foundation, 1947.

Forester, C. S. *The Age of Fighting Sail*. Garden City, N.Y.: Doubleday, 1956.

Fowler, William M., Jr. *Jack Tars and Commodores: The American Navy, 1783–1815*. Boston: Houghton Mifflin, 1984.

Gardiner, Leslie. *The British Admiralty*. Edinburgh: William Blackwood and Sons, 1968.

Gardiner, Robert, ed. *Fleet Battle and Blockade: The French Revolutionary War 1793–1797*. London: Chatham Publishing, 1996.

———. *The Naval War of 1812*. Annapolis: Naval Institute Press, 1998.

———. *Nelson Against Napoleon: From the Nile to Copenhagen, 1798–1801*. London: Chatham Publishing, 1997.

Garitee, Jerome R. *The Republic's Private Navy: The American Privateering Business as Practiced by Baltimore during the War of 1812*. Middletown, Conn.: Wesleyan University Press, 1977.

George, Christopher T. *Terror on the Chesapeake: The War of 1812 on the Bay*. Shippensburg, Pa.: White Mane Books, 2000.

Goodwin, Peter. *The Construction and Fitting of the Sailing Man of War, 1650–1850*. London: Conway Maritime Press, 1987.

Gossett, W. P. *The Lost Ships of the Royal Navy, 1793–1900*. London: Mansell Publishing Limited, 1986.

Graham, Gerald S. *Empire of the North Atlantic: The Maritime Struggle for North America*. Toronto: University of Toronto Press, 1950.

————. *Sea Power and British North America, 1783–1820: A Study in British Colonial Policy*. Cambridge: Harvard University, 1941.

Grimble, Ian. *The Sea Wolf: The Life of Admiral Cochrane*. London: Bland and Briggs, 1978.

Grotius, Hugo. *Commentary on the Law of Prize and Booty*. Trans. Gwladys L. Williams. 1604. Reprint, New York: Oceana Publications, 1964.

————. *The Law of War and Peace*. Trans. Francis W. Kelsey. 1646. Reprint, Indianapolis: Bobbs-Merrill, 1925.

Gruppe, Henry E. *The Frigates*. Amsterdam, N.Y.: Time-Life Books, 1981.

Guttridge, Leonard F., and Jay D. Smith. *The Commodores*. Annapolis: Naval Institute Press, 1969.

Hagan, Kenneth J. *This People's Navy: The Making of American Sea Power*. New York: Free Press, 1991.

————, ed. *In Peace and War: Interpretations of American Naval History, 1775–1984*. 2d ed. Westport, Conn.: Greenwood Press, 1984.

Harding, Richard. *Seapower and Naval Warfare, 1650–1830*. Annapolis: Naval Institute Press, 1999.

Harland, John. *Seamanship in the Age of Sail*. Annapolis: Naval Institute Press, 1996.

Harper, Lawrence A. *The English Navigation Laws*. New York: Columbia University Press, 1939.

Haythornwaite, Phillip. *Nelson's Navy*. London: Osprey Publishing, 1993.

Heckscher, Eli F. *The Continental System: An Economic Interpretation*. Oxford: Clarendon Press, 1922.

Heidler, David S., and Jeanne T. Heidler, eds. *Encyclopedia of the War of 1812*. Santa Barbara, Calif.: ABC-CLIO, 1997.

Henderson, James. *The Frigates: An Account of the Lighter Warships of the Napoleonic Wars, 1793–1815*. 1970. Reprint, London: Leo Cooper, 1994.

————. *Sloops and Brigs: An Account of the Smallest Vessels of the Royal Navy During the Great Wars, 1793–1815*. London: Adlard Coles, 1972.

Hickey, Donald R. *The War of 1812: A Forgotten War*. Urbana: University of Illinois Press, 1989.

Hill, J. R., ed. *The Oxford Illustrated History of the Royal Navy*. New York: Oxford University Press, 1995.

————. *The Prizes of War: The Naval Prize System in the Napoleonic Wars, 1793–1815*. Gloucestershire, U.K.: Sutton Publishing, 1998.

Hirst, Francis W. *Life and Letters of Thomas Jefferson*. New York: Macmillan, 1926.

Ingersoll, Charles J. *History of the Second War Between the United States of America and Great Britain, Declared by Congress the 18th of June, 1812, and Concluded by Peace the 15th of February, 1815*. Philadelphia: Lippincott, Grambo, 1852.

Jackson, Kenneth T. *Atlas of American History.* Rev. ed. New York: Charles Scribner's Sons, 1943.

Jackson, Melvin H. *Privateers in Charleston, 1793–1796: An Account of a French Palatinate in South Carolina.* Washington, D.C.: U.S. Government Printing Office, 1969.

James, William. *A Full and Correct Account of the Chief Naval Operations of the Late War Between Great Britain and the United States of America.* London: T. Egerfor, 1817.

Jones, J. R. *The Anglo-Dutch Wars of the Seventeenth Century.* New York: Longmans, 1996.

Kennedy, Paul. *The Rise and Fall of British Naval Mastery.* New York: Scribner's Sons, 1976.

Kert, Faye Margaret. *Research in Maritime History No. 11—Prize and Prejudice: Privateering and Naval Prize in Atlantic Canada in the War of 1812.* St. John's, Newfoundland: International Maritime Economic History Association, 1997.

King, Dean. *A Sea of Words: A Lexicon and Companion for Patrick O'Brian's Seafaring Tales.* New York: Henry Holt, 1995.

Knox, Dudley W. *History of the United States Navy.* New York: Putnam's Sons, 1936.

Laffin, John. *Brassey's Dictionary of Battle: 3,500 Years of Conflicts, Campaigns, and Wars.* London: Brassey's, 1995.

Langley, Harold D. *A History of Medicine in the Early U.S. Navy.* Baltimore: Johns Hopkins University Press, 1995.

Lavery, Brian. *Nelson's Navy: The Ships, Men, and Organisation, 1793–1815.* 1989. Reprint, Annapolis: Naval Institute Press, 1994.

———. *Shipboard Life and Organization, 1731–1815.* Brookfield, Vt.: Ashgate Publishing (Navy Records Society), 1998.

———. *The Ship of the Line.* Vol. 1, *The Development of the Battlefleet, 1650–1850.* London: Conway Maritime Press, 1983.

Lewis, Emanuel Raymond. *Seacoast Fortifications of the United States, An Introductory History.* 1970. Reprint, Annapolis: Naval Institute Press, 1993.

Lewis, Michael A. *The Navy in Transition, 1814–1864: A Social History.* London: Hodder & Stoughton, 1965.

———. *A Social History of the British Navy, 1793–1815.* London: George Allen and Unwin, 1960.

Lloyd, Christopher. *The Health of Seamen: Selections from the Works of Dr. James Lind, Sir Gilbert Blane, and Dr. Thomas Trotter.* London: Spottiswoode, Ballantyne (Navy Records Society), 1965.

Loffin, John. *Jack Tar: The Story of the British Sailor.* London: Cassell, 1969.

Lord, Walter. *The Dawn's Early Light.* New York: W. W. Norton, 1972.

Lossing, Benson J. *Pictorial Fieldbook of the War of 1812.* New York: Harper and Brothers, 1868.

Ludlum, David M. *Early American Hurricanes, 1492–1870.* Boston: American Meteorological Society, 1963.

Lyon, David. *The Sailing Navy List: All the Ships of the Royal Navy Built, Purchased and Captured—1688–1860.* London: Conway Maritime Press, 1993.

MacGregor, David. *Merchant Sailing Ships, 1775–1875: Their Design and Construction.* Watford, U.K.: Argus Books, 1980.

Mackay, Ruddock F. *Admiral Hawke.* New York: Clarendon Press, 1965.

Mackesy, Piers. *The War for America, 1775–1783.* 1964. Reprint, Lincoln: University of Nebraska Press, 1993.

Maclay, Edgar S. *A History of American Privateers.* New York: D. Appleton & Sons, 1899.

Mahan, A. T. *The Influence of Sea Power upon the French Revolution and Empire, 1793–1812.* 2 vols. Boston: Little, Brown, 1918.

———. *Sea Power in Its Relations to the War of 1812.* 2 vols. Cambridge: Harvard University Press, 1905.

Maloney, Linda M. *The Captain from Connecticut: The Life and Naval Times of Isaac Hull.* Boston: Northeastern University Press, 1986.

Marcus, G. J. *The Age of Nelson: The Royal Navy, 1793–1815.* New York: Viking Press, 1971.

Marrin, Albert. *1812: The War Nobody Won.* New York: Athenaeum, 1985.

Martin, Tyrone G. *A Most Fortunate Ship: A Narrative History of Old Ironsides.* Rev. ed. Annapolis: Naval Institute Press, 1997.

Martin, Winthrop L. *The American Merchant Marine, Its History and Romance from 1620 to 1902.* New York: Charles Scribner's Sons, 1902.

Matloff, Maurice, ed. *American Military History.* Vol. 1, *1775–1902.* 1989. Rev. ed. Conshohocken, Pa.: Combined Books, 1996.

McKee, Christopher. *A Gentlemanly and Honorable Profession: The Creation of the U.S. Naval Officer Corps, 1794–1815.* Annapolis: Naval Institute Press, 1991.

Mitchell, B. R., ed. *European Historical Statistics, 1750–1970.* New York: Columbia University Press, 1975.

Morison, Samuel Eliot, Frederick Merk, and Frank Freidel. *Dissent in Three American Wars.* Cambridge: Harvard University Press, 1970.

Morriss, Roger. *The Royal Dockyards During the Revolutionary and Napoleonic Wars.* Leicester, U.K.: Leicester University Press, 1983.

Mountaine, William. *The Seaman's Vade-Mecum and Defensive War by Sea.* Salem, Mass.: New England & Virginia, 1783.

Norton, Louis Arthur. *Joshua Barney: Hero of the Revolution and 1812.* Annapolis: Naval Institute Press, 2000.

Pack, A. James. *The Man Who Burned the White House: Admiral Sir George Cockburn, 1772–1853.* Annapolis: Naval Institute Press, 1987.

Paine, Ralph D. *The Fight for a Free Sea; a Chronicle of the War of 1812.* New Haven, Conn.: Yale University Press, 1920.

Palmer, Michael A. *Stoddert's War: Naval Operations During the Quasi-War with France, 1798–1801.* Columbia: University of South Carolina Press, 1987.

Paullin, Charles Oscar. *Commodore John Rodgers: Captain, Commodore, and Senior Officer of the American Navy, 1773–1838.* Cleveland: Arthur H. Clark, 1910.

Perkins, Bradford. *Prologue to War: England and the United States, 1805–1812.* Berkeley and Los Angeles: University of California Press, 1961.

Petrie, Donald A. *The Prize Game: Lawful Looting on the High Seas in the Days of Fighting Sail.* Annapolis: Naval Institute Press, 1999.

————, ed. *The Causes of the War of 1812: National Honor or National Interest?* New York: Holt, Rinehart and Winston, 1962.

Pitch, Anthony S. *The Burning of Washington: The British Invasion of 1814.* Annapolis: Naval Institute Press, 1998.

Pitkin, Timothy. *A Statistical View of the Commerce of the United States of America: Its Connection with Agriculture and Manufactures; and an Account of the Public Debt, Revenues, and Expenditures.* New York: James Eastburn, 1817.

Potter, E. B. *The Naval Academy Illustrated History of the United States Navy.* New York: Galahad Books, 1971.

Pratt, Julius W. *Expansionists of 1812.* 1925. Reprint, Gloucester, Mass.: Peter Smith, 1957.

Quimby, Robert S. *The U.S. Army in the War of 1812: An Operational and Command Study.* 2 Vols. East Lansing: Michigan State University Press, 1997.

Rathbone, Julian. *Wellington's War: His Peninsular Dispatches.* London: Michael Joseph, 1984.

Reynolds, Clark G. *Command of the Sea.* New York: William Morrow, 1974.

Richmond, Sir Herbert. *Statesmen and Sea Power.* Oxford: Clarendon Press, 1946.

Rodger, N. A. M. *The Wooden World: An Anatomy of the Georgian Navy.* London: William Collins, 1986.

Roosevelt, Theodore. *The Naval War of 1812.* 1882. Reprint, Annapolis: Naval Institute Press, 1987.

Rutland, Robert A. *James Madison: The Founding Father.* New York: Macmillan, 1987.

Schom, Alan. *Napoleon Bonaparte.* New York: HarperCollins, 1997.

————. *Trafalgar: Countdown to Battle, 1803–1805.* New York: Oxford University Press, 1990.

Schroeder, Paul W. *The Transformation of European Politics, 1763–1848.* New York: Clarendon Press, 1994.

Sheppard, George. *Plunder, Profit, and Paroles: A Social History of the War of 1812 in Upper Canada.* Buffalo, N.Y.: McGill-Queen's University Press, 1994.

Shomette, Donald G. *Flotilla: Battle for the Patuxent.* Solomons, Md.: Calvert Marine Museum Press, 1981.

Skaggs, David Curtis, and Gerard T. Altoff. *A Signal Victory: The Lake Erie Campaign, 1812–1813.* Annapolis: Naval Institute Press, 1997.

Smith, Gene A. *"For the Purposes of Defense": The Politics of the Jeffersonian Gunboat Program.* Newark: University of Delaware Press, 1995.

Snead, Rodman E. *World Atlas of Geomorphic Features.* Huntington, N.Y.: Robert E. Krieger, 1980.

Snider, C. H. J. *Under the Red Jack: Privateers of the Maritime Provinces of Canada in the War of 1812.* London: Martin Hopkinson, 1928.

Sprout, Harold, and Margaret Sprout. *The Rise of American Naval Power, 1776–1918.* 1939. Reprint, Annapolis: Naval Institute Press, 1990.

Stagg, J. C. A. *Mr. Madison's War: Politics, Diplomacy, and Warfare in the Early American Republic.* Princeton, N.J.: Princeton University Press, 1983.

Stephen, Leslie, and Sidney Lee, eds. *Dictionary of National Biography.* Vols. 4 and 20. London: Hansard, 1885–1901.

Symonds, Craig. *The Naval Institute Historical Atlas of the United States Navy.* Annapolis: Naval Institute Press, 1995.

———. *Navalists and Anti-Navalists: The Naval Policy Debate in the United States, 1785–1827.* Newark: University of Delaware Press, 1980.

Tannehill, Ivan Ray. *Hurricanes.* Princeton, N.J.: Princeton University Press, 1952.

Tucker, Spencer C. *The Jeffersonian Gunboat Navy.* Columbia: University of South Carolina Press, 1993.

Tucker, Spencer C., and Frank T. Reuter. *Injured Honor: The Chesapeake-Leopard Affair, June 22, 1807.* Annapolis: Naval Institute Press, 1996.

United States Bureau of the Census. *The Statistical History of the United States from Colonial Times to the Present.* New York: Basic Books, 1976.

Updike, Frank A. *The Diplomacy of the War of 1812.* 1915. Reprint, Gloucester, Mass.: Peter Smith, 1965.

Urdang, Lawrence. *The Timetables of American History.* New York: Simon & Schuster, 1981.

Van Creveld, Martin. *Supplying War.* Cambridge: Cambridge University, 1982.

Vattel, Emmerich de. *The Law of Nations or the Principles of Natural Law.* Trans. Charles G. Fenwick. 1758. Reprint, New York: Oceana Publications, 1964.

Warner, Oliver. *The Life and Letters of Vice-Admiral Lord Collingwood.* London: Oxford University Press, 1968.

Watt, J., E. J. Freeman, and W. F. Bynum, eds. *Starving Sailors: The Influence of Nutrition upon Naval and Maritime History.* Bristol, U.K.: John Wright & Sons, 1981.

Watts, Steven. *The Republic Reborn: War and the Making of Liberal America.* Baltimore: Johns Hopkins Press, 1987.

White, Patrick C. T. *A Nation on Trial: America and the War of 1812.* New York: John Wiley & Sons, 1965.

Whitehorne, Joseph A. *The Battle for Baltimore, 1814.* Baltimore: Nautical and Aviation Publishing Company of America, 1997.

Woodman, Richard. *The Sea Warriors: Fighting Captains and Frigate Warfare in the Age of Nelson.* New York: Carroll and Graf Publishers, 2001.

Index

Allen, Andrew, 194n. 23
Allen, William Henry, 95–96
Amelia Island (Spain), 56, 112, 125, 153–54, 157, 180

Baltimore, failure of British assault on, 122–23
Barney, Joshua, 121
Barrie, Robert, 92, 99; inability to close Chesapeake, 107–8
Battle of the Nile, 165
Baugh, Daniel A., 12
Bermuda, British naval base of, 61, 142
Bladensburg, Battle of, 121
blockade, British development of: American War of Independence, 17–22; Anglo-Dutch Wars, 9–11; blockade of Brest (1759), 13–16; English Civil War, 8–9; France (1793–1802), 161–66; France (1803–1814), 166–75, 189n. 12
blockade, types of: close, 26; commercial or economic, 28; distant, 26; echeloned, 27; limited, 188n. 6; linear, 26, 188n. 6, 188n. 8; military, 1, 24, 26; strategic or national, 1, 24, 26
blockade of 1812–1815: analytical evaluation, 134–60; comparative evaluation, 175–82
blockade theory: evaluative principles, 31–32; legality, 24–26; limitations, 27–29; naval options, 23–24; objectives, 26; response to blockades, 30–31
Blyth, Samuel, 99
Bonaparte, Napoleon, 2; abdication of, 110, 114; Continental System, 173–74; impact of Leipzig, 106; invasion plans, 167; in Italy and Egypt, 165; lack of naval skill, 78, 83

bonded vessels, embargo of 1813–1814, 112
Boulougne, French invasion camp of, 167
Brest, French naval base of, 13–16, 162–63, 170
Broke, Phillip V.: engages *Chesapeake*, 94–95; as squadron commander in 1812, 67–68, 72–73
Burrows, William, 99

Campbell, Hugh G., 126
Canada, as American objective, 3, 43, 132, 144–45
Castlereagh, Viscount Robert, 106
causes of War of 1812, 1–2
charts and sailing hazards, 62
Christie, Ian R., 4, 146
Clowes, William Laird, 3
coasting trade, successful defense of, 99, 102, 118, 125–26, 145–47, 179
Cochrane, Sir Alexander, 114–15; desires revenge for American deprivations in Canada, 120–21; expectation of slave and Indian uprisings, 119; failure at Baltimore, 122; hatred of Americans, 115; performance as commander, 159–60; plans for 1814, 115–16
Cockburn, Sir George, 75, 79; American hatred of, 91; in Chesapeake Bay (1813), 91–93; in Chesapeake Bay (1814), 121–22, 133; Ocracoke raid, 97–98; ordered to blockade southern coasts, 123; organizes Colonial Corps, 119
colonies, French, loss of, 164, 166, 168, 181
commercial blockade (Fox blockade or economic blockade) of 1806, 173; effectiveness of, 174–75
Consolato del Mare, 24

Continental System, 173–74
Convoy Act of 1793, 162–63
Copenhagen, Battles of, 166
Copenhagen mentality in the United
  States, 42
Crouzet, François, 174

Dallas, A. J., 153
Decatur, Stephen, 65, 74
Dent, John H., 74
desertion, 45–46, 73, 92–93
disease: alcohol-related deaths, 190n. 18;
  fever, 54, 56, 98; scurvy, 11–12, 21,
  72–73
distant blockade, failure of (1793–1800),
  165, 177

embargoes: of 1808–1809, 49; of 1812, 49,
  64; of 1813–1814, 104–5, 112–13
Evans, Amos A., 152

fishing fleet, American, 145–47
Fowler, William M., Jr., 66
Fox, Charles James, 173
Fox blockade. *See* commercial blockade
  of 1806
French colonies, loss of, 164, 166, 168,
  181
Fulton, Robert, 105

Gahn, Henry, 100
Glorious First of June, Battle of, 163
Graham, Gerald S., 3–4, 152, 196n. 58
Graves, Samuel, 19–20
Great Britain: admiralty challenged for
  failures, 4, 155; aggressiveness of
  naval officers, 132–33; antiwar
  protests, 67; Caribbean theater,
  60–62, 102; contributing factors to
  blockade weakness summarized, 182;
  disruption of American economy,
  142–47; emphasis on destruction of
  U.S. Navy, 83, 94–95, 103; forbidding
  single combat against American
  heavy frigates, 103; inability to
  contain American navies, 134–35, 137,
  139–42, 157–59; intensification of war,
  74, 76, 81, 87–88; merchant marine,
  48–49, 155; misjudgment of enemy
  capability, 82–83, 133–34; naval
  administration and organization,

44–47; naval losses, 135–38; peace
  initiatives, 106, 132, 155; piecemeal
  development of blockade, 33–34,
  75–76, 85, 90, 117, 151–52, 155–58;
  public reaction to war, 87, 95, 128–29,
  160; reactions to declaration of war,
  50, 64–66, 68–69, 131–32, 155; Treaty
  of Ghent and end of blockade,
  129–30, 155; victory in France, 114,
  160; war planning, 32–33, 81–82,
  102–4, 115–16, 119, 135–38, 158;
  warship availability, 156–59
Great Lakes Theater: Battle of
  Plattsburgh, 125; diversion of assets
  to, 77, 101, 106, 135
Griffith, Edward, 94, 125
Grotius, Hugo, 24–26
Guerre de Course, French, 164, 171–72, 177

Halifax, British naval base of, 19, 60–62,
  64, 77, 102, 135, 142–43, 203n. 29
Hamilton, Paul: fleet in being, 68, 73;
  resignation, 76; stops ransom, 140;
  undelivered orders, 65
Hampton, pillage of, 97
Harding, Richard, 10
Hardy, Thomas, 105–6, 161
Havre de Grace, burning of, 91
Hawke, Sir Edward, 13–16
Hayes, Jonathan, 100
Hickey, Donald, 154
Hood, Alexander Arthur, Lord Bridport,
  162–63, 165
Hotham, Henry, 80; private reports to
  Admiralty, 81; reassigned to blockade
  of New York, 115, 158–59; requests
  reassignment, 104
Hotham, William, 162
Howe, Richard Lord, 162
Hull, Isaac, 67–68, 99, 118

James, William, 3
Jervis, John, Lord St. Vincent, 162,
  165–66
Jones, William: appointment of, 76; on
  commerce raiding, 85, 95–96, 140;
  response to loss of *Chesapeake*, 95

Kennedy, Paul, 4
Kent Island, British seizure of, 98

Lawrence, James, 94
licensing system and trade, 28, 33, 70–71, 100, 113, 147, 153–54, 157, 201n. 70
Lynnhaven Bay, 79, 99

Madison, James: on British barbarity, 121, 124; challenges legality of paper blockade, 117; embargo of 1813–1814, 104–5, 112; preserves merchant marine, 144–45, 180; refusal to compromise on peace terms, 75, 106; strategic planning, 41–44; war message, 1; willingness to compromise on peace terms, 119–20
Mahan, Alfred Thayer, 4, 122–23, 131, 144–45, 199n. 36
Marcus, G. J., 3–4, 146, 195n. 29
marine insurance, increasing rates of, 28, 49, 163, 172, 177, 192n. 29
maritime law, 24–26
Melville, Robert Saunders Dundas, 189n. 13, 191n. 23
merchantmen, losses of: American, 142–47, 180; British, 139–141
merchant vessels: *Chesapeake* (steamship), 112; *Eagle*, 105–6; *Emily*, 85; *Nautilus*, 130
Middleton, Richard, 16–17
Missiessy, Admiral de Burgues, 168
Mobile Bay, defense of, 91–92, 126–27
Monroe, James, 1, 75, 119
Montagu, John, Fourth Earl of Sandwich, 18–21

Napier, Henry Edward: dilemma of prize money, 113; an increasingly harsh war, 97; on New Englanders, 152; risk taking, 5, 133
naval campaigns: Chesapeake Bay (1813), 79, 84–85, 87, 91–93, 96–99, 102–4, 133; Chesapeake Bay (1814), 121–24, 133; Maine (1814), 125, 133, 152; New Orleans (1814–1815), 126–27, 133, 150; Ocracoke, 97–98
naval engagements: *Argus* and *Pelican*, 95; assaults on Mobile Bay, 91–92, 101–2, 126–27; attacks on *Constellation*, 87, 96; attempted sortie by *United States*, *Macedonian*, and *Hornet*, 94–95; capture of *Nautilus* (U.S. warship), 67; capture of *President*, 127; *Chesapeake*

and *Shannon*, 94–95; *Constitution* and *Guerriere*, 72, 136; *Constitution* and *Java*, 76, 132, 136; *Constitution* versus *Cyane* and *Levant*, 130, 136; *Enterprise* and *Boxer*, 99; escape of *Belvidera*, 65; escape of *Constitution*, 67–68; *Essex* and *Alert*, 73, 132; *Essex* versus *Phoebe* and *Cherub*, 111, 136; *Frolic* and *Orpheus*, 111; gunboat skirmishes, 99, 118, 121, 126; *Hornet* and *Peacock*, 87; *Hornet* and *Penguin*, 130; loss of *Asp*, escape of *Scorpion*, 97; *Peacock* and *Epervier*, 117; *President* and *Highflyer*, 99; *United States* and *Macedonian*, 75–76, 136; *Viper* and *Narcissus*, 80; *Vixen* and *Southampton*, 75; *Wasp* and *Avon*, 117–18, 136; *Wasp* and *Frolic*, 74; *Wasp* and *Reindeer*, 117
Navigation Acts, English, 25
Nelson, Horatio, 66, 168–69
New England: British desire to subvert, 70; Cochrane blockades, 117–18; conquest of Machias and Castine, 125, 133; discontent with government, 145; neutral trade, 180; possible commerce with the enemy, 99; receiving center for prizes, 139; unwillingness to make a separate peace, 151–53
Newfoundland squadron, 193n. 12
Nile, Battle of, 165

Ocracoke Island: infrequent blockade 54, 126; raided by Cockburn, 97–98
Oliver, Robert Dudley, 100

Palliser, Sir Hugh, 18–19
peace initiatives: Castlereagh (late 1813), 106; Ghent (1814), 119–21, 145; Russian mediation offered (1813), 87–89; Warren (1812), 74–75, 132
Peace of Amiens, 166
Pigot, Hugh, 119
Porter, David, 67, 111
Prevost, Sir George, 120, 125
privateers, historical usage of, 47–48; during American War of Independence, 21–22; during Anglo-Dutch Wars, 10
privateers, War of 1812: Admiralty opinion, 81–82, 191n. 24; comparison

privateers, War of 1812 (*continued*)
    of American and French raiders, 82;
    continued successes in 1813, 96,
    107–9; continued successes in 1814,
    128, 178; initial successes, 73–74, 77;
    resented by naval officers, 142–43;
    total captures of merchantmen,
    138–42
privateer vessels: *Dart*, 100; *Dolphin*, 107;
    Fortune of War, 126; *Kemp*, 126; *Leo*,
    128; *Lion*, 107; *True-Blooded Yankee*,
    107
prize courts, 77, 143–44
prize money, 46–47, 154, 160

ransom, 113–14, 140, 154
razees, 80
risk assessment, 131–34
Rodgers, John: against maintaining a fleet
    in being, 73; first sortie, 65, 72; second
    sortie, 74
Roosevelt, Theodore, 3
Ross, Robert, 119; 121–22
Rupert, Prince of Bavaria, 8–9

sailing routes and time, 59–60
St. Marys, U.S. Navy station at, 56, 112,
    125–26, 157
Sawyer, Herbert, 65–66, 73–74
Schom, Alan, 166–67
Sherbrooke, Sir John, 125
shipping cycles, 150
Shuldham, Molyneux, 20–21
smuggling, 104–5, 112–13, 154
specie drain, 153–54
Stewart, Charles, 85, 92, 101

technological developments, 12–13;
    16–17; 21–22
terror, as a weapon: applied by Cockburn,
    91; burning of Newark, 203n. 36;
    burning of Washington, 122; burning
    of York, 204n. 47; "Fultons" and
    infernal devices, 105–6; as ordered by
    Cochrane, 116–17, 159–60; public
    reaction, 123–24; as revenge for U.S.
    depredations in Canada, 120–21; used
    at Hampton, 97
Tingey, Thomas, 122
Toulon, 162–63, 168, 170, 210n. 21
Trafalgar, 166–69

Treaty of Ghent, 120–21, 155, 183–84

United States: advantage at Ghent to
    Americans, 125, 155; coastline of, 51;
    condemnation of paper blockade,
    117; Declaration of War, 1–2, 65;
    drops stipulation of impressment for
    peace, 119–20; funding war, 112;
    increased naval strength, 178, 181;
    internal transportation, 58–59;
    merchant marine, 48–49, 132, 144–47,
    180; naval administration and
    organization, 40–41; naval
    appropriations, 76, 87; naval sortie
    rate, 134–35; navalist and antinavalist
    debate, 41–43; peace overtures,
    87–88, 106, 145; success at sea in
    1812, 76–77; summary of results of
    War of 1812, 181; Treaty of Ghent
    ratified, 129–30; war planning, 43–44,
    144
United States, major ports and naval
    facilities: Baltimore, 52, 54, 147–51;
    Boston, 51, 94, 100, 103; Charleston,
    56, 117; New Orleans, 33, 56, 147–51,
    180; New York, 51, 100, 105–6;
    Norfolk, 54; Philadelphia, 52;
    Wilmington, 33, 56; naval facilities,
    41, 60
Upton, Charles, 113

Vattel, Emmerich de, 24–25
Villeneuve, Pierre Charles Jean-Baptiste
    Silvestre de, 168–69

War of 1812, causes of, 1–2
Warren, John Borlase: Admiralty
    criticizes, 80–82; appointment and
    conflicting orders, 69–72, 158; arrival
    in American waters, 73–74; attempt
    on *Adams*, 97; battle and pillaging of
    Hampton, 97; desertion problem, 93;
    early fear of failure, 78; extension of
    blockade to Long Island Sound,
    100–101; last letter of 1813, 108–9;
    performance, 159; proposed blockade
    for 1813, 102–3; reasoning for
    Chesapeake campaign, 103–4;
    relieved of command, 114; standards
    for gunnery, 89–90; urged to destroy
    U.S. Navy, 83–84, 102–4

warships: frigates, 37–38; hired ships, 40; line of battle ships, 36–37; rating system, 35–36, 39; unrated vessels, 38–40
warships, British: *Aeolus*, 67; *Africa*, 67; *Albion*, 111; *Alert*, 73; *Avon*, 118, 136; *Belvidera*, 65, 67; *Boxer*, 99; *Brazen*, 72; *Cherub*, 111; *Colibri*, 72, 102; *Cyane*, 130, 136; *Diamond Rock*, 168; *Dotterel*, 102; *Dragon*, 92, 99; *Epervier*, 117; *Frolic*, 74; *Guerriere*, 67, 72, 74, 136; *Herald*, 101; *Highflyer*, 99; *Java*, 76, 85, 136; *Junon*, 96; *La Hogue* 94; *Levant*, 130, 136; *Macedonian*, 75–76, 136; *Majestic*, 118; *Marlborough*, 79; *Moselle*, 101–2; *Narcissus*, 80, 96; *Nymphe*, 113; *Orpheus*, 111, 119; *Peacock*, 87; *Penguin*, 130; *Phoebe*, 111; *Plantagenet*, 105; *Poictiers*, 74; *Ramillies*, 105–6; *Recruit*, 102; *Reindeer*, 117; *San Domingo*, 87; *Sceptre*, 97, 99, 111; *Shannon*, 67, 94–95; *Southampton*, 75; *Spartan*, 81; *Tenedos*, 94; *Victorious*, 105
warships, United States: *Adams*, 97, 103, 111, 118, 125; *Alert*, 106; *Alligator*, 111, 118; *Argus*, 65, 74, 76, 95–96, 106; *Asp*, 97; *Carolina*, 75; *Chesapeake*, 76, 91, 94–95; *Congress*, 65, 74, 76, 92, 101; *Constellation*, 84–85, 87, 92, 96, 103, 111, 135; *Constitution*, 67–68, 72, 75–76, 85, 101, 106, 117, 127, 130,
136; *Demologus*, 105; *Enterprise*, 80, 99, 111; *Essex*, 65, 73, 111, 136; *Ferret*, 75; *Frolic*, 111; *Gallatin*, 72; *Hornet*, 65, 75, 85, 91, 94, 127, 130; *John Adams*, 65, 106; *Macedonian* (brig), 127, 130; *Macedonian* (frigate), 94–95, 106, 135; *Nautilus*, 65, 67; *Peacock*, 111, 117–18, 127, 130; *President*, 65, 74, 76, 92, 99, 127–28; *Rattlesnake*, 100, 111; *Scorpion*, 97; *Siren*, 94, 99; *Surveyor*, 96; *Tom Bowline*, 127, 130; *United States*, 65, 74, 94, 136; *Viper*, 80; *Vixen*, 75; *Wasp*, 74, 117–18, 136
Washington, burning of, 121–24
weather, effect on blockade: American coasts, 52, 54, 56; *Brazen* dismasted, 72; hurricanes, 58; hurricane season of 1812, 102; loss of *Colibri*, 102; severe winter of 1813, 118; storm at Halifax, 102; summary of weather-related losses, 135–37
Wellesley, Sir Arthur, Duke of Wellington, 3; failure of Royal Navy to protect supply lines, 107; little fear of French navy, 78; logistical needs in Iberian Peninsula, 69; naval discipline, 45–46; specie drain, 153
Woodfine, Peter, 11

Yeo, James, 75

In 1995 Wade G. Dudley left the private sector to pursue the twin roles of teacher and historian. After earning a master's degree in maritime history and nautical archaeology from East Carolina University, he received his doctorate from the University of Alabama at Tuscaloosa. Since earning his Ph.D. in 1999, Dr. Dudley has served as a visiting assistant professor at East Carolina University.

A writer of both fiction and nonfiction, Dr. Dudley specializes in military and naval history. For future publications, he has researched topics ranging from Sir John de Hawkwood (the leader of a fourteenth-century band of mercenaries) to the Yom Kippur War of 1973. And, of course, his study of naval warfare blockade theory continues.

A father, grandfather, and a dedicated husband of nearly thirty years, Dr. Dudley uses his dwindling leisure time to imbibe tremendous quantities of military and science fiction. He has also been known to push miniature soldiers across a table or counters across a map to simulate the great and small battles of history.

The Naval Institute Press is the book-publishing arm of the U.S. Naval Institute, a private, nonprofit, membership society for sea service professionals and others who share an interest in naval and maritime affairs. Established in 1873 at the U.S. Naval Academy in Annapolis, Maryland, where its offices remain today, the Naval Institute has members worldwide.

Members of the Naval Institute support the education programs of the society and receive the influential monthly magazine *Proceedings* and discounts on fine nautical prints and on ship and aircraft photos. They also have access to the transcripts of the Institute's Oral History Program and get discounted admission to any of the Institute-sponsored seminars offered around the country.

The Naval Institute also publishes *Naval History* magazine. This colorful bimonthly is filled with entertaining and thought-provoking articles, first-person reminiscences, and dramatic art and photography. Members receive a discount on *Naval History* subscriptions.

The Naval Institute's book-publishing program, begun in 1898 with basic guides to naval practices, has broadened its scope to include books of more general interest. Now the Naval Institute Press publishes about one hundred titles each year, ranging from how-to books on boating and navigation to battle histories, biographies, ship and aircraft guides, and novels. Institute members receive significant discounts on the Press's more than eight hundred books in print.

Full-time students are eligible for special half-price membership rates. Life memberships are also available.

For a free catalog describing Naval Institute Press books currently available, and for further information about subscribing to *Naval History* magazine or about joining the U.S. Naval Institute, please write to:

Membership Department
U.S. Naval Institute
291 Wood Road
Annapolis, MD 21402-5034
Telephone: (800) 233-8764
Fax: (410) 269-7940
Web address: www.usni.org